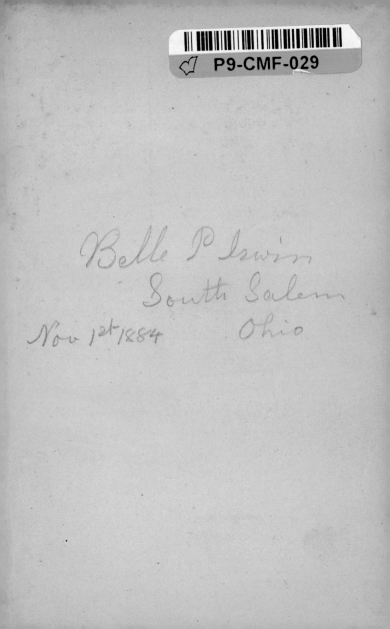

Belle P Irwin
South Salem
Nov 1st 1884   Ohio

CHAUTAUQUA EDITION

HISTORIES OF

CYRUS THE GREAT

AND

ALEXANDER THE GREAT

BY

JACOB ABBOTT

WITH REVISIONS AND AN APPENDIX
BY LYMAN ABBOTT

NEW YORK
HARPER & BROTHERS, FRANKLIN SQUARE

GENERAL PREFACE

FOR THE

CHAUTAUQUA EDITION

FOR any comprehensive knowledge of history some acquaintance with the lives of Cyrus and Alexander is essential; since the conquest of Cyrus has been well characterized as the starting-point of European life, and the conquest of Alexander prepared the way for that spread of Grecian literature and philosophy which were themselves preparations for the spread of Christianity. Moreover, as individuals, Cyrus stands out clearly as the representative of the East, Alexander of the West.

In preparing this edition of my father's volumes, at the request of Dr. Vincent, regard has been had to making a cheap edition for popular use: it is, therefore, printed from the original plates; such errors as were discoverable in them have been corrected, but these were very few in number.

The additional matter, gathered from a wide range of modern authorities—the result of researches in the East since the original histories were written—are incorporated in brief notes in an Appendix, where also the student will find references to English authorities easily accessible in all of the larger libraries, and many of them to be found in any good school or town library.   In using the volume, the reader is recommended, after finishing each chapter, to turn to the Appendix, read the notes there, and perhaps connect them with the chapter by pencil memoranda at the appropriate page, for future convenience.

L. A.

CORNWALL-ON-HUDSON, N. Y.

PERSIAN EMPIRE.

Longitude East from Ferro

HISTORY

OF

CYRUS THE GREAT

BY JACOB ABBOTT.

With Engravings.

NEW YORK:

HARPER & BROTHERS, PUBLISHERS,

FRANKLIN SQUARE.

PREFACE.

ONE special object which the author of this series has had in view, in the plan and method which he has followed in the preparation of the successive volumes, has been to adapt them to the purposes of text-books in schools. The study of a *general compend* of history, such as is frequently used as a text-book, is highly useful, if it comes in at the right stage of education, when the mind is sufficiently matured, and has acquired sufficient preliminary knowledge to understand and appreciate so condensed a generalization as a summary of the whole history of a nation contained in an ordinary volume must necessarily be. Without this degree of maturity of mind, and this preparation, the study of such a work will be, as it too frequently is, a mere mechanical committing to memory of names, and dates, and phrases, which awaken no interest, communicate no ideas, and impart no useful knowledge to the mind.

A class of ordinary pupils, who have not yet

become much acquainted with history, would, accordingly, be more benefited by having their attention concentrated, at first, on detached and separate topics, such as those which form the subjects, respectively, of these volumes. By studying thus fully the history of individual monarchs, or the narratives of single events, they can go more fully into detail ; they conceive of the transactions described as realities; their reflecting and reasoning powers are occupied on what they read; they take notice of the motives of conduct, of the gradual development of character, the good or ill desert of actions, and of the connection of causes and consequences, both in respect to the influence of wisdom and virtue on the one hand, and, on the other, of folly and crime. In a word, their *minds* and *hearts* are occupied instead of merely their memories. They reason, they sympathize, they pity, they approve, and they condemn. They enjoy the real and true pleasure which constitutes the charm of historical study for minds that are mature ; and they acquire a taste for truth instead of fiction, which will tend to direct their reading into proper channels in all future years.

The use of these works, therefore, as textbooks in classes, has been kept continually in mind in the preparation of them. The running index on the tops of the pages is intended to serve instead of questions. These captions can be used in their present form as *topics*, in respect to which, when announced in the class, the pupils are to repeat substantially what is said on the page; or, on the other hand, questions in form, if that mode is preferred, can be readily framed from them by the teacher. In all the volumes, a very regular system of division into chapters is observed, which will greatly facilitate the assignment of lessons.

CONTENTS.

Chapter		Page
I.	HERODOTUS AND XENOPHON	13
II.	THE BIRTH OF CYRUS	37
III.	THE VISIT TO MEDIA	68
IV.	CRŒSUS	101
V.	ACCESSION OF CYRUS TO THE THRONE	124
VI.	THE ORACLES	144
VII.	THE CONQUEST OF LYDIA	164
VIII.	THE CONQUEST OF BABYLON	187
IX.	THE RESTORATION OF THE JEWS	207
X.	THE STORY OF PANTHEA	226
XI.	CONVERSATIONS	253
XII.	THE DEATH OF CYRUS	270

ENGRAVINGS.

	Pag.
MAP OF THE PERSIAN EMPIRE	*Frontispiece.*
THE EXPOSURE OF THE INFANT	48
CYRUS'S HUNTING	90
THE SECRET CORRESPONDENCE	132
THE SIEGE OF SARDIS	179
RAISING JEREMIAH FROM THE DUNGEON	219
THE WAR-CHARIOT OF ABRADATES	242

CYRUS THE GREAT.

CHAPTER I.

HERODOTUS AND XENOPHON.

CYRUS was the founder of the ancient Persian empire—a monarchy, perhaps, the most wealthy and magnificent which the world has ever seen. Of that strange and incomprehensible principle of human nature, under the influence of which vast masses of men, notwithstanding the universal instinct of aversion to control, combine, under certain circumstances, by millions and millions, to maintain, for many successive centuries, the representatives of some one great family in a condition of exalted, and absolute, and utterly irresponsible ascendency over themselves, while they toil for them, watch over them, submit to endless and most humiliating privations in their behalf, and commit, if commanded to do so, the most inexcusable and atrocious crimes to sustain the demigods

2

they have thus made in their lofty estate, we have, in the case of this Persian monarchy, one of the most extraordinary exhibitions.

The Persian monarchy appears, in fact, even as we look back upon it from this remote distance both of space and of time, as a very vast wave of human power and grandeur. It swelled up among the populations of Asia, between the Persian Gulf and the Caspian Sea, about five hundred years before Christ, and rolled on in undiminished magnitude and glory for many centuries. It bore upon its crest the royal line of Astyages and his successors. Cyrus was, however, the first of the princes whom it held up conspicuously to the admiration of the world, and he rode so gracefully and gallantly on the lofty crest that mankind have given him the credit of raising and sustaining the magnificent billow on which he was borne. How far we are to consider him as founding the monarchy, or the monarchy as raising and illustrating him, will appear more fully in the course of this narrative.

Cotemporaneous with this Persian monarchy in the East, there flourished in the West the small but very efficient and vigorous republics of Greece The Greeks had a written

B.C. 550.] HERODOTUS AND XENOPHON 15

The republics of Greece.   Written characters Greek and Persian

character for their language which could be
easily and rapidly executed, while the ordinary
language of the Persians was scarcely written
at all There was, it is true, in this latter nation, a certain learned character, which was
used by the priests for their mystic records,
and also for certain sacred books which constituted the only national archives. It was, however, only slowly and with difficulty that this
character could be penned, and, when penned,
it was unintelligible to the great mass of the
population. For this reason, among others,
the Greeks wrote narratives of the great events
which occurred in their day, which narratives
they so embellished and adorned by the picturesque lights and shades in which their genius
enabled them to present the scenes and characters described as to make them universally admired, while the surrounding nations produced
nothing but formal governmental records, not
worth to the community at large the toil and labor necessary to decipher them and make them
intelligible. Thus the Greek writers became
the historians, not only of their own republics,
but also of all the nations around them ; and
with such admirable genius and power did they
fulfill this function, that, while the records of all

16   CYRUS THE GREAT. [B.C. 550.

Preservation of the Greek language.   Herodotus and Xenophon

other nations cotemporary with them have been almost entirely neglected and forgotten, the language of the Greeks has been preserved among mankind, with infinite labor and toil, by successive generations of scholars, in every civilized nation, for two thousand years, solely in order that men may continue to read these tales.

Two Greek historians have given us a narrative of the events connected with the life of Cyrus—Herodotus and Xenophon. These writers disagree very materially in the statements which they make, and modern readers are divided in opinion on the question which to believe. In order to present this question fairly to the minds of our readers, we must commence this volume with some account of these two authorities, whose guidance, conflicting as it is, furnishes all the light which we have to follow

Herodotus was a philosopher and scholar Xenophon was a great general. The one spent his life in solitary study, or in visiting various countries in the pursuit of knowledge; the other distinguished himself in the command of armies, and in distant military expeditions, which he conducted with great energy and skill. They were both, by birth, men of wealth and high station, so that they occupied, from the beginning, conspicuous positions in society; and as they were both energetic and enterprising in character, they were led, each, to a very romantic and adventurous career, the one in his travels, the other in his campaigns, so that their personal history and their exploits attracted great attention even while they lived.

Herodotus was born in the year 484 before Christ, which was about fifty years after the death of the Cyrus whose history forms the subject of this volume. He was born in the Grecian state of Caria, in Asia Minor, and in the city of Halicarnassus. Caria, as may be seen from the map at the commencement of this volume, was in the southwestern part of Asia Minor, near the shores of the Ægean Sea. Herodotus became a student at a very early age. It was the custom in Greece, at that time, to give to young men of his rank a good intellectual education. In other nations, the training of the young men, in wealthy and powerful families, was confined almost exclusively to the use of arms, to horsemanship, to athletic feats, and other such accomplishments as would give them a manly and graceful personal bearing, and enable them to excel in the various friendly contests of the public games, as well as prepare

B

them to maintain their ground against their
enemies in personal combats on the field of
battle. The Greeks, without neglecting these
things, taught their young men also to read and
to write, explained to them the structure and
the philosophy of language, and trained them
to the study of the poets, the orators, and the
historians which their country had produced.
Thus a general taste for intellectual pursuits
and pleasures was diffused throughout the community. Public affairs were discussed, before
large audiences assembled for the purpose, by
orators who felt a great pride and pleasure in
the exercise of the power which they had acquired of persuading, convincing, or exciting
the mighty masses that listened to them; and
at the great public celebrations which were customary in those days, in addition to the wrestlings, the races, the games, and the military
spectacles, there were certain literary entertainments provided, which constituted an essential
part of the public pleasures. Tragedies were
acted, poems recited, odes and lyrics sung, and
narratives of martial enterprises and exploits,
and geographical and historical descriptions of
neighboring nations, were read to vast throngs
of listeners, who, having been accustomed from

infancy to witness such performances, and to hear them applauded, had learned to appreciate and enjoy them. Of course, these literary exhibitions would make impressions, more or less strong, on different minds, as the mental temperaments and characters of individuals varied. They seem to have exerted a very powerful influence on the mind of Herodotus in his early years. He was inspired, when very young, with a great zeal and ardor for the attainment of knowledge; and as he advanced toward maturity, he began to be ambitious of making new discoveries, with a view of communicating to his countrymen, in these great public assemblies, what he should thus acquire. Accordingly, as soon as he arrived at a suitable age, he resolved to set out upon a tour into foreign countries, and to bring back a report of what he should see and hear.

The intercourse of nations was, in those days, mainly carried on over the waters of the Mediterranean Sea; and in times of peace, almost the only mode of communication was by the ships and the caravans of the merchants who traded from country to country, both by sea and on the land. In fact, the knowledge which one country possessed of the geography and the

manners and customs of another, was almost
wholly confined to the reports which these merchants circulated. When military expeditions
invaded a territory, the commanders, or the
writers who accompanied them, often wrote
descriptions of the scenes which they witnessed
in their campaigns, and described briefly the
countries through which they passed. These
cases were, however, comparatively rare; and
yet, when they occurred, they furnished ac
counts better authenticated, and more to be relied upon, and expressed, moreover, in a more
systematic and regular form, than the reports
of the merchants, though the information which
was derived from both these sources combined
was very insufficient, and tended to excite more
curiosity than it gratified. Herodotus, therefore, conceived that, in thoroughly exploring the
countries on the shores of the Mediterranean
and in the interior of Asia, examining their geographical position, inquiring into their history,
their institutions, their manners, customs, and
laws, and writing the results for the entertainment and instruction of his countrymen, he had
an ample field before him for the exercise of all
his powers.

He went first to Egypt   Egypt had been,

until that time, closely shut up from the rest
of mankind by the jealousy and watchfulness
of the government. But now, on account of
some recent political changes, which will be
hereafter more particularly alluded to, the way
was opened for travelers from other countries
to come in. Herodotus was the first to avail
himself of this opportunity. He spent some
time in the country, and made himself minutely
acquainted with its history, its antiquities, its
political and social condition at the time of his
visit, and with all the other points in respect
to which he supposed that his countrymen
would wish to be informed. He took copious
notes of all that he saw. From Egypt he
went eastward into Libya, and thence he traveled slowly along the whole southern shore of
the Mediterranean Sea as far as to the Straits of
Gibraltar, noting, with great care, every thing
which presented itself to his own personal observation, and availing himself of every possible source of information in respect to all other
points of importance for the object which he
had in view.

The Straits of Gibraltar were the ends of the
earth toward the westward in those ancient
days, and our traveler accordingly, after reach-

22   Cyrus the Great. [B.C. 450

Route of Herodotus in Asia.   His return to Greece

ing them, returned again to the eastward. He
visited Tyre, and the cities of Phœnicia, on the
eastern coast of the Mediterranean Sea, and
thence went still further eastward to Assyria
and Babylon.   It was here that he obtained
the materials for what he has written in respect
to the Medes and Persians, and to the history
of Cyrus.   After spending some time in these
countries, he went on by land still further to
the eastward, into the heart of Asia.   The
country of Scythia was considered as at "the
end of the earth" in this direction.   Herodotus
penetrated for some distance into the almost
trackless wilds of this remote land, until he
found that he had gone as far from the great
center of light and power on the shores of the
Ægean Sea as he could expect the curiosity
of his countrymen to follow him.   He passed
thence round toward the north, and came down
through the countries north of the Danube into
Greece, by way of the Epirus and Macedon
To make such a journey as this was, in fact
in those days, almost to explore the whole known
world.

It ought, however, here to be stated, that
many modern scholars, who have examined,
with great care, the accounts which Herodotus

has given of what he saw and heard in his
wanderings, doubt very seriously whether his
journeys were really as extended as he pre-
tends.   As his object was to read what he was
intending to write at great public assemblies
in Greece, he was, of course, under every possible inducement to make his narrative as interesting as possible, and not to detract at all
from whatever there might be extraordinary
either in the extent of his wanderings or in
the wonderfulness of the objects and scenes
which he saw, or in the romantic nature of the
adventures which he met with in his protracted
tour.   Cicero, in lauding him as a writer, says
that he was the first who evinced the power to
adorn a historical narrative.   Between adorn-
ing and *embellishing*, the line is not to be very
distinctly marked; and Herodotus has often
been accused of having drawn more from his
fancy than from any other source, in respect to
a large portion of what he relates and describes.
Some do not believe that he ever even entered
half the countries which he professes to have
thoroughly explored, while others find, in the
minuteness of his specifications, something like
conclusive proof that he related only what he
actually saw.   In a word, the question of his

credibility has been discussed by successive
generations of scholars ever since his day, and
strong parties have been formed who have gone
to extremes in the opinions they have taken;
so that, while some confer upon him the title
of the father of *history*, others say it would be
more in accordance with his merits to call him
the father of *lies*. In controversies like this,
and, in fact, in all controversies, it is more
agreeable to the mass of mankind to take sides
strongly with one party or the other, and either
to believe or disbelieve one or the other fully
and cordially. There is a class of minds, however, more calm and better balanced than the
rest, who can deny themselves this pleasure,
and who see that often, in the most bitter and
decided controversies, the truth lies between.
By this class of minds it has been generally
supposed that the narratives of Herodotus are
substantially true, though in many cases highly
colored and embellished, or, as Cicero called it,
adorned, as, in fact, they inevitably must have
been under the circumstances in which they
were written.

We can not follow minutely the circumstances of the subsequent life of Herodotus.
He became involved in some political disturb-

ances and difficulties in his native state after his return, in consequence of which he retired, partly a fugitive and partly an exile, to the island of Samos, which is at a little distance from Caria, and not far from the shore. Here he lived for some time in seclusion, occupied in writing out his history. He divided it into nine books, to which, respectively, the names of the nine Muses were afterward given, to designate them. The island of Samos, where this great literary work was performed, is very near to Patmos, where, a few hundred years later, the Evangelist John, in a similar retirement, and in the use of the same language and character, wrote the Book of Revelation.

When a few of the first books of his history were completed, Herodotus went with the manuscript to Olympia, at the great celebration of the 81st Olympiad. The Olympiads were periods recurring at intervals of about four years. By means of them the Greeks reckoned their time. The Olympiads were celebrated as they occurred, with games, shows, spectacles, and parades, which were conducted on so magnificent a scale that vast crowds were accustomed to assemble from every part of Greece to witness and join in them. They were held at

Olympia, a city on the western side of Greece. Nothing now remains to mark the spot but some acres of confused and unintelligible ruins

The personal fame of Herodotus and of his travels had preceded him, and when he arrived at Olympia he found the curiosity and eagerness of the people to listen to his narratives extreme. He read copious extracts from his accounts, so far as he had written them, to the vast assemblies which convened to hear him, and they were received with unbounded applause; and inasmuch as these assemblies comprised nearly all the statesmen, the generals, the philosophers, and the scholars of Greece, applause expressed by them became at once universal renown. Herodotus was greatly gratified at the interest which his countrymen took in his narratives, and he determined thenceforth to devote his time assiduously to the continuation and completion of his work.

It was twelve years, however, before his plan was finally accomplished. He then repaired to Athens, at the time of a grand festive celebration which was held in that city, and there he appeared in public again, and read extended portions of the additional books that he had written. The admiration and applause which his work now elicited was even greater than before. In deciding upon the passages to be read, Herodotus selected such as would be most likely to excite the interest of his Grecian hearers, and many of them were glowing accounts of Grecian exploits in former wars which had been waged in the countries which he had visited. To expect that, under such circumstances, Herodotus should have made his history wholly impartial, would be to suppose the historian not human.

The Athenians were greatly pleased with the narratives which Herodotus thus read to them of their own and of their ancestors' exploits. They considered him a national benefactor for having made such a record of their deeds, and, in addition to the unbounded applause which they bestowed upon him, they made him a public grant of a large sum of money. During the remainder of his life Herodotus continued to enjoy the high degree of literary renown which his writings had acquired for him—a renown which has since been extended and increased, rather than diminished, by the lapse of time.

As for Xenophon, the other great historian of Cyrus, it has already been said that he was a military commander, and his life was accord-

ingly spent in a very different manner from
that of his great competitor for historic fame.
He was born at Athens, about thirty years after
the birth of Herodotus, so that he was but a
child while Herodotus was in the midst of his
career.   When he was about twenty-two years
of age, he joined a celebrated military expedition which was formed in Greece, for the purpose of proceeding to Asia Minor to enter into
the service of the governor of that country.
The name of this governor was Cyrus ; and to
distinguish him from Cyrus the Great, whose
history is to form the subject of this volume,
and who lived about one hundred and fifty years
before him, he is commonly called Cyrus the
Younger.

This expedition was headed by a Grecian
general named Clearchus.   The soldiers and
the subordinate officers of the expedition did
not know for what special service it was designed, as Cyrus had a treasonable and guilty
object in view, and he kept it accordingly concealed, even from the agents who were to aid
him in the execution of it.   His plan was to
make war upon and dethrone his brother Artaxerxes, then king of Persia, and consequently
his sovereign.   Cyrus was a very young man,

but he was a man of a very energetic and accomplished character, and of unbounded ambition When his father died, it was arranged
that Artaxerxes, the older son, should succeed
him Cyrus was extremely unwilling to submit to this supremacy of his brother. His mother was an artful and unprincipled woman, and
Cyrus, being the youngest of her children, was
her favorite. She encouraged him in his ambitious designs ; and so desperate was Cyrus
himself in his determination to accomplish
them, that it is said he attempted to assassinate his brother on the day of his coronation.
His attempt was discovered, and it failed. His
brother, however, instead of punishing him for
the treason, had the generosity to pardon him,
and sent him to his government in Asia Minor.
Cyrus immediately turned all his thoughts to
the plan of raising an army and making war
upon his brother, in order to gain forcible possession of his throne. That he might have a
plausible pretext for making the necessary military preparations, he pretended to have a quarrel
with one of his neighbors, and wrote, hypocrit-
ically, many letters to the king, affecting solicitude for his safety, and asking aid. The
king was thus deceived, and made no prepara

tions to resist the force which Cyrus was assembling, not having the remotest suspicion
that its destiny was Babylon.

The auxiliary army which came from Greece,
to enter into Cyrus's service under these circumstances, consisted of about thirteen thousand men. He had, it was said, a hundred
thousand men besides; but so celebrated were
the Greeks in those days for their courage,
their discipline, their powers of endurance, and
their indomitable tenacity and energy, that Cyrus very properly considered this corps as the
flower of his army. Xenophon was one of the
younger Grecian generals. The army crossed
the Hellespont, and entered Asia Minor, and,
passing across the country, reached at last the
famous pass of Cilicia, in the southwestern part
of the country—a narrow defile between the
mountains and the sea, which opens the only
passage in that quarter toward the Persian regions beyond. Here the suspicions which the
Greeks had been for some time inclined to feel,
that they were going to make war upon the
Persian monarch himself, were confirmed, and
they refused to proceed. Their unwillingness,
however, did not arise from any compunctions
of conscience about the guilt of treason, or the

wickedness of helping an ungrateful and unprincipled wretch, whose forfeited life had once
been given to him by his brother, in making
war upon and destroying his benefactor. Soldiers have never, in any age of the world, any
thing to do with compunctions of conscience
in respect to the work which their commanders give them to perform. The Greeks were
perfectly willing to serve in this or in any other
undertaking; but, since it was rebellion and
treason that was asked of them, they considered it as specially hazardous, and so they concluded that they were entitled to extra pay.
Cyrus made no objection to this demand; an
arrangement was made accordingly, and the
army went on.

Artaxerxes assembled suddenly the whole
force of his empire on the plains of Babylon—
an immense army, consisting, it is said, of over
a million of men. Such vast forces occupy,
necessarily, a wide extent of country, even
when drawn up in battle array. So great, in
fact, was the extent occupied in this case, that
the Greeks, who conquered all that part of the
king's forces which was directly opposed to
them, supposed, when night came, at the close
of the day of battle, that Cyrus had been every

where victorious; and they were only unde-
ceived when, the next day, messengers came
from the Persian camp to inform them that Cyrus's whole force, excepting themselves, was
defeated and dispersed, and that Cyrus himself
was slain, and to summon them to surrender at
once and unconditionally to the conquerors.

The Greeks refused to surrender. They formed themselves immediately into a compact and
solid body, fortified themselves as well as they
could in their position, and prepared for a desperate defense. There were about ten thousand of
them left, and the Persians seem to have considered them too formidable to be attacked. The
Persians entered into negotiations with them, offering them certain terms on which they would
be allowed to return peaceably into Greece
These negotiations were protracted from day to
day for two or three weeks, the Persians treach-
erously using toward them a friendly tone, and
evincing a disposition to treat them in a liberal
and generous manner. This threw the Greeks
off their guard, and finally the Persians contrived to get Clearchus and the leading Greek generals into their power at a feast, and then they
seized and murdered them, or, as they would
perhaps term it, *executed* them as rebels and

traitors. When this was reported in the Grecian camp, the whole army was thrown at first into the utmost consternation. They found themselves two thousand miles from home, in the heart of a hostile country, with an enemy nearly a hundred times their own number close upon them, while they themselves were without provisions, without horses, without money; and there were deep rivers, and rugged mountains, and every other possible physical obstacle to be surmounted, before they could reach their own frontiers. If they surrendered to their enemies, a hopeless and most miserable slavery was their inevitable doom.

Under these circumstances, Xenophon, according to his own story, called together the surviving officers in the camp, urged them not to despair, and recommended that immediate measures should be taken for commencing a march toward Greece. He proposed that they should elect commanders to take the places of those who had been killed, and that, under their new organization, they should immediately set out on their return. These plans were adopted. He himself was chosen as the commanding general, and under his guidance the whole force was conducted safely through the count-

C

34   CYRUS THE GREAT.   [B.C. 402

Retreat of the Ten Thousand.   Xenophon's retirement

less difficulties and dangers which beset their
way, though they had to defend themselves, at
every step of their progress, from an enemy so
vastly more numerous than they, and which
was hanging on their flanks and on their rear,
and making the most incessant efforts to surround and capture them. This retreat occupied two hundred and fifteen days. It has always been considered as one of the greatest military achievements that has ever been performed It is called in history the Retreat of the
Ten Thousand. Xenophon acquired by it a
double immortality. He led the army, and thus
attained to a military renown which will never
fade ; and he afterward wrote a narrative of
the exploit, which has given him an equally
extended and permanent literary fame.

Some time after this, Xenophon returned
again to Asia as a military commander, and
distinguished himself in other campaigns. He
acquired a large fortune, too, in these wars,
and at length retired to a villa, which :.o built
and adorned magnificently, in the neighborhood
of Olympia, where Herodotus had acquired so
extended a fame by reading his histories. It
was probably, in some degree, through the influence of the success which had attended the

labors of Herodotus in this field, that Xenophon
was induced to enter it.   He devoted the later
years of his life to writing various historical
memoirs, the two most impo tant of which that
have come down to modern times are, first, the
narrative of his own expedition, under Cyrus
the Younger, and, secondly, a sort of romance
or tale founded on the history of Cyrus the
Great. This last is called the Cyropædia ; and
it is from this work, and from the history written by Herodotus, that nearly all our knowledge of the great Persian monarch is derived.

The question how far the stories which Herodotus and Xenophon have told us in relating
the history of the great Persian king are true,
is of less importance than one would at first
imagine ; for the case is one of those numerous
instances in which the narrative itself, which
genius has written, has had far greater influence on mankind than the events themselves
exerted which the narrative professes to record.
It is now far more important for us to know
what the story is which has for eighteen hundred years been read and listened to by every
generation of men, than what the actual events
were in which the tale thus told had its origin.
This consideration applies very extensively to

history, and especially to ancient history. The events themselves have long since ceased to be of any great interest or importance to readers of the present day; but the *accounts*, whether they are fictitious or real, partial or impartial, honestly true or embellished and colored, since they have been so widely circulated in every age and in every nation, and have impressed themselves so universally and so permanently in the mind and memory of the whole human race, and have penetrated into and colored the literature of every civilized people, it becomes now necessary that every well-informed man should understand. In a word, the real Cyrus is now a far less important personage to mankind than the Cyrus of Herodotus and Xenophon, and it is, accordingly, their story which the author proposes to relate in this volume. The reader will understand, therefore, that the end and aim of the work is not to guarantee an exact and certain account of Cyrus as he actually lived and acted, but only to give a true and faithful summary of the story which for the last two thousand years has been in circulation respecting him among mankind.

CHAPTER II.

THE BIRTH OF CYRUS.

THERE are records coming down to us from the very earliest times of three several kingdoms situated in the heart of Asia—Assyria, Media, and Persia, the two latter of which, at the period when they first emerge indistinctly into view, were more or less connected with and dependent upon the former. Astyages was the King of Media; Cambyses was the name of the ruling prince or magistrate of Persia. Cambyses married Mandane, the daughter of Astyages, and Cyrus was their son. In recounting the circumstances of his birth, Herodotus relates, with all seriousness, the following very extraordinary story:

While Mandane was a maiden, living at her father's palace and home in Media, Astyages awoke one morning terrified by a dream. He had dreamed of a great inundation, which over-whelmed and destroyed his capital, and sub-merged a large part of his kingdom. The great rivers of that country were liable to very de-

structive floods, and there would have been nothing extraordinary or alarming in the king's imagination being haunted, during his sleep, by the
image of such a calamity, were it not that, in
this case, the deluge of water which produced
such disastrous results seemed to be, in some
mysterious way, connected with his daughter,
so that the dream appeared to portend some
great calamity which was to originate in her.
He thought it perhaps indicated that after her
marriage she should have a son who would rebel against him and seize the supreme power,
thus overwhelming his kingdom as the inundation had done which he had seen in his dream.

To guard against this imagined danger, Astyages determined that his daughter should not
be married in Media, but that she should be
provided with a husband in some foreign land,
so as to be taken away from Media altogether.
He finally selected Cambyses, the king of Persia, for her husband.   Persia was at that time
a comparatively small and circumscribed dominion, and Cambyses, though he seems to
have been the supreme ruler of it, was very far
beneath Astyages in rank and power.   The distance between the two countries was considerable, and the institutions and customs of the

people of Persia were simple and rude, little
likely to awaken or encourage in the minds of
their princes any treasonable or ambitious designs. Astyages thought, therefore, that in
sending Mandane there to be the wife of the
king, he had taken effectual precautions to
guard against the danger portended by his
dream.

Mandane was accordingly married, and conducted by her husband to her new home. About
a year afterward her father had another dream.
He dreamed that a vine proceeded from his
daughter, and, growing rapidly and luxuriantly
while he was regarding it, extended itself over
the whole land. Now the vine being a symbol
of beneficence and plenty, Astyages might have
considered this vision as an omen of good ; still,
as it was good which was to be derived in some
way from his daughter, it naturally awakened
his fears anew that he was doomed to find a
rival and competitor for the possession of his
kingdom in Mandane's son and heir. He called together his soothsayers, related his dream to
them, and asked for their interpretation. They
decided that it meant that Mandane would have
a son who would one day become a king.

Astyages was now seriously alarmed, and he

sent for Mandane to come home, ostensibly be
cause he wished her to pay a visit to her father
and to her native land, but really for the purpose of having her in his power, that he might
destroy her child so soon as one should be born.

Mandane came to Media, and was established by her father in a residence near his palace,
and such officers and domestics were put in
charge of her household as Astyages could
rely upon to do whatever he should command.
Things being thus arranged, a few months passed away, and then Mandane's child was born.

Immediately on hearing of the event, Astyages sent for a certain officer of his court, an
unscrupulous and hardened man, who possessed, as he supposed, enough of depraved and
reckless resolution for the commission of any
crime, and addressed him as follows:

"I have sent for you, Harpagus, to commit
to your charge a business of very great importance. I confide fully in your principles of obedience and fidelity, and depend upon your doing, yourself, with your own hands, the work
that I require. If you fail to do it, or if you
attempt to evade it by putting it off upon others, you will suffer severely. I wish you to
take Mandane's child to your own house and

put him to death. You may accomplish the object in any mode you please, and you may arrange the circumstances of the burial of the body, or the disposal of it in any other way, as you think best; the essential thing is, that you see to it, yourself, that the child is killed."

Harpagus replied that whatever the king might command it was his duty to do, and that, as his master had never hitherto had occasion to censure his conduct, he should not find him wanting now. Harpagus then went to receive the infant. The attendants of Mandane had been ordered to deliver it to him. Not at all suspecting the object for which the child was thus taken away, but naturally supposing, on the other hand, that it was for the purpose of some visit, they arrayed their unconscious charge in the most highly-wrought and costly of the robes which Mandane, his mother, had for many months been interested in preparing for him, and then gave him up to the custody of Harpagus, expecting, doubtless, that he would be very speedily returned to their care.

Although Harpagus had expressed a ready willingness to obey the cruel behest of the king at the time of receiving it, he manifested, as soon as he received the child, an extreme de-

gree of anxiety and distress. He immediately
sent for a herdsman named Mitridates to come
to him. In the mean time, he took the child
home to his house, and in a very excited and
agitated manner related to his wife what had
passed. He laid the child down in the apartment, leaving it neglected and alone, while he
conversed with his wife in a hurried and anx
ious manner in respect to the dreadful situation
in which he found himself placed. She asked
him what he intended to do. He replied that he
certainly should not, himself, destroy the child.
"It is the son of Mandane," said he. "She
is the king's daughter. If the king should die,
Mandane would succeed him, and then what
terrible danger would impend over me if she
should know me to have been the slayer of her
son!" Harpagus said, moreover, that he did
not dare absolutely to disobey the orders of the
king so far as to save the child's life, and that
he had sent for a herdsman, whose pastures extended to wild and desolate forests and mount.
ains — the gloomy haunts of wild beasts and
birds of prey—intending to give the child to
him, with orders to carry it into those solitudes
and abandon it there. His name was Mitridates.

While they were speaking this herdsman

came in. He found Harpagus and his wife talking thus together, with countenances expressive of anxiety and distress, while the child, uneasy under the confinement and inconveniences of its splendid dress, and terrified at the strangeness of the scene and the circumstances around it, and perhaps, moreover, experiencing some dawning and embryo emotions of resentment at being laid down in neglect, cried aloud and incessantly. Harpagus gave the astonished herdsman his charge. He, afraid, as Harpagus had been in the presence of Astyages, to evince any hesitation in respect to obeying the orders of his superior, whatever they might be, took up the child and bore it away.

He carried it to his hut. It so happened that his wife, whose name was Spaco, had at that very time a new-born child, but it was dead. Her dead son had, in fact, been born during the absence of Mitridates. He had been extremely unwilling to leave his home at such a time, but the summons of Harpagus must, he knew, be obeyed. His wife, too, not knowing what could have occasioned so sudden and urgent a call, had to bear, all the day, a burden of anxiety and solicitude in respect to her husband, in addition to her disappointment and grief at the loss of her child. Her anxiety and grief were changed for a little time into astonishment and curiosity at seeing the beautiful babe, so magnificently dressed, which her husband brought to her, and at hearing his extraordinary story.

He said that when he first entered the house of Harpagus and saw the child lying there, and heard the directions which Harpagus gave him to carry it into the mountains and leave it to die, he supposed that the babe belonged to some of the domestics of the household, and that Harpagus wished to have it destroyed in order to be relieved of a burden. The richness, however, of the infant's dress, and the deep anxiety and sorrow which was indicated by the countenances and by the conversation of Harpagus and his wife, and which seemed altogether too earnest to be excited by the concern which they would probably feel for any servant's offspring, appeared at the time, he said, inconsistent with that supposition, and perplexed and bewildered him. He said, moreover, that in the end, Harpagus had sent a man with him a part of the way when he left the house, and that this man had given him a full explanation of the case. The child was the son of Mandane, the daugh-

ter of the king, and he was to be destroyed by
the orders of Astyages himself, for fear that at
some future period he might attempt to usurp
the throne.

They who know any thing of the feelings of
a mother under the circumstances in which
Spaco was placed, can imagine with what emotions she received the little sufferer, now nearly
exhausted by abstinence, fatigue, and fear, from
her husband's hands, and the heartfelt pleasure
with which she drew him to her bosom, to comfort and relieve him. In an hour she was, as
it were, herself his mother, and she began to
plead hard with her husband for his life.

Mitridates said that the child could not possibly be saved. Harpagus had been most earnest and positive in his orders, and he was coming himself to see that they had been executed.
He would demand, undoubtedly, to see the body
of the child, to assure himself that it was actually dead. Spaco, instead of being convinced
by her husband's reasoning, only became more
and more earnest in her desires that the child
might be saved. She rose from her couch
and clasped her husband's knees, and begged
him with the most earnest entreaties and with
many tears to grant her request. Her husband

4

was, however, inexorable. He said that if he
were to yield, and attempt to save the child
from its doom, Harpagus would most certainly know that his orders had been disobeyed,
and then their own lives would be forfeited,
and the child itself sacrificed after all, in the
end.

The thought then occurred to Spaco that
her own dead child might be substituted for the
living one, and be exposed in the mountains in
its stead. She proposed this plan, and, after
much anxious doubt and hesitation, the herdsman consented to adopt it. They took off the
splendid robes which adorned the living child,
and put them on the corpse, each equally unconscious of the change. The little limbs of
the son of Mandane were then more simply
clothed in the coarse and scanty covering which
belonged to the new character which he was
now to assume, and then the babe was restored to its place in Spaco's bosom. Mitridates
placed his own dead child, completely disguised
as it was by the royal robes it wore, in the little
basket or cradle in which the other had been
brought, and, accompanied by an attendant,
whom he was to leave in the forest to keep
watch over the body, he went away to seek

THE EXPOSURE OF THE INFANT.

some wild and desolate solitude in which to leave it exposed.

Three days passed away, during which the attendant whom the herdsman had left in the forest watched near the body to prevent its being devoured by wild beasts or birds of prey, and at the end of that time he brought it home. The herdsman then went to Harpagus to inform him that the child was dead, and, in proof that it was really so, he said that if Harpagus would come to his hut he could see the body. Harpagus sent some messenger in whom he could confide to make the observation. The herdsman exhibited the dead child to him, and he was satisfied. He reported the result of his mission to Harpagus, and Harpagus then ordered the body to be buried. The child of Mandane, whom we may call Cyrus, since that was the name which he subsequently received, was brought up in the herdsman's hut, and passed every where for Spaco's child.

Harpagus, after receiving the report of his messenger, then informed Astyages that his orders had been executed, and that the child was dead. A trusty messenger, he said, whom he had sent for the purpose, had seen the body. Although the king had been so earnest to have

D

the deed performed, he found that, after all, the knowledge that his orders had been obeyed gave him very little satisfaction. The fears, prompted by his selfishness and ambition, which had led him to commit the crime, gave place, when it had been perpetrated, to remorse for his unnatural cruelty. Mandane mourned incessantly the death of her innocent babe, and loaded her father with reproaches for having destroyed it, which he found it very hard to bear. In the end, he repented bitterly of what he had done.

The secret of the child's preservation remained concealed for about ten years. It was then discovered in the following manner:

Cyrus, like Alexander, Cæsar, William the Conqueror, Napoleon, and other commanding minds, who obtained a great ascendency over masses of men in their maturer years, evinced his dawning superiority at a very early period of his boyhood. He took the lead of his playmates in their sports, and made them submit to his regulations and decisions. Not only did the peasants' boys in the little hamlet where his reputed father lived thus yield the precedence to him, but sometimes, when the sons of men of rank and station came out from the city

to join them in their plays, even then Cyrus
was the acknowledged head.   One day the son
of an officer of King Astyages's court—his father's name was Artembaris—came out, with
other boys from the city, to join these village
boys in their sports.   They were playing *king*.
Cyrus was the king.   Herodotus says that the
other boys *chose* him as such.   It was, however,
probably such a sort of choice as that by which
kings and emperors are made among men, a
yielding more or less voluntary on the part of
the subjects to the resolute and determined energy with which the aspirant places himself
upon the throne.

During the progress of the play, a quarrel
arose between Cyrus and the son of Artemba-
is.   The latter would not obey, and Cyrus
beat him.   He went home and complained bitterly to his father.   The father went to **Asty-**
ages to protest against such an indignity offered
to his son by a peasant boy, and demanded that
the little tyrant should be punished.   Probably
far the larger portion of intelligent readers of
history consider the whole story as a romance ;
but if we look upon it as in any respect true,
we must conclude that the Median monarchy
must have been, at that time, in a very rude

and simple condition indeed, to allow of the submission of such a question as this to the personal adjudication of the reigning king.

However this may be, Herodotus states that
Artembaris went to the palace of Astyages,
taking his son with him, to offer proofs of the
violence of which the herdsman's son had been
guilty, by showing the contusions and bruises
that had been produced by the blows. "Is this
the treatment," he asked, indignantly, of the
king, when he had completed his statement,
"that my boy is to receive from the son of one
of your slaves?"

Astyages seemed to be convinced that Artembaris had just cause to complain, and he
sent for Mitridates and his son to come to him
in the city. When they arrived, Cyrus advanced into the presence of the king with that courageous and manly bearing which romance writers are so fond of ascribing to boys of noble
birth, whatever may have been the circumstances of their early training. Astyages was
much struck with his appearance and air. He,
however, sternly laid to his charge the accusa-
tion which Artembaris had brought against
him. Pointing to Artembaris's son, all bruised
and swollen as he was, he asked, "Is that the

way that you, a mere herdsman's boy, dare to
treat the son of one of my nobles ?"

The little prince looked up into his stern
judge's face with an undaunted expression of
countenance, which, considering the circumstances of the case, and the smallness of the
scale on which this embryo heroism was represented, was partly ludicrous and partly sublime.
" My lord," said he, " what I have done I am
able to justify. I did punish this boy, and I
had a right to do so. I was king, and he was
my subject, and he would not obey me. If you
think that for this I deserve punishment myself,
here I am ; I am ready to suffer it."

If Astyages had been struck with the appearance and manner of Cyrus at the commencement of the interview, his admiration was awakened far more strongly now, at hearing such
words, uttered, too, in so exalted a tone, from
such a child. He remained a long time silent.
At last he told Artembaris and his son that
they might retire. He would take the affair,
he said, into his own hands, and dispose of it in
a just and proper manner. Astyages then took
the herdsman aside, and asked him, in an earnest tone, whose boy that was, and where he
had obtained him.

Mitridates was terrified. He replied, however, that the boy was his own son, and that his mother was still living at home, in the hut where they all resided. There seems to have been something, however, in his appearance and manner, while making these assertions, which led Astyages not to believe what he said. He was convinced that there was some unexplained mystery in respect to the origin of the boy, which the herdsman was willfully withholding. He assumed a displeased and threatening air, and ordered in his guards to take Mitridates into custody. The terrified herdsman then said that he would explain all, and he accordingly related honestly the whole story.

Astyages was greatly rejoiced to find that the child was alive. One would suppose it to be almost inconsistent with this feeling that he should be angry with Harpagus for not having destroyed it. It would seem, in fact, that Harpagus was not amenable to serious censure, in any view of the subject, for he had taken what he had a right to consider very effectual measures for carrying the orders of the king into faithful execution. But Astyages seems to have been one of those inhuman monsters which the possession and long-continued exercise of

despotic power have so often made, who take a
calm, quiet, and deliberate satisfaction in tor-
turing to death any wretched victim whom they
can have any pretext for destroying, especially
if they can invent some new means of torment
to give a fresh piquancy to their pleasure.
These monsters do not act from passion. Men
are sometimes inclined to palliate great cruelties and crimes which are perpetrated under the
influence of sudden anger, or from the terrible
impulse of those impetuous and uncontrollable
emotions of the human soul which, when once
excited, seem to make men insane; but the
crimes of a tyrant are not of this kind. They
are the calm, deliberate, and sometimes carefully economized gratifications of a nature essentially malign.

When, therefore, Astyages learned that Harpagus had failed of literally obeying his command to destroy, with his own hand, the infant
which had been given him, although he was
pleased with the consequences which had resulted from it, he immediately perceived that
there was another pleasure besides that he was
to derive from the transaction, namely, that of
gratifying his own imperious and ungovernable
will by taking vengeance on him who had failed.

56   CYRUS THE GREAT. [B.C 589.

Interview between Astyages and Harpagus.   Explanation of Harpagus

even in so slight a degree, of fulfilling its dictates.   In a word, he was glad that the child
was saved, but he did not consider that that
was any reason why he should not have the
pleasure of punishing the man who saved him.

Thus, far from being transported by any sudden and violent feeling of resentment to an in-
considerate act of revenge, Astyages began,
calmly and coolly, and with a deliberate malignity more worthy of a demon than of a man,
to consider how he could best accomplish the
purpose he had in view.   When, at length, his
plan was formed, he sent for Harpagus to come
to him.   Harpagus came.   The king began
the conversation by asking Harpagus what
method he had employed for destroying the
child of Mandane, which he, the king, had delivered to him some years before.   Harpagus
replied by stating the exact truth.   He said
that, as soon as he had received the infant, he
began immediately to consider by what means
he could effect its destruction without involving
himself in the guilt of murder; that, finally,
he had determined upon employing the herdsman Mitridates to expose it in the forest till it
should perish of hunger and cold; and, in order
to be sure that the king's behest was fully

obeyed, he charged the herdsman, he said, to keep strict watch near the child till it was dead, and then to bring home the body. He had then sent a confidential messenger from his own household to see the body and provide for its interment. He solemnly assured the king, in conclusion, that this was the real truth, and that the child was actually destroyed in the manner he had described.

The king then, with an appearance of great satisfaction and pleasure, informed Harpagus that the child had not been destroyed after all, and he related to him the circumstances of its having been exchanged for the dead child of Spaco, and brought up in the herdsman's hut. He informed him, too, of the singular manner in which the fact that the infant had been pre-served, and was still alive, had been discovered. He told Harpagus, moreover, that he was greatly rejoiced at this discovery. "After he was dead, as I supposed," said he, "I bitterly repented of having given orders to destroy him I could not bear my daughter's grief, or the reproaches which she incessantly uttered against me. But the child is alive, and all is well; and I am going to give a grand entertainment as a festival of rejoicing on the occasion."

Astyages then requested Harpagus to send his son, who was about thirteen years of age, to the palace, to be a companion to Cyrus, and, inviting him very specially to come to the enter-tainment, he dismissed him with many marks of attention and honor. Harpagus went home, trembling at the thought of the imminent dan-ger which he had incurred, and of the narrow escape by which he had been saved from it. He called his son, directed him to prepare him-self to go to the king, and dismissed him with many charges in respect to his behavior, both toward the king and toward Cyrus. He related to his wife the conversation which had taken place between himself and Astyages, and she re-joiced with him in the apparently happy issue of an affair which might well have been ex-pected to have been their ruin.

The sequel of the story is too horrible to be told, and yet too essential to a right understand-ing of the influences and effects produced on human nature by the possession and exercise of despotic and irresponsible power to be omit-ted. Harpagus came to the festival. It was a grand entertainment. Harpagus was placed in a conspicuous position at the table. A great variety of dishes were brought in and set before the different guests, and were eaten without question. Toward the close of the feast, Astyages asked Harpagus what he thought of his fare. Harpagus, half terrified with some mysterious presentiment of danger, expressed himself well pleased with it. Astyages then told him there was plenty more of the same kind, and ordered the attendants to bring the basket in. They came accordingly, and uncovered a basket before the wretched guest, which contained, as he saw when he looked into it, the head, and hands, and feet of his son. Astyages asked him to help himself to whatever part he liked!

The most astonishing part of the story is yet to be told. It relates to the action of Harpagus in such an emergency. He looked as composed and placid as if nothing unusual had occurred. The king asked him if he knew what he had been eating. He said that he did; and that whatever was agreeable to the will of the king was always pleasing to him!!

It is hard to say whether despotic power exerts its worst and most direful influences on those who wield it, or on those who have it to bear; on its masters, or on its slaves.

After the first feelings of pleasure which As-

tyages experienced in being relieved from the
sense of guilt which oppressed his mind so long
as he supposed that his orders for the murder
of his infant grandchild had been obeyed, his
former uneasiness lest the child should in future years become his rival and competitor for
the possession of the Median throne, which had
been the motive originally instigating him to
the commission of the crime, returned in some
measure again, and he began to consider wheth
er it was not incumbent on him to take some
measures to guard against such a result. The
end of his deliberations was, that he concluded
to send for the magi, or soothsayers, as he had
done in the case of his dream, and obtain their
judgment on the affair in the new aspect which
it had now assumed.

When the magi had heard the king's narrative of the circumstances under which the discovery of the child's preservation had been
made. through complaints which had been pro-
ferred against him on account of the manner in
which he had exercised the prerogatives of a
king among his playmates, they decided at once
that Astyages had no cause for any further ap-
prehensions in respect to the dreams which had
disturbed him previous to his grandchild's birth

" He has been a king," they said, " and the danger is over. It is true that he has been a monarch only in play, but that is enough to satisfy and fulfill the presages of the vision. Occurrences very slight and trifling in themselves are often found to accomplish what seemed of very serious magnitude and moment, as portended. Your grandchild has been a king, and he will never reign again. You have, therefore, no further cause to fear, and may send him to his parents in Persia with perfect safety."

The king determined to adopt this advice He ordered the soothsayers, however, not to remit their assiduity and vigilance, and if any signs or omens should appear to indicate approaching danger, he charged them to give him immediate warning. This they faithfully promised to do. They felt, they said, a personal interest in doing it; for Cyrus being a Persian prince, his accession to the Median throne would involve the subjection of the Medes to the Persian dominion, a result which they wished on every account to avoid. So, promising to watch vigilantly for every indication of danger, they left the presence of the king. The king then sent for Cyrus.

It seems that Cyrus, though astonished at the great and mysterious changes which had taken place in his condition, was still ignorant of his true history. Astyages now told him that he was to go into Persia. " You will rejoin there," said he, " your true parents, who, you will find, are of very different rank in life from the herdsman whom you have lived with thus far. You will make the journey unde the charge and escort of persons that I have appointed for the purpose. They will explain to you, on the way, the mystery in which your parentage and birth seems to you at present enveloped. You will find that I was induced many years ago, by the influence of an untoward dream, to treat you injuriously. But all has ended well, and you can now go in peace to your proper home."

As soon as the preparations for the journey could be made, Cyrus set out, under the care of the party appointed to conduct him, and went to Persia. His parents were at first dumb with astonishment, and were then overwhelmed with gladness and joy at seeing their much-loved and long-lost babe reappear, as if from the dead, in the form of this tall and handsome boy, with health, intelligence, and happiness beaming in his countenance. They overwhelmed him with caresses, and the heart of Mandane, especially, was filled with pride and pleasure.

As soon as Cyrus became somewhat settled in his new home, his parents began to make arrangements for giving him as complete an education as the means and opportunities of those days afforded.

Xenophon, in his narrative of the early life of Cyrus, gives a minute, and, in some respects quite an extraordinary account of the mode of life led in Cambyses's court. The sons of all the nobles and officers of the court were educated together, within the precincts of the royal palaces, or, rather, they spent their time together there, occupied in various pursuits and avocations, which were intended to train them for the duties of future life, though there was very little of what would be considered, in modern times, as education. They were not generally taught to read, nor could they, in fact, since there were no books, have used that art if they had acquired it. The only intellectual instruction which they seem to have received was what was called learning justice. The boys had certain teachers, who explained to them, more or less formally, the general principles of

64   CYRUS THE GREAT.   [B.C. 588.

Cyrus a judge.   His decision in that capacity

right and wrong, the injunctions and prohibitions of the laws, and the obligations resulting from them, and the rules by which controversies between man and man, arising in the various relations of life, should be settled. The boys were also trained to apply these principles and rules to the cases which occurred among themselves, each acting as judge in turn, to discuss and decide the questions that arose from time to time, either from real transactions as they occurred, or from hypothetical cases invented to put their powers to the test. To stimulate the exercise of their powers, they were rewarded when they decided right, and punished when they decided wrong. Cyrus himself was punished on one occasion for a wrong decision, under the following circumstances :

A bigger boy took away the coat of a smaller boy than himself, because it was larger than his own, and gave him his own smaller coat instead. The smaller boy complained of the wrong, and the case was referred to Cyrus for his adjudication. After hearing the case, Cyrus decided that each boy should keep the coat that fitted him. The teacher condemned this as a very unjust decision. "When you are called upon," said he, "to consider a question

of what fits best, then you should determine as
you have done in this case; but when you are
appointed to decide whose each coat is, and to
adjudge it to the proper owner, then you are to
consider what constitutes right possession, and
whether he who takes a thing by force from one
who is weaker than himself, should have it, or
whether he who made it or purchased it should
be protected in his property. You have decided against law, and in favor of violence and
wrong." Cyrus's sentence was thus condemned, and he was punished for not reasoning more
soundly.

The boys at this Persian court were trained
to many manly exercises. They were taught
to wrestle and to run. They were instructed
in the use of such arms as were employed in
those times, and rendered dexterous in the use
of them by daily exercises. They were taught
to put their skill in practice, too, in hunting
excursions, which they took, by turns, with the
king, in the neighboring forest and mountains.
On these occasions, they were armed with a
bow, and a quiver of arrows, a shield, a small
sword or dagger, which was worn at the side
in a sort of scabbard, and two javelins. One
of these was intended to be thrown, the other

E

to be retained in the hand, for use in close
combat, in case the wild beast, in his despera-
tion, should advance to a personal rencounter.
These hunting expeditions were considered extremely important as a part of the system
of youthful training. They were often long
and fatiguing. The young men became inured, by means of them, to toil, and privation,
and exposure. They had to make long marches, to encounter great dangers, to engage in
desperate conflicts, and to submit sometimes
to the inconveniences of hunger and thirst, as
well as exposure to the extremes of heat and
cold, and to the violence of storms. All this
was considered as precisely the right sort of
discipline to make them good soldiers in their
future martial campaigns.

Cyrus was not, himself, at this time, old
enough to take a very active part in these se-
verer services, as they belonged to a somewhat
advanced stage of Persian education, and he
was yet not quite twelve years old. He was
a very beautiful boy, tall and graceful in form,
and his countenance was striking and expressive. He was very frank and open in his disposition and character, speaking honestly, and
without fear, the sentiments of his heart, in

any presence and on all occasions. He was extremely kind hearted, and amiable, too, in his disposition, averse to saying or doing any thing which could give pain to those around him. In fact, the openness and cordiality of his address and manners, and the unaffected ingenuousness and sincerity which character- ized his disposition, made him a universal fa- vorite. His frankness, his childish simplicity, his vivacity, his personal grace and beauty, and his generous and self-sacrificing spirit, rendered him the object of general admiration through- out the court, and filled Mandane's heart with maternal gladness and pride.

68   Cyrus the Great   [B.C. 587

Astyages sends for Cyrus.   Cyrus goes to Media

Chapter III.

The Visit to Media.

WHEN Cyrus was about twelve years old,
if the narrative which Xenophon gives of
his history is true, he was invited by his grandfather Astyages to make a visit to Media.   As
he was about ten years of age, according to Herodotus, when he was restored to his parents,
he could have been residing only two years in
Persia when he received this invitation.   During this period, Astyages had received, through
Mandane and others, very glowing descriptions
of the intelligence and vivacity of the young
prince, and he naturally felt a desire to see him
once more.   In fact, Cyrus's personal attract-
iveness and beauty, joined to a certain frank
and noble generosity of spirit which he seems
to have manifested in his earliest years, made
him a universal favorite at home, and the reports of these qualities, and of the various say-
ings and doings on Cyrus's part, by which his
disposition and character were revealed, awakened strongly in the mind of Astyages that kind

of interest which a grandfather is always very
prone to feel in a handsome and precocious
grandchild.

As Cyrus had been sent to Persia as soon as
his true rank had been discovered, he had had
no opportunities of seeing the splendor of royal
life in Media, and the manners and habits of
the Persians were very plain and simple.   Cyrus was accordingly very much impressed with
the magnificence of the scenes to which he was
introduced when he arrived in Media, and with
the gayeties and luxuries, the pomp and display, and the spectacles and parades in which
the Median court abounded.   Astyages himself
took great pleasure in witnessing and increasing his little grandson's admiration for these
wonders.   It is one of the most extraordinary
and beautiful of the provisions which God has
made for securing the continuance of human
happiness to the very end of life, that we can
renew, through sympathy with children, the
pleasures which, for ourselves alone, had long
since, through repetition and satiety, lost their
charm.   The rides, the walks, the flowers gathered by the road-side, the rambles among peb-
bles on the beach, the songs, the games, and
even the little picture-book of childish tales,

which have utterly and entirely lost their power to affect the mind even of middle life, directly and alone, regain their magic influence, and call up vividly all the old emotions, even to the heart of decrepit age, when it seeks these enjoyments in companionship and sympathy with children or grandchildren beloved. By giving to us this capacity for renewing our own sensitiveness to the impressions of pleasure through sympathy with childhood, God has provided a true and effectual remedy for the satiety and insensibility of age. Let any one who is in the decline of years, whose time passes but heavily away, and who supposes that nothing can awaken interest in his mind or give him pleasure, make the experiment of taking children to a ride or to a concert, or to see a menagerie or a museum, and he will find that there is a way by which he can again enjoy very highly the pleasures which he had supposed were for him forever exhausted and gone.

This was the result, at all events, in the case of Astyages and Cyrus. The monarch took a new pleasure in the luxuries and splendors which had long since lost their charm for him, in observing their influence and effect upon the mind of his little grandson. Cyrus, as we have already said, was very frank and open in his disposition, and spoke with the utmost freedom of every thing that he saw. He was, of course, a privileged person, and could always say what the feeling of the moment and his own childish conceptions prompted, without danger. He had, however, according to the account which Xenophon gives, a great deal of good sense, as well as of sprightliness and brilliancy; so that, while his remarks, through their originality and point, attracted every one's attention, there was a native politeness and sense of propriety which restrained him from saying any thing to give pain. Even when he disapproved of and condemned what he saw in the arrangements of his grandfather's court or household, he did it in such a manner—so ingenuous, good-natured, and unassuming, that it amused all and offended none.

In fact, on the very first interview which Astyages had with Cyrus, an instance of the boy's readiness and tact occurred, which impressed his grandfather very much in his favor. The Persians, as has been already remarked, were accustomed to dress very plainly, while, on the other hand, at the Median court the superior officers, and especially the king, were always very splendidly adorned. Accordingly, when

Cyrus was introduced into his grandfather's presence, he was quite dazzled with the display. The king wore a purple robe, very richly adorned, with a belt and collars, which were embroidered highly, and set with precious stones. He had bracelets, too, upon his wrists, of the most costly character. He wore flowing locks of artificial hair, and his face was painted, after the Median manner. Cyrus gazed upon this gay spectacle for a few moments in silence, and then exclaimed, "Why, mother! what a handsome man my grandfather is!"

Such an exclamation, of course, made great amusement both for the king himself and for the others who were present; and at length, Mandane, somewhat indiscreetly, it must be confessed, asked Cyrus which of the two he thought the handsomest, his father or his grandfather. Cyrus escaped from the danger of deciding such a formidable question by saying that his father was the handsomest man in Persia, but his grandfather was the handsomest of all the Medes he had ever seen. Astyages was even more pleased by this proof of his grandson's adroitness and good sense than he had been with the compliment which the boy had paid to him; and thenceforward Cyrus became an established favorite, and did and said, in his grandfather's presence, almost whatever he pleased.

When the first childish feelings of excitement and curiosity had subsided, Cyrus seemed to attach very little value to the fine clothes and gay trappings with which his grandfather was disposed to adorn him, and to all the other external marks of parade and display, which were generally so much prized among the Medes. He was much more inclined to continue in his former habits of plain dress and frugal means than to imitate Median ostentation and luxury. There was one pleasure, however, to be found in Media, which in Persia he had never enjoyed, that he prized very highly. That was the pleasure of learning to ride on horseback. The Persians, it seems, either because their country was a rough and mountainous region, or for some other cause, were very little accustomed to ride. They had very few horses, and there were no bodies of cavalry in their armies. The young men, therefore, were not trained to the art of horsemanship. Even in their hunting excursions they went always on foot, and were accustomed to make long marches through the forests and among the

mountains in this manner, loaded heavily, too,
all the time, with the burden of arms and pro·
visions which they were obliged to carry.   It
was, therefore, a new pleasure to Cyrus to
mount a horse.   Horsemanship was a great art
among the Medes.   Their horses were beautiful
and fleet, and splendidly caparisoned.   Astyages
provided for Cyrus the best animals which could
be procured, and the boy was very proud and
happy in exercising himself in the new accomplishment which he thus had the opportunity
to acquire.   To ride is always a great source
of pleasure to boys; but in that period of the
world, when physical strength was so much
more important and more highly valued than
at present, horsemanship was a vastly greater
source of gratification than it is now.   Cyrus
felt that he had, at a single leap, quadrupled
his power, and thus risen at once to a far higher
rank in the scale of being than he had occupied
before; for, as soon as he had once learned to
be at home in the saddle, and to subject the
spirit and the power of his horse to his own
will, the courage, the strength, and the speed
of the animal became, in fact, almost personal
acquisitions of his own.   He felt, accordingly,
when he was galloping over the plains, or pur·

suing deer in the park, or running over the race-course with his companions, as if it was some newly-acquired strength and speed of his own that he was exercising, and which, by some magic power, was attended by no toilsome exertion, and followed by no fatigue.

The various officers and servants in Astyages's household, as well as Astyages himself, soon began to feel a strong interest in the young prince. Each took a pleasure in explaining to him what pertained to their several departments, and in teaching him whatever he desired to learn. The attendant highest in rank in such a household was the cup-bearer. He had the charge of the tables and the wine, and all the general arrangements of the palace seem to have been under his direction. The cup-bearer in Astyages's court was a Sacian. He was, however, less a friend to Cyrus than the rest. There was nothing within the range of his official duties that he could teach the boy; and Cyrus did not like his wine. Besides, when Astyages was engaged, it was the cup-bearer's duty to guard him from interruption, and at such times he often had occasion to restrain the young prince from the liberty of entering his grandfather's apartments as often as he pleased.

At one of the entertainments which Astyages gave in his palace, Cyrus and Mandane were invited; and Astyages, in order to gratify the young prince as highly as possible, set before him a great variety of dishes—meats, and sauces, and delicacies of every kind—all served in costly vessels, and with great parade and ceremony. He supposed that Cyrus would have been enraptured with the luxury and splendor of the entertainment. He did not, however, seem much pleased. Astyages asked him the reason, and whether the feast which he saw before him was not a much finer one than he had been accustomed to see in Persia. Cyrus said, in reply, that it seemed to him to be very troublesome to have to eat a little of so many separate things. In Persia they managed, he thought, a great deal better. "And how do you manage in Persia?" asked Astyages. "Why, in Persia," replied Cyrus, "we have plain bread and meat, and eat it when we are hungry; so we get health and strength, and have very little trouble." Astyages laughed at this simplicity, and told Cyrus that he might, if he preferred it, live on plain bread and meat while he remained in Media, and then he would return to Persia in as good health as he came.

B.C. 587.]   VISIT TO MEDIA.   **77**

Cyrus and the Sacian cup-bearer.   Cyrus slights him.

Cyrus was satisfied; he, however, asked his grandfather if he would give him all those things which had been set before him, to dispose of as he thought proper; and on his grandfather's assenting, he began to call the various attendants up to the table, and to distribute the costly dishes to them, in return, as he said, for their various kindnesses to him. "This," said he to one, "is for you, because you take pains to teach me to ride; this," to another, "for you, because you gave me a javelin; this to you, because you serve my grandfather well and faithfully; and this to you, because you honor my mother." Thus he went on until he had distributed all that he had received, though he omitted, as it seemed designedly, to give any thing to the Sacian cup-bearer. This Sacian being an officer of high rank, of tall and handsome figure, and beautifully dressed, was the most conspicuous attendant at the feast, and could not, therefore, have been accidentally passed by. Astyages accordingly asked Cyrus why he had not given any thing to the Sacian —the servant whom, as he said, he liked better than all the others.

"And what is the reason," asked Cyrus, in reply, "that this Sacian is such a favorite with you?"

" Have you not observed," replied Astyages,
" how gracefully and elegantly he pours out
the wine for me, and then hands me the cup ?"

The Sacian was, in fact, uncommonly ac
complished in respect to the personal grace and
dexterity for which cup-bearers in those days
were most highly valued, and which constitute,
in fact, so essential a part of the qualifications
of a master of ceremonies at a royal court in
every age.   Cyrus, however, instead of yielding
to this argument, said, in reply, that he could
come into the room and pour out the wine as
well as the Sacian could do it, and he asked his
grandfather to allow him to try.   Astyages consented.   Cyrus then took the goblet of wine,
and went out.   In a moment he came in again,
stepping grandly, as he entered, in mimicry of
the Sacian, and with a countenance of assumed
gravity and self-importance, which imitated so
well the air and manner of the cup-bearer as
greatly to amuse the whole company assem
bled.   Cyrus advanced thus toward the king,
and presented him with the cup, imitating, with
the grace and dexterity natural to childhood,
all the ceremonies which he had seen the cup-
bearer himself perform, except that of tasting
the wine.   The king and Mandane laughed

heartily. Cyrus then, throwing off his assumed character, jumped up into his grandfather's lap and kissed him, and turning to the cup-bearer, he said, "Now, Sacian, you are ruined. I shall get my grandfather to appoint me in your place. I can hand the wine as well as you, and without tasting it myself at all."

"But why did you not taste it?" asked Astyages; "you should have performed that part of the duty as well as the rest."

It was, in fact, a very essential part of the duty of a cup-bearer to taste the wine that he offered before presenting it to the king. He did this, however, not by putting the cup to his lips, but by pouring out a little of it into the palm of his hand. This custom was adopted by these ancient despots to guard against the danger of being poisoned; for such a danger would of course be very much diminished by requiring the officer who had the custody of the wine, and without whose knowledge no foreign substance could well be introduced into it, always to drink a portion of it himself immediately before tendering it to the king.

To Astyages's question why he had not tasted the wine, Cyrus replied that he was afraid it was poisoned. "What led you to imagine that

it was poisoned?" asked his grandfather. "Because," said Cyrus, "it was poisoned the other
day, when you made a feast for your friends,
on your birth-day. I knew by the effects. It
made you all crazy. The things that you do
not allow us boys to do, you did yourselves,
for you were very rude and noisy; you all
bawled together, so that nobody could hear or
understand what any other person said. Pres-
ently you went to singing in a very ridiculous
manner, and when a singer ended his song, you
applauded him, and declared that he had sung
admirably, though nobody had paid attention.
You went to telling stories, too, each one of
his own accord, without succeeding in making
any body listen to him. Finally, you got up
and began to dance, but it was out of all rule
and measure; you could not even stand erect
and steadily. Then, you all seemed to forget
who and what you were. The guests paid no
regard to you as their king, but treated you in
a very familiar and disrespectful manner, and
you treated them in the same way; so I thought
that the wine that produced these effects must
have been poisoned."

Of course, Cyrus did not seriously mean that
he thought the wine had been actually poison-

ed. He was old enough to understand its nature and effects. He undoubtedly intended his reply as a playful satire upon the intemperate excesses of his grandfather's court.

"But have not you ever seen such things before?" asked Astyages. "Does not your father ever drink wine until it makes him merry?"

"No," replied Cyrus, "indeed he does not. He drinks only when he is thirsty, and then only enough for his thirst, and so he is not harmed." He then added, in a contemptuous tone, "He has no Sacian cup-bearer, you may depend, about *him*."

"What is the reason, my son," here asked Mandane, "why you dislike this Sacian so much?"

"Why, every time that I want to come and see my grandfather," replied Cyrus, "this teazing man always stops me, and will not let me come in. I wish, grandfather, you would let me have the rule over him just for three days."

"Why, what would you do to him?" asked Astyages.

"I would treat him as he treats me now," replied Cyrus. "I would stand at the door, as he does when I want to come in, and when he was coming for his dinner, I would stop him

F

and say, 'You can not come in now : he is busy with some men.'"

In saying this, Cyrus imitated, in a very ludicrous manner, the gravity and dignity of the Sacian's air and manner.

"Then," he continued, "when he came to supper, I would say, 'He is bathing now; you must come some other time ;' or else, 'He is going to sleep, and you will disturb him.' So I would torment him all the time, as he now torments me, in keeping me out when I want to come and see you."

Such conversation as this, half playful, half earnest, of course amused Astyages and Mandane very much, as well as all the other listeners. There is a certain charm in the simplicity and confiding frankness of childhood, when it is honest and sincere, which in Cyrus's case was heightened by his personal grace and beauty He became, in fact, more and more a favorite the longer he remained. At length, the indulgence and the attentions which he received began to produce, in some degree, their usual injurious effects. Cyrus became too talkative, and sometimes he appeared a little vain. Still, there was so much true kindness of heart, such consideration for the feelings of others, and so

respectful a regard for his grandfather, his mother, and his uncle,* that his faults were over-
looked, and he was the life and soul of the company in all the social gatherings which took
place in the palaces of the king.

At length the time arrived for Mandane to
return to Persia. Astyages proposed that she
should leave Cyrus in Media, to be educated
there under his grandfather's charge. Mandane
replied that she was willing to gratify her father in every thing, but she thought it would
be very hard to leave Cyrus behind, unless he
was willing, of his own accord, to stay. Astyages then proposed the subject to Cyrus himself. "If you will stay," said he, "the Sacian
shall no longer have power to keep you from
coming in to see me; you shall come whenever
you choose. Then, besides, you shall have the
use of all my horses, and of as many more as
you please, and when you go home at last you
shall take as many as you wish with you.

---

* The uncle here referred to was Mandane's brother. His
name was Cyaxares. He was at this time a royal prince, the
heir apparent to the throne. He figures very conspicuously
in the subsequent portions of Xenophon's history as Astyages's successor on the throne. Herodotus does not mention
him at all, but makes Cyrus himself the direct successor of
Astyages

Then you may have all the animals in the park
to hunt.   You can pursue them on horseback,
and shoot them with bows and arrows, or kill
them with javelins, as men do with wild beasts
in the woods.   I will provide boys of your own
age to play with you, and to ride and hunt with
you, and will have all sorts of arms made of
suitable size for you to use; and if there is
any thing else that you should want at any
time, you will only have to ask me for it, and
I will immediately provide it."

The pleasure of riding and of hunting in the
park was very captivating to Cyrus's mind, and
he consented to stay.   He represented to his
mother that it would be of great advantage to
him, on his final return to Persia, to be a skill-
ful and powerful horseman, as that would at
once give him the superiority over all the Persian youths, for they were very little accustomed to ride.   His mother had some fears lest, by
too long a residence in the Median court, her
son should acquire the luxurious habits, and
proud and haughty manners, which would be
constantly before him in his grandfather's example; but Cyrus said that his grandfather,
being imperious himself, required all around
him to be submissive, and that Mandane need

not fear but that he would return at last as du-
tiful and docile as ever. It was decided, therefore, that Cyrus should stay, while his mother,
bidding her child and her father farewell, went
back to Persia.

After his mother was gone, Cyrus endear-
ed himself very strongly to all persons at his
grandfather's court by the nobleness and generosity of character which he evinced, more and
more, as his mind was gradually developed.
He applied himself with great diligence to acquiring the various accomplishments and arts
then most highly prized, such as leaping, vault-
ing, racing, riding, throwing the javelin, and
drawing the bow. In the friendly contests
which took place among the boys, to test their
comparative excellence in these exercises, Cyrus would challenge those whom he knew to be
superior to himself, and allow them to enjoy
the pleasure of victory, while he was satisfied,
himself, with the superior stimulus to exertion
which he derived from coming thus into comparison with attainments higher than his own.
He pressed forward boldly and ardently, undertaking every thing which promised to be, by
any possibility, within his power ; and, far from
being disconcerted and discouraged at his mis-

takes and failures, he always joined merrily in
the 'augh which they occasioned, and renewed
his attempts with as much ardor and alacrity as before. Thus he made great and rapid
progress, and learned first to equal and then
to surpass one after another of his companions, and all without exciting any jealousy or
envy.

It was a great amusement both to him and
to the other boys, his playmates, to hunt the
animals in the park, especially the deer. The
park was a somewhat extensive domain, but
the animals were soon very much diminished
by the slaughter which the boys made among
them.   Astyages endeavored to supply their
places by procuring more.   At length, however, all the sources of supply that were con-
veniently at hand were exhausted; and Cyrus,
then finding that his grandfather was put to no
little trouble to obtain tame animals for his
park, proposed, one day, that he should be allowed to go out into the forests, to hunt the
wild beasts with the men. "There are animals enough there, grandfather," said Cyrus,
"and I shall consider them all just as if you
had procured them expressly for me."

In fact, by this time Cyrus had grown up to be

a tall and handsome young man, with strength and vigor sufficient, under favorable circumstances, to endure the fatigues and exposures of real hunting. As his person had become developed, his mind and manners, too, had undergone a change. The gayety, the thoughtfulness, the self-confidence, and talkative vivacity of his childhood had disappeared, and he was fast becoming reserved, sedate, deliberate, and cautious. He no longer entertained his grandfather's company by his mimicry, his repartees, and his childish wit. He was silent; he observed, he listened, he shrank from publicity, and spoke, when he spoke at all, in subdued and gentle tones. Instead of crowding forward eagerly into his grandfather's presence on all occasions, seasonable and unseasonable, as he had done before, he now became, of his own accord, very much afraid of occasioning trouble or interruption. He did not any longer need a Sacian to restrain him, but became, as Xenophon expresses it, a Sacian to himself, taking great care not to go into his grandfather's apartments without previously ascertaining that the king was disengaged; so that he and the Sacian now became very great friends.

This being the state of the case, Astyages

consented that Cyrus should go out with his son
Cyaxares into the forests to hunt at the next
opportunity.   The party set out, when the time
arrived, on horseback, the hearts of Cyrus and
his companions bounding, when they mounted
their steeds, with feelings of elation and pride.
There were certain attendants and guards appointed to keep near to Cyrus, and to help him
in the rough and rocky parts of the country,
and to protect him from the dangers to which,
if left alone, he would doubtless have been exposed.   Cyrus talked with these attendants, as
they rode along, of the mode of hunting, of the
difficulties of hunting, the characters and the
habits of the various wild beasts, and of the
dangers to be shunned.   His attendants told
him that the dangerous beasts were bears, lions,
tigers, boars, and leopards; that such animals
as these often attacked and killed men, and that
he must avoid them; but that stags, wild goats,
wild sheep, and wild asses were harmless, and
that he could hunt such animals as they as
much as he pleased.   They told him, moreover,
that steep, rocky, and broken ground was more
dangerous to the huntsman than any beasts,
however ferocious; for riders, off their guard,
driving impetuously over such ways, were often

CYRUS'S HUNTING.

thrown from their horses, or fell with them over precipices or into chasms, and were killed.

Cyrus listened very attentively to these in structions, with every disposition to give heed to them; but when he came to the trial, he found that the ardor and impetuosity of the chase drove all considerations of prudence wholly from his mind. When the men got into the forest, those that were with Cyrus roused a stag, and all set off eagerly in pursuit, Cyrus at the head. Away went the stag over rough and dangerous ground. The rest of the party turned aside, or followed cautiously, while Cyrus urged his horse forward in the wildest excitement, thinking of nothing, and seeing nothing but the stag bounding before him. The horse came to a chasm which he was obliged to leap. But the distance was too great; he came down upon his knees, threw Cyrus violently forward almost over his head, and then, with a bound and a scramble, recovered his feet and went on. Cyrus clung tenaciously to the horse's mane, and at length succeeded in getting back to the saddle, though, for a moment, his life was in the most imminent danger. His attendants were extremely terrified, though he himself seemed to experience no feeling but the

pleasurable excitement of the chase ; for, as
soon as the obstacle was cleared, he pressed on
with new impetuosity after the stag, overtook
him, and killed him with his javelin. Then,
alighting from his horse, he stood by the side of
his victim, to wait the coming up of the party,
his countenance beaming with an expression
of triumph and delight.

His attendants, however, on their arrival,
instead of applauding his exploit, or seeming to
share his pleasure, sharply reproved him for his
recklessness and daring. He had entirely disregarded their instructions, and they threatened
to report him to his grandfather. Cyrus looked
perplexed and uneasy. The excitement and
the pleasure of victory and success were struggling in his mind against his dread of his grandfather's displeasure. Just at this instant he
heard a new halloo. Another party in the
neighborhood had roused fresh game. All Cyrus's returning sense of duty was blown at once
to the winds. He sprang to his horse with a
shout of wild enthusiasm, and rode off toward
the scene of action. The game which had been
started, a furious wild boar, just then issued
from a thicket directly before him. Cyrus, instead of shunning the danger, as he ought to

have done, in obedience to the orders of those
to whom his grandfather had intrusted him,
dashed on to meet the boar at full speed, and
aimed so true a thrust with his javelin against
the beast as to transfix him in the forehead.
The boar fell, and lay upon the ground in dying
struggles, while Cyrus's heart was filled with
joy and triumph even greater than before.

When Cyaxares came up, he reproved Cyrus
anew for running such risks. Cyrus received
the reproaches meekly, and then asked Cyaxares to give him the two animals that he had
killed; he wanted to carry them home to his
grandfather.

"By no means," said Cyaxares; "your grandfather would be very much displeased to know
what you had done. He would not only condemn you for acting thus, but he would reprove
us too, severely, for allowing you to do so."

"Let him punish me," said Cyrus, "if he
wishes, after I have shown him the stag and
the boar, and you may punish me too, if you
think best; but do let me show them to him."

Cyaxares consented, and Cyrus made arrangements to have the bodies of the beasts
and the bloody javelins carried home. Cyrus
then presented the carcasses to his grandfather,

7

saying that it was some game which he had
taken for him.   The javelins he did not exhibit
directly, but he laid them down in a place
where his grandfather would see them.   Astyages thanked him for his presents, but he said
he had no such need of presents of game as to
wish his grandson to expose himself to such imminent dangers to take it.

"Well, grandfather," said Cyrus, "if you do
not want the meat, give it to me, and I will
divide it among my friends."   Astyages agreed
to this, and Cyrus divided his booty among his
companions, the boys, who had before hunted
with him in the park.   They, of course, took
their several portions home, each one carrying
with his share of the gift a glowing account of
the valor and prowess of the giver.   It was not
generosity which led Cyrus thus to give away
the fruits of his toil, but a desire to widen and
extend his fame.

When Cyrus was about fifteen or sixteen
years old, his uncle Cyaxares was married,
and, in celebrating his nuptials, he formed a
great hunting party, to go to the frontiers between Media and Assyria to hunt there, where
it was said that game of all kinds was very
plentiful, as it usually was, in fact, in those

days, in the neighborhood of disturbed and un-
settled frontiers.   The very causes which made
such a region as this a safe and frequented
haunt for wild beasts, made it unsafe for men,
and Cyaxares did not consider it prudent to
venture on his excursion without a considerable
force to attend him.   His hunting party formed,
therefore, quite a little army.   They set out
from home with great pomp and ceremony, and
proceeded to the frontiers in regular organization and order, like a body of troops on a march.
There was a squadron of horsemen, who were to
hunt the beasts in the open parts of the forest,
and a considerable detachment of light-armed
footmen also, who were to rouse the game, and
drive them out of their lurking places in the
glens and thickets.   Cyrus accompanied this
expedition.

When Cyaxares reached the frontiers, he
concluded, instead of contenting himself and his
party with hunting wild beasts, to make an
incursion for plunder into the Assyrian territory, that being, as Zenophon expresses it, a
more noble enterprise than the other.   The nobleness, it seems, consisted in the greater immi-
nence of the danger, in having to contend with
armed men instead of ferocious brutes, and in

the higher value of the prizes which they would obtain in case of success. The idea of there being any injustice or wrong in this wanton and unprovoked aggression upon the territories of a neighboring nation seems not to have entered the mind either of the royal robber himself or of his historian.

Cyrus distinguished himself very conspicuously in this expedition, as he had done in the hunting excursion before; and when, at length, this nuptial party returned home, loaded with booty, the tidings of Cyrus's exploits went to Persia. Cambyses thought that if his son was beginning to take part, as a soldier, in military campaigns, it was time for him to be recalled. He accordingly sent for him, and Cyrus began to make preparations for his return.

The day of his departure was a day of great sadness and sorrow among all his companions in Media, and, in fact, among all the members of his grandfather's household. They accompanied him for some distance on his way, and took leave of him, at last, with much regret and many tears. Cyrus distributed among them, as they left him, the various articles of value which he possessed, such as his arms, and ornaments of various kinds, and costly articles of dress. He gave his Median robe, at last, to a certain youth whom he said he loved the best of all. The name of this special favorite was Araspes. As these his friends parted from him, Cyrus took his leave of them, one by one, as they returned, with many proofs of his affection for them, and with a very sad and heavy heart.

The boys and young men who had received these presents took them home, but they were so valuable, that they or their parents, supposing that they were given under a momentary impulse of feeling, and that they ought to be returned, sent them all to Astyages. Astyages sent them to Persia, to be restored to Cyrus. Cyrus sent them all back again to his grandfather, with a request that he would distribute them again to those to whom Cyrus had originally given them, "which," said he, "grandfather, you must do, if you wish me ever to come to Media again with pleasure and not with shame."

Such is the story which Xenophon gives of Cyrus's visit to Media, and in its romantic and incredible details it is a specimen of the whole narrative which this author has given of his hero's life. It is not, at the present day, supposed

G

that these, and the many similar stories with which Xenophon's books are filled, are true histo‧ry. It is not even thought that Xenophon real‧ly intended to offer his narrative as history, but rather as an historical romance—a fiction found‧ed on fact, written to amuse the warriors of his times, and to serve as a vehicle for inculcating such principles of philosophy, of morals, and of military science as seemed to him worthy of the attention of his countrymen. The story has no air of reality about it from beginning to end, but only a sort of poetical fitness of one part to another, much more like the contrived coincidences of a romance writer than like the real events and transactions of actual life. A very large portion of the work consists of long discourses on military, moral, and often meta‧physical philosophy, made by generals in coun‧cil, or commanders in conversation with each other when going into battle. The occurrences and incidents out of which these conversations arise always take place just as they are wanted, and arrange themselves in a manner to produce the highest dramatic effect; like the stag, the broken ground, and the wild boar in Cyrus's hunting, which came, one after another, to fur‧nish the hero with poetical occasions for display‧

ing his juvenile bravery, and to produce the most picturesque and poetical grouping of incidents and events. Xenophon too, like other writers of romances, makes his hero a model of military virtue and magnanimity, according to the ideas of the times. He displays superhuman sagacity in circumventing his foes, he performs prodigies of valor, he forms the most sentimental attachments, and receives with a romantic confidence the adhesions of men who come over to his side from the enemy, and who, being traitors to old friends, would seem to be only worthy of suspicion and distrust in being received by new ones. Every thing, however, results well; all whom he confides in prove worthy; all whom he distrusts prove base. All his friends are generous and noble, and all his enemies treacherous and cruel. Every prediction which he makes is verified, and all his enterprises succeed; or if, in any respect, there occurs a partial failure, the incident is always of such a character as to heighten the impression which is made by the final and triumphant success.

Such being the character of Xenophon's tale, or rather drama, we shall content ourselves, after giving this specimen of it, with adding,

Herodotus more trustworthy than Xenophon.

in some subsequent chapters, a few other scenes
and incidents drawn from his narrative.   In the
mean time, in relating the great leading events
of Cyrus's life, we shall take Herodotus for our
guide, by following his more sober, and, probably, more trustworthy record.

CHAPTER IV.

CRŒSUS.

THE scene of our narrative must now be
changed, for a time, from Persia and Media, in the East, to Asia Minor, in the West,
where the great Crœsus, originally King of
Lydia, was at this time gradually extending
his empire along the shores of the Ægean Sea.
The name of Crœsus is associated in the minds
of men with the idea of boundless wealth, the
phrase " as rich as Crœsus" having been a common proverb in all the modern languages of
Europe for many centuries. It was to this
Crœsus, king of Lydia, whose story we are
about to relate, that the proverb alludes.

The country of Lydia, over which this famous sovereign originally ruled, was in the
western part of Asia Minor, bordering on the
Ægean Sea. Crœsus himself belonged to a
dynasty, or race of kings, called the Mermnadæ. The founder of this line was Gyges, who
displaced the dynasty which preceded him and
established his own by a revolution effected in

a very remarkable manner.   The circumstances were as follows:

The name of the last monarch of the old dynasty—the one, namely, whom Gyges displaced—was Candaules.   Gyges was a household servant in Candaules's family—a sort of slave, in fact, and yet, as such slaves often were in those rude days, a personal favorite and boon companion of his master.   Candaules was a dissolute and unprincipled tyrant.   He had, however, a very beautiful and modest wife, whose name was Nyssia.   Candaules was very proud of the beauty of his queen, and was always extolling it, though, as the event proved, he could not have felt for her any true and honest affection.   In some of his revels with Gyges, when he was boasting of Nyssia's charms, he said that the beauty of her form and figure, when unrobed, was even more exquisite than that of her features; and, finally, the monster, growing more and more excited, and having rendered himself still more of a brute than he was by nature by the influence of wine, declared that Gyges should see for himself.   He would conceal him, he said, in the queen's bed-chamber, while she was undressing for the night.   Gyges remonstrated very earnestly against this proposal. It would be doing the innocent queen, he said, a great wrong. He assured the king, too, that he believed fully all that he said about Nyssia's beauty, without applying such a test, and he begged him not to insist upon a proposal with which it would be criminal to comply.

The king, however, did insist upon it, and Gyges was compelled to yield. Whatever is offered as a favor by a half-intoxicated despot to an humble inferior, it would be death to refuse. Gyges allowed himself to be placed behind a half-opened door of the king's apartment, when the king retired to it for the night. There he was to remain while the queen began to un robe herself for retiring, with a strict injunction to withdraw at a certain time which the king designated, and with the utmost caution, so as to prevent being observed by the queen. Gyges did as he was ordered. The beautiful queen laid aside her garments and made her toilet for the night with all the quiet composure and confidence which a woman might be expected to feel while in so sacred and inviolable a sanctuary, and in the presence and under the guardianship of her husband. Just as she was about to retire to rest, some movement

alarmed her. It was Gyges going away. She
saw him. She instantly understood the case.
She was overwhelmed with indignation and
shame. She, however, suppressed and concealed her emotions; she spoke to Candaules in her
usual tone of voice, and he, on his part, secretly rejoiced in the adroit and successful manner
in which his little contrivance had been carried
into execution.

The next morning Nyssia sent, by some of
her confidential messengers, for Gyges to come
to her. He came, with some forebodings, perhaps, but without any direct reason for believ-
ing that what he had done had been discovered.
Nyssia, however, informed him that she knew
all, and that either he or her husband must die.
Gyges earnestly remonstrated against this decision, and supplicated forgiveness. He explained the circumstances under which the act
had been performed, which seemed, at least so
far as he was concerned, to palliate the deed.
The queen was, however, fixed and decided.
It was wholly inconsistent with her ideas of
womanly delicacy that there should be two living men who had both been admitted to her
bedchamber. "The king," she said, "by what
he has done, has forfeited his claims to me and

resigned me to you. If you will kill him, seize his kingdom, and make me your wife, all shall be well; otherwise you must prepare to die."

From this hard alternative, Gyges chose to assassinate the king, and to make the lovely object before him his own. The excitement of indignation and resentment which glowed upon her cheek, and with which her bosom was heaving, made her more beautiful than ever. "How shall our purpose be accomplished?" asked Gyges. "The deed," she replied, "shall be perpetrated in the very place which was the scene of the dishonor done to me. I will admit you into our bedchamber in my turn, and you shall kill Candaules in his bed."

When night came, Nyssia stationed Gyges again behind the same door where the king had placed him. He had a dagger in his hand. He waited there till Candaules was asleep. Then at a signal given him by the queen, he entered, and stabbed the husband in his bed. He married Nyssia, and possessed himself of the kingdom After this, he and his successors reigned for many years over the kingdom of Lydia, constituting the dynasty of the Mermnadæ, from which, in process of time, King Crœsus descended.

The successive sovereigns of this dynasty gradually extended the Lydian power over the countries around them. The name of Crœsus's father, who was the monarch that immediately preceded him, was Alyattes. Alyattes waged war toward the southward, into the territories of the city of Miletus. He made annual incursions into the country of the Milesians for plunder, always taking care, however, while he seized all the movable property that he could find, to leave the villages and towns, and all the hamlets of the laborers without injury. The reason for this was, that he did not wish to drive away the population, but to encourage them to remain and cultivate their lands, so that there might be new flocks and herds, and new stores of corn, and fruit, and wine, for him to plunder from in succeeding years. At last, on one of these marauding excursions, some fires which were accidentally set in a field spread into a neighboring town, and destroyed, among other buildings, a temple consecrated to Minerva. After this, Alyattes found himself quite unsuccessful in all his expeditions and campaigns. He sent to a famous oracle to ask the reason.

"You can expect no more success," replied

the oracle, "until you rebuild the temple that you have destroyed."

But how could he rebuild the temple? The site was in the enemy's country. His men could not build an edifice and defend themselves, at the same time, from the attacks of their foes. He concluded to demand a truce of the Milesians until the reconstruction should be completed, and he sent embassadors to Miletus, accordingly, to make the proposal.

The proposition for a truce resulted in a permanent peace, by means of a very singular stratagem which Thrasybulus, the king of Miletus, practiced upon Alyattes. It seems that Alyattes supposed that Thrasybulus had been reduced to great distress by the loss and destruction of provisions and stores in various parts of the country, and that he would soon be forced to yield up his kingdom. This was, in fact, the case; but Thrasybulus determined to disguise his real condition, and to destroy, by an artifice, all the hopes which Alyattes had formed from the supposed scarcity in the city. When the herald whom Alyattes sent to Miletus was about to arrive, Thrasybulus collected all the corn, and grain, and other provisions which he could command, and had them heaped

up in a public part of the city, where the herald
was to be received, so as to present indications
of the most ample abundance of food. He col·
lected a large body of his soldiers, too, and gave
them leave to feast themselves without restric-
tion on what he had thus gathered. Accordingly, when the herald came in to deliver his
message, he found the whole city given up to
feasting and revelry, and he saw stores of provisions at hand, which were in process of being
distributed and consumed with the most prodigal profusion. The herald reported this state
of things to Alyattes. Alyattes then gave up
all hopes of reducing Miletus by famine, and
made a permanent peace, binding himself to its
stipulations by a very solemn treaty. To celebrate the event, too, he built two temples to
Minerva instead of one.

A story is related by Herodotus of a remark·
able escape made by Arion at sea, which oc·
curred during the reign of Alyattes, the father
of Crœsus. We will give the story as Herod·
otus relates it, leaving the reader to judge for
himself whether such tales were probably true,
or were only introduced by Herodotus into his
narrative to make his histories more entertaining to the Grecian assemblies to whom he read

them. Arion was a celebrated singer. He had been making a tour in Sicily and in the southern part of Italy, where he had acquired considerable wealth, and he was now returning to Corinth. He embarked at Tarentum, which is a city in the southern part of Italy, in a Corinthian vessel, and put to sea. When the sailors found that they had him in their power, they determined to rob and murder him. They accordingly seized his gold and silver, and then told him that he might either kill himself or jump overboard into the sea. One or the other he must do. If he would kill himself on board the vessel, they would give him decent burial when they reached the shore.

Arion seemed at first at a loss how to decide in so hard an alternative. At length he told the sailors that he would throw himself into the sea, but he asked permission to sing them one of his songs before he took the fatal plunge. They consented. He accordingly went into the cabin, and spent some time in dressing himself magnificently in the splendid and richly-ornamented robes in which he had been accustomed to appear upon the stage. At length he reappeared, and took his position on the side of the ship, with his harp in his hand. He sang

8

his song, accompanying himself upon the harp,
and then, when he had finished his performance, he leaped into the sea. The seamen divided their plunder and pursued their voyage.

Arion, however, instead of being drowned,
was taken up by a dolphin that had been charm-
ed by his song, and was borne by him to Tænarus, which is the promontory formed by the
southern extremity of the Peloponnesus. There
Arion landed in safety. From Tænarus he proceeded to Corinth, wearing the same dress in
which he had plunged into the sea. On his arrival, he complained to the king of the crime
which the sailors had committed, and narrated
his wonderful escape. The king did not believe him, but put him in prison to wait until
the ship should arrive. When at last the vessel came, the king summoned the sailors into
his presence, and asked them if they knew any
thing of Arion. Arion himself had been previously placed in an adjoining room, ready to
be called in as soon as his presence was required. The mariners answered to the question
which the king put to them, that they had seen
Arion in Tarentum, and that they had left him
there. Arion was then himself called in. His
sudden appearance, clothed as he was in the

same dress in which the mariners had seen him
leap into the sea, so terrified the conscience-
stricken criminals, that they confessed their
guilt, and were all punished by the king. A
marble statue, representing a man seated upon
a dolphin, was erected at Tænarus to commemorate this event, where it remained for centuries afterward, a monument of the wonder which
Arion had achieved.

At length Alyattes died and Crœsus succeeded him. Crœsus extended still further the
power and fame of the Lydian empire, and was
for a time very successful in all his military
schemes. By looking upon the map, the reader will see that the Ægean Sea, along the
coasts of Asia Minor, is studded with islands.
These islands were in those days very fertile
and beautiful, and were densely inhabited by a
commercial and maritime people, who possessed
a multitude of ships, and were very powerful in
all the adjacent seas. Of course their land
forces were very few, whether of horse or of
foot, as the habits and manners of such a sea
going people were all foreign to modes of war
fare required in land campaigns. On the sea,
however, these islanders were supreme.

Crœsus formed a scheme for attacking these

islands and bringing them under his sway, and he began to make preparations for building and equipping a fleet for this purpose, though, of course, his subjects were as unused to the sea as the nautical islanders were to military oper- ations on the land. While he was making these preparations, a certain philosopher was visiting at his court: he was one of the seven wise men of Greece, who had recently come from the Peloponnesus. Crœsus asked him if there was any news from that country. "I heard," said the philosopher, "that the inhab- itants of the islands were preparing to invade your dominions with a squadron of ten thou- sand horse." Crœsus, who supposed that the philosopher was serious, appeared greatly pleas- ed and elated at the prospect of his sea-faring enemies attempting to meet him as a body of cavalry. "No doubt," said the philosopher, after a little pause, "you would be pleased to have those sailors attempt to contend with you on horseback; but do you not suppose that they will be equally pleased at the prospect of en- countering Lydian landsmen on the ocean?"

Crœsus perceived the absurdity of his plan, and abandoned the attempt to execute it.

Crœsus acquired the enormous wealth for

which he was so celebrated from the golden
sands of the River Pactolus, which flowed
through his kingdom. The river brought the
particles of gold, in grains, and globules, and
flakes, from the mountains above, and the ser
vants and slaves of Crœsus washed the sands,
and thus separated the heavier deposit of the
metal. In respect to the origin of the gold,
however, the people who lived upon the banks
of the river had a different explanation from the
simple one that the waters brought down the
treasure from the mountain ravines. They had
a story that, ages before, a certain king, named
Midas, rendered some service to a god, who, in
return, offered to grant him any favor that he
might ask. Midas asked that the power might
be granted him to turn whatever he touched
into gold. The power was bestowed, and Midas, after changing various objects around him
into gold until he was satisfied, began to find
his new acquisition a source of great inconven-
ience and danger. His clothes, his food, and
even his drink, were changed to gold when he
touched them. He found that he was about to
starve in the midst of a world of treasure, and
he implored the god to take back the fatal gift.
The god directed him to go and bathe in the

H

Pactolus, and he should be restored to his former condition. Midas did so, and was saved, but not without transforming a great portion of the sands of the stream into gold during the process of his restoration.

Crœsus thus attained quite speedily to a very high degree of wealth, prosperity, and renown His dominions were widely extended; his palaces were full of treasures; his court was a scene of unexampled magnificence and splendor. While in the enjoyment of all this grandeur, he was visited by Solon, the celebrated Grecian law-giver, who was traveling in that part of the world to observe the institutions and customs of different states. Crœsus received Solon with great distinction, and showed him all his treasures. At last he one day said to him, "You have traveled, Solon, over many countries, and have studied, with a great deal of attention and care, all that you have seen. I have heard great commendations of your wisdom, and I should like very much to know who, of all the persons you have ever known, has seemed to you most fortunate and happy."

The king had no doubt that the answer would be that he himself was the one.

"I think," replied Solon, after a pause, "that

Tellus, an Athenian citizen, was the most fortunate and happy man I have ever known."

"Tellus, an Athenian!" repeated Crœsus, surprised. "What was there in his case which you consider so remarkable?"

"He was a peaceful and quiet citizen of Athens," said Solon. "He lived happily with his family, under a most excellent government, enjoying for many years all the pleasures of domestic life. He had several amiable and virtuous children, who all grew up to maturity, and loved and honored their parents as long as they lived. At length, when his life was drawing toward its natural termination, a war broke out with a neighboring nation, and Tellus went with the army to defend his country. He aided very essentially in the defeat of the enemy, but fell, at last, on the field of battle. His countrymen greatly lamented his death. They buried him publicly where he fell, with every circumstance of honor."

Solon was proceeding to recount the domestic and social virtues of Tellus, and the peaceful happiness which he enjoyed as the result of them, when Crœsus interrupted him to ask who, next to Tellus, he considered the most fortunate and happy man.

Solon, after a little farther reflection, mentioned two brothers, Cleobis and Bito, private persons among the Greeks, who were celebrated for their great personal strength, and also for their devoted attachment to their mother. He related to Crœsus a story of a feat they performed on one occasion, when their mother, at the celebration of some public festival, was going some miles to a temple, in a car to be drawn by oxen. There happened to be some delay in bringing the oxen, while the mother was waiting in the car. As the oxen did not come, the young men took hold of the pole of the car themselves, and walked off at their case with the load, amid the acclamations of the spectators, while their mother's heart was filled with exultation and pride.

Crœsus here interrupted the philosopher again, and expressed his surprise that he should place private men, like those whom he had named, who possessed no wealth, or prominence, or power, before a monarch like him, occupying a station of such high authority and renown, and possessing such boundless treasures.

"Crœsus," replied Solon, "I see you now, indeed, at the height of human power and grandeur. You reign supreme over many nations.

and you are in the enjoyment of unbounded affluence. and every species of luxury and splendor. I can not, however, decide whether I am to consider you a fortunate and happy man, until I know how all this is to end. If we consider seventy years as the allotted period of life, you have a large portion of your existence yet to come, and we can not with certainty pronounce any man happy till his life is ended."

This conversation with Solon made a deep impression upon Crœsus's mind, as was afterward proved in a remarkable manner; but the impression was not a pleasant or a salutary one. The king, however, suppressed for the time the resentment which the presentation of these unwelcome truths awakened within him, though he treated Solon afterward with indifference and neglect, so that the philosopher soon found it best to withdraw.

Crœsus had two sons. One was deaf and dumb. The other was a young man of uncommon promise, and, of course, as he only could succeed his father in the government of the kingdom, he was naturally an object of the king's particular attention and care. His name was Atys. He was unmarried. He was, however, old enough to have the command of a con

siderable body of troops, and he had often distinguished himself in the Lydian campaigns. One
night the king had a dream about Atys which
greatly alarmed him. He dreamed that his
son was destined to die of a wound received
from the point of an iron spear. The king was
made very uneasy by this ominous dream. He
determined at once to take every precaution in
his power to avert the threatened danger. He
immediately detached Atys from his command
in the army, and made provision for his marriage. He then very carefully collected all
the darts, javelins, and every other iron-pointed
weapon that he could find about the palace, and
caused them to be deposited carefully in a secure place, where there could be no danger even
of an accidental injury from them.

About that time there appeared at the court
of Crœsus a stranger from Phrygia, a neighboring state, who presented himself at the palace and asked for protection. He was a prince
of the royal family of Phrygia, and his name
was Adrastus. He had had the misfortune
by some unhappy accident, to kill his brother;
his father, in consequence of it, had banished
him from his native land, and he was now home-
less, friendless, and destitute.

Crœsus received him kindly. "Your family have always been my friends," said he, "and I am glad of the opportunity to make some return by extending my protection to any member of it suffering misfortune. You shall reside in my palace, and all your wants shall be supplied. Come in, and forget the calamity which has befallen you, instead of distressing yourself with it as if it had been a crime."

Thus Crœsus received the unfortunate Adrastus into his household. After the prince had been domiciliated in his new home for some time, messengers came from Mysia, a neighboring state, saying that a wild boar of enormous size and unusual ferocity had come down from the mountains, and was lurking in the cultivated country, in thickets and glens, from which, at night, he made great havoc among the flocks and herds, and asking that Crœsus would send his son, with a band of hunters and a pack of dogs, to help them destroy the common enemy Crœsus consented immediately to send the dogs and the men, but he said that he could not send his son. "My son," he added, "has been lately married, and his time and attention are employed about other things."

When, however, Atys himself heard of this

reply, he remonstrated very earnestly against it, and begged his father to allow him to go. "What will the world think of me," said he, "if I shut myself up to these effeminate pursuits and enjoyments, and shun those dangers and toils which other men consider it their highest honor to share? What will my fellow-citizens think of me, and how shall I appear in the eyes of my wife? She will despise me."

Crœsus then explained to his son the reason why he had been so careful to avoid exposing him to danger. He related to him the dream which had alarmed him. "It is on that account," said he, "that I am so anxious about you. You are, in fact, my only son, for your speechless brother can never be my heir."

Atys said, in reply, that he was not surprised, under those circumstances, at his father's anxiety; but he maintained that this was a case to which his caution could not properly apply. "You dreamed," he said, "that I should be killed by a weapon pointed with iron; but a boar has no such weapon. If the dream had portended that I was to perish by a tusk or a tooth, you might reasonably have restrained me from going to hunt a wild beast: but iron-pointed instruments are the weapons of men, and we

B.C. 545.] CRŒSUS. 121

Atys joins the expedition.   He is killed by Adrastus

are not going, in this expedition, to contend with men."

The king, partly convinced, perhaps, by the arguments which Atys offered, and partly over-borne by the urgency of his request, finally consented to his request and allowed him to go. He consigned him, however, to the special care of Adrastus, who was likewise to accompany the expedition, charging Adrastus to keep constantly by his side, and to watch over him with the utmost vigilance and fidelity.

The band of huntsmen was organized, the dogs prepared, and the train departed. Very soon afterward, a messenger came back from the hunting ground, breathless, and with a countenance of extreme concern and terror, bringing the dreadful tidings that Atys was dead. Adrastus himself had killed him. In the ardor of the chase, while the huntsmen had surrounded the boar, and were each intent on his own personal danger while in close combat with such a monster, and all were hurling darts and javelins at their ferocious foe, the spear of Adrastus missed its aim, and entered the body of the unhappy prince. He bled to death on the spot.

Soon after the messenger had made known

these terrible tidings, the hunting train, transformed now into a funeral procession, appeared,
bearing the dead body of the king's son, and
followed by the wretched Adrastus himself, who
was wringing his hands, and crying out incessantly in accents and exclamations of despair.
He begged the king to kill him at once, over
the body of his son, and thus put an end to the
unutterable agony that he endured.   This second calamity was more, he said, than he could
bear.   He had killed before his own brother,
and now he had murdered the son of his greatest benefactor and friend.

Crœsus, though overwhelmed with anguish,
was disarmed of all resentment at witnessing
Adrastus's suffering.   He endeavored to soothe
and quiet the agitation which the unhappy man
endured, but it was in vain.   Adrastus could
not be calmed.   Crœsus then ordered the body
of his son to be buried with proper honors.   The
funeral services were performed with great and
solemn ceremonies, and when the body was interred, the household of Crœsus returned to the
palace, which was now, in spite of all its splendor, shrouded in gloom.   That night—at midnight—Adrastus, finding his mental anguish
insupportable, retired from his apartment to

the place where Atys had been buried, and killed himself over the grave.

Solon was wise in saying that he could not tell whether wealth and grandeur were to be accounted as happiness till he saw how they would end. Crœsus was plunged into inconsolable grief, and into extreme dejection and misery for a period of two years, in consequence of this calamity, and yet this calamity was only the beginning of the end.

124   Cyrus the Great. [B.C. 560

Change in the character of Cyrus.   His ambition

Chapter V.

Accession of Cyrus to the Throne.

WHILE Crœsus had thus, on his side of the River Halys—which was the stream that marked the boundary between the Lydian empire on the west and the Persian and Assyrian dominions on the east—been employed in building up his grand structure of outward magnificence and splendor, and in contending, within, against an overwhelming tide of domestic misery and woe, great changes had taken place in the situation and prospects of Cyrus. From being an artless and generous-minded child, he had become a calculating, ambitious, and aspiring man, and he was preparing to take his part in the great public contests and struggles of the day, with the same eagerness for self-aggrandizement, and the same unconcern for the welfare and happiness of others, which always characterizes the spirit of ambition and love of power.

Although it is by no means certain that what Xenophon relates of his visit to his grandfather

Astyages is meant for a true narrative of facts,
it is not at all improbable that such a visit
might have been made, and that occurrences,
somewhat similar, at least, to those which his
narrative records, may have taken place. It
may seem strange to the reader that a man who
should, at one time, wish to put his grandchild
to death, should, at another, be disposed to treat
him with such a profusion of kindness and attention. There is nothing, however, really extraordinary in this. Nothing is more fluctuat-
ing than the caprice of a despot. Man, accustomed from infancy to govern those around him
by his own impetuous will, never learns self-
control. He gives himself up to the dominion
of the passing animal emotions of the hour. It
may be jealousy, it may be revenge, it may be
parental fondness, it may be hate, it may be
love—whatever the feeling is that the various
incidents of life, as they occur, or the influences, irritating or exhilarating, which are produced by food or wine, awaken in his mind, he
follows its impulse blindly and without reserve.
He loads a favorite with kindness and caresses
at one hour, and directs his assassination the
next. He imagines that his infant grandchild
is to become his rival, and he deliberately **or**

9

ders him to be left in a gloomy forest alone, to die of cold and hunger. When the imaginary danger has passed away, he seeks amusement in making the same grandchild his plaything, and overwhelms him with favors bestowed solely for the gratification of the giver, under the influence of an affection almost as purely animal as that of a lioness for her young.

Favors of such a sort can awaken no permanent gratitude in any heart, and thus it is quite possible that Cyrus might have evinced, during the simple and guileless days of his childhood, a deep veneration and affection for his grandfather, and yet, in subsequent years, when he had arrived at full maturity, have learned to regard him simply in the light of a great political potentate, as likely as any other potentate around him to become his rival or his enemy.

This was, at all events, the result. Cyrus, on his return to Persia, grew rapidly in strength and stature, and soon became highly distinguished for his personal grace, his winning manners, and for the various martial accomplishments which he had acquired in Media and in which he excelled almost all his companions. He gained, as such princes always do, a vast ascendency over the minds of all around him. As he advanced toward maturity, his mind passed from its interest in games, and hunting, and athletic sports, to plans of war, of conquest, and of extended dominion.

In the mean time, Harpagus, though he had, at the time when he endured the horrid punishment which Astyages inflicted upon him, expressed no resentment, still he had secretly felt an extreme indignation and anger, and he had now, for fifteen years, been nourishing covert schemes and plans for revenge. He remained all this time in the court of Astyages, and was apparently his friend. He was, however, in heart a most bitter and implacable enemy. He was looking continually for a plan or prospect which should promise some hope of affording him his long-desired revenge. His eyes were naturally turned toward Cyrus. He kept up a communication with him so far as it was possible, for Astyages watched very closely what passed between the two countries, being always suspicious of plots against his government and crown. Harpagus, however, contrived to evade this vigilance in some degree. He made continual reports to Cyrus of the tyranny and misgovernment of Astyages, and of the defenselessness of the realm of Media, and he endeavored

to stimulate his rising ambition to the desire of
one day possessing for himself both the Median
and Persian throne.

In fact, Persia was not then independent of
Media. It was more or less connected with the
government of Astyages, so that Cambyses, the
chief ruler of Persia, Cyrus's father, is called
sometimes a king and sometimes a *satrap*,
which last title is equivalent to that of viceroy
or governor general. Whatever his true and
proper title may have been, Persia was a Median dependency, and Cyrus, therefore, in forming plans for gaining possession of the Median
throne, would consider himself as rather endeavoring to rise to the supreme command in his
own native country, than as projecting any
scheme for foreign conquest.

Harpagus, too, looked upon the subject in the
same light. Accordingly, in pushing forward
his plots toward their execution, he operated in
Media as well as Persia. He ascertained, by
diligent and sagacious, but by very covert inquiries, who were discontented and ill at ease
under the dominion of Astyages, and by sympa-
thizing with and encouraging them, he increas
ed their discontent and insubmission. Whenever Astyages, in the exercise of his tyranny,

inflicted an injury upon a powerful subject, Harpagus espoused the cause of the injured man, condemned, with him, the intolerable oppression of the king, and thus fixed and perpetuated his enmity. At the same time, he took pains to collect and to disseminate among the Medes all the information which he could obtain favorable to Cyrus, in respect to his talents, his character, and his just and generous spirit, so that, at length, the ascendency of Astyages, through the instrumentality of these measures, was very extensively undermined, and the way was rapidly becoming prepared for Cyrus's accession to power.

During all this time, moreover, Harpagus was personally very deferential and obsequious to Astyages, and professed an unbounded devotedness to his interests. He maintained a high rank at court and in the army, and Astyages relied upon him as one of the most obedient and submissive of his servants, without entertaining any suspicion whatever of his true designs.

At length a favorable occasion arose, as Harpagus thought, for the execution of his plans. It was at a time when Astyages had been guilty of some unusual acts of tyranny and oppression, by which he had produced extensive dissatis-

I

faction among his people.   Harpagus communi-
nicated, very cautiously, to the principal men
around him, the designs that he had long been
forming for deposing Astyages and elevating
Cyrus in his place.   He found them favorably
inclined to the plan.   The way being thus prepared, the next thing was to contrive some secret way of communicating with Cyrus.   As
the proposal which he was going to make was
that Cyrus should come into Media with as
great a force as he could command, and head
an insurrection against the government of Astyages, it would, of course, be death to him to
have it discovered.   He did not dare to trust
the message to any living messenger, for fear
of betrayal ; nor was it safe to send a letter
by any ordinary mode of transmission, lest the
letter should be intercepted by some of Astyages's spies, and thus the whole plot be discovered.   He finally adopted the following very extraordinary plan :

He wrote a letter to Cyrus, and then taking
a hare, which some of his huntsmen had caught
for him, he opened the body and concealed the
letter within.   He then sewed up the skin
again in the most careful manner, so that no
signs of the incision should remain.   He deliv-

THE SECRET CORRESPONDENCE.

ered this hare, together with some nets and other hunting apparatus, to certain trustworthy servants, on whom he thought he could rely, charging them to deliver the hare into Cyrus's own hands, and to say that it came from Harpagus, and that it was the request of Harpagus that Cyrus should open it himself and alone. Harpagus concluded that this mode of making the communication was safe; for, in case the persons to whom the hare was intrusted were to be seen by any of the spies or other persons employed by Astyages on the frontiers, they would consider them as hunters returning from the chase with their game, and would never think of examining the body of a hare, in the hands of such a party, in search after a clandestine correspondence.

The plan was perfectly successful. The men passed into Persia without any suspicion. They delivered the hare to Cyrus, with their message. He opened the hare, and found the letter. It was in substance as follows:

"It is plain, Cyrus, that you are a favorite of Heaven, and that you are destined to a great and glorious career. You could not otherwise have escaped, in so miraculous a manner, the

snares set for you in your infancy.   Astyages
meditated your death, and he took such measures to effect it as would seem to have made
your destruction sure.   You were saved by the
special interposition of Heaven.   You are aware
by what extraordinary incidents you were preserved and discovered, and what great and unusual prosperity has since attended you.   You
know, too, what cruel punishments Astyages
inflicted upon me, for my humanity in saving
you.   The time has now come for retribution.
From this time the authority and the dominions
of Astyages may be yours.   Persuade the Persians to revolt.   Put yourself at the head of an
army and march into Media.   I shall probably
myself be appointed to command the army sent
out to oppose you.   If so, we will join our forces
when we meet, and I will enter your service.
I have conferred with the leading nobles in Media, and they are all ready to espouse your
cause.   You may rely upon finding every thing
thus prepared for you here; come, therefore.
without any delay."

Cyrus was thrown into a fever of excitement
and agitation on reading this letter.   He determined to accede to Harpagus's proposal.   He

revolved in his mind for some time the measures by which he could raise the necessary
force. Of course he could not openly announce
his plan and enlist an army to effect it, for any
avowed and public movement of that kind
would be immediately made known to Astyages, who, by being thus forewarned of his enemies' designs, might take effectual measures to
circumvent them. He determined to resort to
deceit, or, as he called it, stratagem; nor did
he probably have any distinct perception of the
wrongfulness of such a mode of proceeding.
The demon of war upholds and justifies falsehood and treachery, in all its forms, on the part
of his votaries. He always applauds a forgery, a
false pretense, or a lie: he calls it a stratagem.

Cyrus had a letter prepared, in the form of a
commission from Astyages, appointing him commander of a body of Persian forces to be raised
for the service of the king. Cyrus read the
fabricated document in the public assembly of
the Persians, and called upon all the warriors
to join him. When they were organized, he
ordered them to assemble on a certain day, at
a place that he named, each one provided with
a woodman's ax. When they were thus mus-
tered, he marched them into a forest, and set

them at work to clear a piece of ground. The army toiled all day, felling the trees, and piling them up to be burned. They cleared in this way, as Herodotus states, a piece of ground eighteen or twenty furlongs in extent. Cyrus kept them thus engaged in severe and incessant toil all the day, giving them, too, only coarse food and little rest. At night he dismissed them, commanding them to assemble again the second day.

On the second day, when they came together, they found a great banquet prepared for them, and Cyrus directed them to devote the day to feasting and making merry. There was an abundance of meats of all kinds, and rich wines in great profusion. The soldiers gave themselves up for the whole day to merriment and revelry. The toils and the hard fare of the day before had prepared them very effectually to enjoy the rest and the luxuries of this festival. They spent the hours in feasting about their camp-fires and reclining on the grass, where they amused themselves and one another by relating tales, or joining in merry songs and dances. At last, in the evening, Cyrus called them together, and asked them which day they had liked the best. They replied that there was nothing at all to like in the one, and nothing to be disliked in the other. They had had, on the first day, hard work and bad fare, and on the second, uninterrupted ease and the most luxurious pleasures.

"It is indeed so," said Cyrus, "and you have your destiny in your own hands to make your lives pass like either of these days, just as you choose. If you will follow me, you will enjoy ease, abundance, and luxury. If you refuse, you must remain as you are, and toil on as you do now, and endure your present privations and hardships to the end of your days." He then explained to them his designs. He told them that although Media was a great and powerful kingdom, still that they were as good soldiers as the Medes, and with the arrangements and preparations which he had made, they were sure of victory.

The soldiers received this proposal with great enthusiasm and joy. They declared themselves ready to follow Cyrus wherever he should lead them, and the whole body immediately commenced making preparations for the expedition Astyages was, of course, soon informed of these proceedings. He sent an order to Cyrus, summoning him immediately into his presence

Cyrus sent back word, in reply, that Astyages
would probably see him sooner than he wished,
and went on vigorously with his preparations
When all was ready, the army marched, and,
crossing the frontiers, they entered into Media.

In the mean time, Astyages had collected a
large force, and, as had been anticipated by the
conspirators, he put it under the command of
Harpagus. Harpagus made known his design
of going over to Cyrus as soon as he should
meet him, to as large a portion of the army as
he thought it prudent to admit to his confidence; the rest knew nothing of the plan; and
thus the Median army advanced to meet the
invaders, a part of the troops with minds intent
on resolutely meeting and repelling their enemies, while the rest were secretly preparing to
go over at once to their side.

When the battle was joined, the honest part
of the Median army fought valian. y at first,
but soon, thunderstruck and utterly confounded
at seeing themselves abandoned and betrayed
by a large body of their comrades, they were
easily overpowered by the triumphant Persians.
Some were taken prisoners; some fled back to
Astyages; and others, following the example of
the deserters, went over to Cyrus's camp and

swelled the numbers of his train. Cyrus, thus re-enforced by the accessions he had received, and encouraged by the flight or dispersion of all who still wished to oppose him, began to advance toward the capital.

Astyages, when he heard of the defection of Harpagus and of the discomfiture of his army, was thrown into a perfect phrensy of rage and hate. The long-dreaded prediction of his dream seemed now about to be fulfilled, and the magi, who had taught him that when Cyrus had once been made king of the boys in sport, there was no longer any danger of his aspiring to regal power, had proved themselves false. They had either intentionally deceived him, or they were ignorant themselves, and in that case they were worthless impostors. Although the danger from Cyrus's approach was imminent in the extreme, Astyages could not take any measures for guarding against it until he had first gratified the despotic cruelty of his nature by taking vengeance on these false pretenders. He directed to have them all seized and brought before him, and then, having upbraided them with bitter reproaches for their false predictions, he ordered them all to be crucified.

He then adopted the most decisive measures

140 CYRUS THE GREAT. [B.C.560

Defeat and capture of Astyages.   Interview with Harpagus

for raising an army. He ordered every man capable of bearing arms to come forward, and then, putting himself at the head of the immense force which he had thus raised, he advanced to meet his enemy. He supposed, no doubt, that he was sure of victory; but he underrated the power which the discipline, the resolution, the concentration, and the terrible energy of Cyrus's troops gave to their formidable array. He was defeated. His army was totally cut to pieces, and he himself was taken prisoner.

Harpagus was present when he was taken, and he exulted in revengeful triumph over the fallen tyrant's ruin. Astyages was filled with rage and despair. Harpagus asked him what he thought now of the supper in which he had compelled a father to feed on the flesh of his child. Astyages, in reply, asked Harpagus whether he thought that the success of Cyrus was owing to what he had done. Harpagus replied that it was, and exultingly explained to Astyages the plots he had formed, and the preparations which he had made for Cyrus's invasion, so that Astyages might see that his destruction had been effected by Harpagus alone, in terrible retribution for the atrocious crime which

B.C. 560.]   ACCESSION.   141

Cyrus King of Media and Persia.   Confinement of Astyages.

he had committed so many years before, and for which the vengeance of the sufferer had slumbered, during the long interval, only to be more complete and overwhelming at last.

Astyages told Harpagus that he was a miserable wretch, the most foolish and most wicked of mankind. He was the most foolish, for having plotted to put power into another's hands which it would have been just as easy for him to have secured and retained in his own; and he was the most wicked, for having betrayed his country, and delivered it over to a foreign power, merely to gratify his own private revenge.

The result of this battle was the complete overthrow of the power and kingdom of Astyages, and the establishment of Cyrus on the throne of the united kingdom of Media and Persia. Cyrus treated his grandfather with kindness after his victory over him. He kept him confined, it is true, but it was probably that indirect and qualified sort of confinement which is all that is usually enforced in the case of princes and kings. In such cases, some extensive and often sumptuous residence is assigned to the illustrious prisoner, with grounds sufficiently extensive to afford every necessary

10

range for recreation and exercise, and with
bodies of troops for keepers, which have much
more the form and appearance of military
guards of honor attending on a prince, than of
jailers confining a prisoner. It was probably
in such an imprisonment as this that Astyages
passed the remainder of his days. The people,
having been wearied with his despotic tyranny,
rejoiced in his downfall, and acquiesced very
readily in the milder and more equitable government of Cyrus.

Astyages came to his death many years afterward, in a somewhat remarkable manner.
Cyrus sent for him to come into Persia, where
he was himself then residing. The officer who
had Astyages in charge, conducted him, on the
way, into a desolate wilderness, where he perished of fatigue, exposure, and hunger. It was
supposed that this was done in obedience to secret orders from Cyrus, who perhaps found the
charge of such a prisoner a burden. The officer, however, was cruelly punished for the act;
but even this may have been only for appearances, to divert the minds of men from all suspicion that Cyrus could himself have been an
accomplice in such a crime.

The whole revolution which has been describ-

ed in this chapter, from its first inception to its
final accomplishment, was effected in a very
short period of time, and Cyrus thus found himself very unexpectedly and suddenly elevated to
a throne.

Harpagus continued in his service, and became subsequently one of his most celebrated
generals.

Chapter VI.

The Oracles.

AS soon as Cyrus had become established on his throne as King of the Medes and Persians, his influence and power began to extend westward toward the confines of the empire of Croesus, king of Lydia. Croesus was aroused from the dejection and stupor into which the death of his son had plunged him, as related in a former chapter, by this threatening danger. He began to consider very earnestly what he could do to avert it.

The River Halys, a great river of Asia Minor, which flows northward into the Black Sea, was the eastern boundary of the Lydian empire. Croesus began to entertain the design of raising an army and crossing the Halys, to invade the empire of Cyrus, thinking that that would perhaps be safer policy than to wait for Cyrus to cross the Halys, and bring the war upon him. Still, the enterprise of invading Persia was a vast undertaking, and the responsibility great of being the aggressor in the contest. After carefully considering the subject in all its aspects, Crœsus found himself still perplexed and undecided.

The Greeks had a method of looking into futurity, and of ascertaining, as they imagined, by supernatural means, the course of future events, which was peculiar to that people; at least no other nation seems ever to have practiced it in the precise form which prevailed among them. It was by means of the oracles. There were four or five localities in the Grecian countries which possessed, as the people thought, the property of inspiring persons who visited them, or of giving to some natural object certain supernatural powers by which future events could be foretold. The three most important of these oracles were situated respectively at Delphi, at Dodona, and at the Oasis of Jupiter Ammon.

Delphi was a small town built in a sort of valley, shaped like an amphitheater, on the southern side of Mount Parnassus. Mount Parnassus is north of the Peloponnesus, not very far from the shores of the Gulf of Corinth. Delphi was in a picturesque and romantic situation, with the mountain behind it, and steep, precipitous rocks descending to the level coun-

K

try before.   These precipices answered instead
of walls to defend the temple and the town.
In very early times a cavern or fissure in the
rocks was discovered at Delphi, from which
there issued a stream of gaseous vapor, which
produced strange effects on those who inhaled
it.   It was supposed to inspire them.   People
resorted to the place to obtain the benefit of
these inspirations, and of the knowledge which
they imagined they could obtain by means of
them.   Finally, a temple was built, and a
priestess resided constantly in it, to inhale the
vapor and give the responses.   When she gave
her answers to those who came to consult the
oracle, she sat upon a sort of three-legged stool,
which was called the sacred tripod.   These
stools were greatly celebrated as a very important part of the sacred apparatus of the place.
This oracle became at last so renowned, that
the greatest potentates, and even kings, came
from great distances to consult it, and they
made very rich and costly presents at the shrine
when they came.   These presents, it was supposed, tended to induce the god who presided
over the oracle to give to those who made them
favorable and auspicious replies.   The deity that
dictated the predictions of this oracle was Apollo

B.C. 547.] THE ORACLES. 147

The oracle of Dodona. The two black doves

There was another circumstance, besides the existence of the cave, which signalized the locality where this oracle was situated. The people believed that this spot was the exact center of the earth, which of course they considered as one vast plain. There was an ancient story that Jupiter, in order to determine the central point of creation, liberated two eagles at the same time, in opposite quarters of the heavens, that they might fly toward one another, and so mark the middle point by the place of their meeting. They met at Delphi.

Another of the most celebrated oracles was at Dodona. Dodona was northwest of Delphi, in the Epirus, which was a country in the western part of what is now Turkey in Europe, and on the shores of the Adriatic Sea. The origin of the oracle at Dodona was, as the priestesses there told Herodotus, as follows: In very ancient times, two black doves were set at liberty in Thebes, which was a very venerable and sacred city of Egypt. One flew toward the north and the other toward the west. The former crossed the Mediterranean, and then continued its flight over the Peloponnesus, and over all the southern provinces of Greece, until it reached Dodona. There it alighted on a beech-tree, and said, in a human voice, that that spot was divinely appointed for the seat of a sacred oracle. The other dove flew to the Oasis of Jupiter Ammon.

There were three priestesses at Dodona in the days of Herodotus. Their names were Promenea, Timarete, and Nicandre. The answers of the oracle were, for a time, obtained by the priestesses from some appearances which they observed in the sacred beech on which the dove alighted, when the tree was agitated by the wind. In later times, however, the responses were obtained in a still more singular manner. There was a brazen statue of a man, holding a whip in his hand. The whip had three lashes, which were formed of brazen chains. At the end of each chain was an *astragalus*, as it was called, which was a row of little knots or knobs, such as were commonly appended to the lashes of whips used in those days for scourging criminals.

These heavy lashes hung suspended in the hand of the statue over a great brazen caldron, in such a manner that the wind would impel them, from time to time, against its sides, causing the caldron to ring and resound like a gong. There was, however, something in this reso nance supernatural and divine; for, though it was not loud, it was very long continued, when once the margin of the caldron was touched, however gently, by the lashes. In fact, it was commonly said that if touched in the morning, it would be night before the reverberations would have died entirely away. Such a belief could be very easily sustained among the common people; for a large, open-mouthed vessel like the Dodona caldron, with thin sides formed of sonorous metal, might be kept in a state of continual vibration by the wind alone.

They who wished to consult this oracle came with rich presents both for the priestesses and for the shrine, and when they had made the offerings, and performed the preliminary ceremonies required, they propounded their questions to the priestesses, who obtained the replies by interpreting, according to certain rules which they had formed, the sounds emitted by the mysterious gong.

The second black dove which took its flight from Thebes alighted, as we have already said, in the Oasis of Jupiter Ammon. This oasis was a small fertile spot in the midst of the deserts of Africa, west of Egypt, about a hundred miles from the Nile, and somewhat nearer than that to the Mediterranean Sea. It was first discovered in the following manner: A certain king was marching across the deserts, and his army, having exhausted their supplies of water, were on the point of perishing with thirst, when a ram mysteriously appeared, and took a position before them as their guide. They followed him, and at length came suddenly upon a green and fertile valley, many miles in length. The ram conducted them into this valley, and then suddenly vanished, and a copious fountain of water sprung up in the place where he had stood. The king, in gratitude for this divine interposition, consecrated the spot and built a temple upon it, which was called the temple of Jupiter Ammon. The dove alighted here, and ever afterward the oracles delivered by the priests of this temple were considered as divinely inspired.

These three were the most important oracles. There were, however, many others of subordinate consequence, each of which had its own peculiar ceremonies, all senseless and absurd At one there was a sort of oven-shaped cave in the rocks, the spot being inclosed by an artificial wall. The cave was about six feet wide and eight feet deep. The descent into it was by a ladder   Previously to consulting this oracle certain ceremonies were necessary, which it required several days to perform.   The applicant was to offer sacrifices to many different deities, and to purify himself in various ways. He was then conducted to a stream in the neighborhood of the oracle, where he was to be anointed and washed.   Then he drank a certain magical water, called the water of forgetfulness, which made him forget all previous sorrows and cares.   Afterward he drank of another enchanted cup, which contained the water of remembrance; this was to make him remember all that should be communicated to him in the cave.   He then descended the ladder, and received within the cave the responses of the oracle.

At another of these oracles, which was situated in Attica, the magic virtue was supposed to reside in a certain marble statue, carved in honor of an ancient and celebrated prophet, and placed in a temple.   Whoever wished to consult this oracle must abstain from wine for three days, and from food of every kind for twenty-four hours preceding the application. He was then to offer a ram as a sacrifice; and afterward, taking the skin of the ram from the

152   CYRUS THE GREAT. [B.C. 547

Crœsus puts the oracles to the test.   Manner of doing it

carcass, he was to spread it out before the statue,
and lie down upon it to sleep. The answers of
the oracle came to him in his dreams.

But to return to Crœsus. He wished to ascertain, by consulting some of these oracles,
what the result of his proposed invasion of the
dominions of Cyrus would be, in case he should
undertake it; and in order to determine which
of the various oracles were most worthy of reliance, he conceived the plan of putting them
all to a preliminary test. He effected this object in the following manner:

He dispatched a number of messengers from
Sardis, his capital, sending one to each of the
various oracles. He directed these messengers
to make their several journeys with all convenient dispatch; but, in order to provide for any
cases of accidental detention or delay, he allowed them all one hundred days to reach their
several places of destination. On the hundredth
day from the time of their leaving Sardis, they
were all to make applications to the oracles,
and inquire what Crœsus, king of Lydia, was
doing at that time. Of course he did not tell
them what he should be doing; and as the oracles themselves could not possibly know how he
was employed by any human powers, their an-

swers would seem to test the validity of their claims to powers divine.

Crœsus kept the reckoning of the days himself with great care, and at the hour appointed on the hundredth day, he employed himself in boiling the flesh of a turtle and of a lamb together in a brazen vessel. The vessel was covered with a lid, which was also of brass. He then awaited the return of the messengers They came in due time, one after another, bringing the replies which they had severally obtained. The replies were all unsatisfactory, except that of the oracle at Delphi. This answer was in verse, as, in fact, the responses of that oracle always were. The priestess who sat upon the tripod was accustomed to give the replies in an incoherent and half-intelligible manner, as impostors are very apt to do in uttering prophecies, and then the attendant priests and secretaries wrote them out in verse.

The verse which the messenger brought back from the Delphic tripod was in Greek; but some idea of its style, and the import of it, is conveyed by the following imitation:

> " I number the sands, I measure the sea,
> What's hidden to others is known to me.
> The lamb and the turtle are simmering slow.
> With brass above them and brass below."

Of course, Crœsus decided that the Delphic oracle was the one that he must rely upon for guidance in respect to his projected campaign. And he now began to prepare to consult it in a manner corresponding with the vast importance of the subject, and with his own boundless wealth. He provided the most extraordinary and sumptuous presents. Some of these treasures were to be deposited in the temple, as sacred gifts, for permanent preservation there. Others were to be offered as a burnt sacrifice in honor of the god. Among the latter, besides an incredible number of living victims, he caused to be prepared a great number of couches, magnificently decorated with silver and gold, and goblets and other vessels of gold, and dresses of various kinds richly embroidered, and numerous other articles, all intended to be used in the ceremonies preliminary to his application to the oracle. When the time arrived, a vast concourse of people assembled to witness the spectacle. The animals were sacrificed, and the people feasted on the flesh; and when these ceremonies were concluded, the couches, the goblets, the utensils of every kind, the dresses— every thing, in short, which had been used on the occasion, were heaped up into one great sac-

rificial pile, and set on fire. Every thing that
was combustible was consumed, while the gold
was melted, and ran into plates of great size,
which were afterward taken out from the ashes.
Thus it was the workmanship only of these articles which was destroyed and lost by the fire.
The gold, in which the chief value consisted,
was saved. It was gold from the Pactolus.

Besides these articles, there were others
made, far more magnificent and costly, for the
temple itself. There was a silver cistern or
tank, large enough to hold three thousand gal-
lons of wine. This tank was to be used by the
inhabitants of Delphi in their great festivals.
There was also a smaller cistern, or immense
goblet, as it might, perhaps, more properly be
called, which was made of gold. There were
also many other smaller presents, such as basins,
vases, and statues, all of silver and gold, and
of the most costly workmanship. The gold,
too, which had been taken from the fire, was
cast again, a part of it being formed into the
image of a lion, and the rest into large plates
of metal for the lion to stand upon. The image
was then set up upon the plates, within the precincts of the temple.

There was one piece of statuary which Cr∝

s¹s presented to the oracle at Delphi, which was,
in some respects, more extraordinary than any
of the rest. It was called the bread-maker. It
was an image representing a woman, a servant
in the household of Crœsus, whose business it
was to bake the bread. The reason that induced Crœsus to honor this bread-maker with
a statue of gold was, that on one occasion during his childhood she had saved his life. The
mother of Crœsus died when he was young,
and his father married a second time. The
second wife wished to have some one of *her*
children, instead of Crœsus, succeed to her husband's throne. In order, therefore, to remove
Crœsus out of the way, she prepared some
poison and gave it to the bread-maker, instruct-
ing her to put it into the bread which Crœsus
was to eat. The bread-maker received the poison and promised to obey. But, instead of doing
so, she revealed the intended murder to Crœsus,
and gave the poison to the queen's own children.
In gratitude for this fidelity to him, Crœsus,
when he came to the throne, caused this statue
to be made, and now he placed it at Delphi,
where he supposed it would forever remain.
The memory of his faithful servant was indeed
immortalized by the measure, though the statue

itself, as well as all these other treasures, in process of time disappeared.   In fact, statues of brass or of marble generally make far more durable monuments than statues of gold ; and no structure or object of art is likely to be very permanent among mankind unless the workmanship is worth more than the material.

Crœsus did not proceed himself to Delphi with these presents, but sent them by the hands of trusty messengers, who were instructed to perform the ceremonies required. to offer the gifts, and then to make inquiries of the oracle in the following terms.

·· Crœsus, the sovereign of Lydia and of various other kingdoms, in return for the wisdom which has marked your former declarations, has sent you these gifts.   He now furthermore desires to know whether it is safe for him to proceed against the Persians, and if so, whether it is best for him to seek the assistance of any allies."

The answer was as follows :

" If Crœsus crosses the Halys, and prosecutes a war with Persia, a mighty empire will be overthrown.   It will be best for him to form an alliance with the most powerful states of Greece."

Crœsus was extremely pleased with this re-

11

sponse.   He immediately resolved on undertaking the expedition against Cyrus; and to
express his gratitude for so favorable an answer
to his questions, he sent to Delphi to inquire
what was the number of inhabitants in the city,
and, when the answer was reported to him, he
sent a present of a sum of money to every one.
The Delphians, in their turn, conferred special
privileges and honors upon the Lydians and
upon Crœsus in respect to their oracle, giving
them the precedence in all future consultations,
and conferring upon them other marks of distinction and honor.

At the time when Crœsus sent his present
to the inhabitants of Delphi, he took the opportunity to address another inquiry to the oracle,
which was, whether his power would ever decline.   The oracle replied in a couplet of Greek
verse, similar in its style to the one recorded on
the previous occasion.

It was as follows:

" Whene'er a mule shall mount upon the Median throne,
    Then, and not till then, shall great Crœsus fear to lose
    his own."

This answer pleased the king quite as much
as the former one had done.   The allusion to
the contingency of a mule's reigning in Media

he very naturally regarded as only a rhetorical
and mystical mode of expressing an utter im
possibility. Crœsus considered himself and the
continuance of his power as perfectly secure.
He was fully confirmed in his determination to
organize his expedition without any delay, and
to proceed immediately to the proper measures
for obtaining the Grecian alliance and aid which
the oracle had recommended. The plans which
he formed, and the events which resulted, will
be described in subsequent chapters.

In respect to these Grecian oracles, it is
proper here to state, that there has been much
discussion among scholars on the question how
they were enabled to maintain, for so long a
period, so extended a credit among a people as
intellectual and well informed as the Greeks.
It was doubtless by means of a variety of contrivances and influences that this end was attained. There is a natural love of the marvelous among the humbler classes in all countries,
which leads them to be very ready to believe
in what is mystic and supernatural ; and they
accordingly exaggerate and color such real incidents as occur under any strange or remarkable circumstances, and invest any unusual
phenomena which they witness with a mirac-

ulous or supernatural interest. The cave at
Delphi might really have emitted gases which
would produce quite striking effects upon those
who inhaled them; and how easy it would be
for those who witnessed these effects to imagine
that some divine and miraculous powers must
exist in the aërial current which produced them.
The priests and priestesses, who inhabited the
temples in which these oracles were contained,
had, of course, a strong interest in keeping up
the belief of their reality in the minds of the
community; so were, in fact, all the inhabitants of the cities which sprung up around them.
They derived their support from the visitors
who frequented these places, and they contrived
various ways for drawing contributions, both
of money and gifts, from all who came. In
one case there was a sacred stream near an oracle, where persons, on permission from the
priests, were allowed to bathe. After the bathing, they were expected to throw pieces of
money into the stream. What afterward, in
such cases, became of the money, it is not difficult to imagine.

Nor is it necessary to suppose that all these
priests and priestesses were impostors. Hav
ing been trained up from infancy to believe that

B.C. 547.] THE ORACLES. 161

Whether the priests were impostors.   Answers of the oracles

the inspirations were real, they would continue
to look upon them as such all their lives. Even
at the present day we shall all, if we closely
scrutinize our mental habits, find ourselves continuing to take for granted, in our maturer
years, what we inconsiderately imbibed or were
erroneously taught in infancy, and that, often,
in cases where the most obvious dictates of reason, or even the plain testimony of our senses,
might show us that our notions are false. The
priests and priestesses, therefore, who imposed
on the rest of mankind, may have been as honestly and as deep in the delusion themselves as
any of their dupes.

The answers of the oracles were generally
vague and indefinite, and susceptible of almost
any interpretation, according to the result.
Whenever the event corresponded with the prediction, or could be made to correspond with it
by the ingenuity of the commentators, the story of the coincidence would, of course, be every
where spread abroad, becoming more striking
and more exact at each repetition. Where
there was a failure, it would not be direct and
absolute, on account of the vagueness and in-
definiteness of the response, and there would
therefore be no interest felt in hearing or in cir-

L

culating the story. The cases, thus, which would tend to establish the truth of the oracle, would be universally known and remembered, while those of a contrary bearing would be speedily forgotten.

There is no doubt, however, that in many cases the responses were given in collusion with the one who consulted the oracle, for the purpose of deceiving others. For example, let us suppose that Crœsus wished to establish strongly the credibility of the Delphic oracle in the minds of his countrymen, in order to encourage them to enlist in his armies, and to engage in the enterprise which he was contemplating against Cyrus with resolution and confidence; it would have been easy for him to have let the priestess at Delphi know what he was doing on the day when he sent to inquire, and thus himself to have directed her answer. Then, when his messengers returned, he would appeal to the answer as proof of the reality of the inspiration which seemed to furnish it. Alexander the Great certainly did, in this way, act in collusion with the priests at the temple of Jupiter Ammon.

The fact that there have been so many and

Is there any revelation truly divine?

such successful cases of falsehood and imposture among mankind in respect to revelations from Heaven, is no indication, as some superficially suppose, that no revelation is true, but is, on the other hand, strong evidence to the contrary. The Author of human existence has given no instincts in vain ; and the universal tendency of mankind to believe in the supernatural, to look into an unseen world, to seek, and to imagine that they find, revelations from Heaven, and to expect a continuance of existence after this earthly life is over, is the strongest possible natural evidence that there is an unseen world ; that man may have true communications with it ; that a personal deity reigns, who approves and disapproves of human conduct, and that there is a future state of being In this point of view, the absurd oracles of Greece, and the universal credence which they obtained, constitute strong evidence that there is somewhere to be found inspiration and prophecy really divine.

CHAPTER VII.

THE CONQUEST OF LYDIA.

THERE were, in fact, three inducements
which combined their influence on the mind
of Crœsus, in leading him to cross the Halys,
and invade the dominions of the Medes and
Persians : first, he was ambitious to extend his
own empire ; secondly, he feared that if he did
not attack Cyrus, Cyrus would himself cross
the Halys and attack him ; and, thirdly, he felt
under some obligation to consider himself the
ally of Astyages, and thus bound to espouse his
cause, and to aid him in putting down, if possible, the usurpation of Cyrus, and in recovering
his throne.   He felt under this obligation because Astyages was his brother-in-law ; for the
latter had married, many years before, a daughter of Alyattes, who was the father of Crœsus.
This, as Crœsus thought, gave him a just title
to interfere between the dethroned king and the
rebel who had dethroned him.   Under the influence of all these reasons combined, and encouraged by the responses of the oracle, he determined on attempting the invasion.

The first measure which he adopted was to
form an alliance with the most powerful of the
states of Greece, as he had been directed to do
by the oracle. After much inquiry and consideration, he concluded that the Lacedæmonian
state was the most powerful. Their chief city
was Sparta, in the Peloponnesus. They were
a warlike, stern, and indomitable race of men,
capable of bearing every possible hardship, and
of enduring every degree of fatigue and toil, and
they desired nothing but military glory for their
reward. This was a species of wages which it
was very easy to pay; much more easy to furnish than coin, even for Crœsus, notwithstanding the abundant supplies of gold which he was
accustomed to obtain from the sands of the Pactolus.

Crœsus sent embassadors to Sparta to inform the people of the plans which he contem-
plated, and to ask their aid. He had been instructed, he said, by the oracle at Delphi, to
seek the alliance of the most powerful of the
states of Greece, and he accordingly made application to them. They were gratified with
the compliment implied in selecting them, and
acceded readily to his proposal. Besides, they
were already on very friendly terms with Crœ-

sus; for, some years before, they had sent to
him to procure some gold for a statue which
they had occasion to erect, offering to give an
equivalent for the value of it in such productions as their country afforded. Crœsus supplied them with the gold that they needed, but
generously refused to receive any return.

In the mean time, Crœsus went on, energetically, at Sardis, making the preparations for
his campaign. One of his counselors, whose
name was Sardaris, ventured, one day, strongly
to dissuade him from undertaking the expedition. "You have nothing to gain by it," said
he, "if you succeed, and every thing to lose if
you fail. Consider what sort of people these
Persians are whom you are going to combat.
They live in the most rude and simple manner,
without luxuries, without pleasures, without
wealth. If you conquer their country, you will
find nothing in it worth bringing away. On
the other hand, if they conquer you, they will
come like a vast band of plunderers into Lydia,
where there is every thing to tempt and reward
them. I counsel you to leave them alone, and
to remain on this side the Halys, thankful if
Cyrus will be contented to remain on the
other."

B.C. 546.] CONQUEST OF LYDIA. 167

The army begins to march. Thales the Milesian

But Crœsus was not in a mood of mind to be persuaded by such reasoning.

When all things were ready, the army commenced its march and moved eastward, through one province of Asia Minor after another, until they reached the Halys. This river is a considerable stream, which rises in the interior of the country, and flows northward into the Euxine Sea. The army encamped on the banks of it, and some plan was to be formed for crossing the stream. In accomplishing this object, Crœsus was aided by a very celebrated engineer who accompanied his army, named Thales. Thales was a native of Miletus, and is generally called in history, Thales the Milesian. He was a very able mathematician and calculator, and many accounts remain of the discoveries and performances by which he acquired his renown.

For example, in the course of his travels, he at one time visited Egypt, and while there, he contrived a very simple way of measuring the height of the pyramids. He set up a pole on the plain in an upright position, and then measured the pole and also its shadow. He also measured the length of the shadow of the pyramid. He then calculated the height of the

pyramid by this proportion : as the length of
shadow of the pole is to that of the pole itself,
so is the length of the shadow of the pyramid
to its height.

Thales was an astronomer as well as a philosopher and engineer. He learned more exactly the true length of the year than it had
been known before ; and he also made some
calculations of eclipses, at least so far as to
predict the year in which they would happen
One eclipse which he predicted happened to occur on the day of a great battle between two
contending armies. It was cloudy, so that the
combatants could not see the sun. This circumstance, however, which concealed the eclipse
itself, only made the darkness which was caused
by it the more intense. The armies were much
terrified at this sudden cessation of the light
of day, and supposed it to be a warning from
heaven that they should desist from the combat.

Thales the Milesian was the author of several of the geometrical theorems and demon-
strations now included in the Elements of
Euclid. The celebrated fifth proposition of
the first book, so famous among all the modern
nations of Europe as the great stumbling block
in the way of beginners in the study of geom-

etry, was his. The discovery of the truth expressed in this proposition, and of the complicated demonstration which establishes it, was certainly a much greater mathematical performance than the measuring of the altitude of the pyramids by their shadow.

But to return to Crœsus. Thales undertook the work of transporting the army across the river. He examined the banks, and found, at length, a spot where the land was low and level for some distance from the stream. He caused the army to be brought up to the river at this point, and to be encamped there, as near to the bank as possible, and in as compact a form He then employed a vast number of laborers to cut a new channel for the waters, behind the army, leading out from the river above, and rejoining it again at a little distance below. When this channel was finished, he turned the river into its new course, and then the army passed without difficulty over the former bed of the stream.

The Halys being thus passed, Crœsus moved on in the direction of Media. But he soon found that he had not far to go to find his enemy. Cyrus had heard of his plans through deserters and spies, and he had for some time

been advancing to meet him. One after the
other of the nations through whose dominions
he had passed, he had subjected to his sway,
or, at least, brought under his influence by
treaties and alliances, and had received from
them all re-enforcements to swell the numbers
of his army. One nation only remained—the
Babylonians. They were on the side of Crœsus. They were jealous of the growing power
of the Medes and Persians, and had made a
league with Crœsus, promising to aid him in
the war. The other nations of the East were
in alliance with Cyrus, and he was slowly
moving on, at the head of an immense combined
force, toward the Halys, at the very time when
Crœsus was crossing the stream.

The scouts, therefore, that preceded the army
of Crœsus on its march, soon began to fall back
into the camp, with intelligence that there was
a large armed force coming on to meet them,
the advancing columns filling all the roads, and
threatening to overwhelm them. The scouts
from the army of Cyrus carried back similar
intelligence to him. The two armies accordingly halted and began to prepare for battle
The place of their meeting was called Pteria
It was in the province of Cappadocia, and toward the eastern part of Asia Minor

A great battle was fought at Pteria. It was continued all day, and remained undecided when the sun went down. The combatants separated when it became dark, and each withdrew from the field. Each king found, it seems, that his antagonist was more formidable than he had imagined, and on the morning after the battle they both seemed inclined to remain in their respective encampments, without evincing any disposition to renew the contest.

Crœsus, in fact, seems to have considered that he was fortunate in having so far repulsed the formidable invasion which Cyrus had been intending for him. He considered Cyrus's army as repulsed, since they had withdrawn from the field, and showed no disposition to return to it. He had no doubt that Cyrus would now go back to Media again, having found how well prepared Crœsus had been to receive him. For himself, he concluded that he ought to be satisfied with the advantage which he had already gained, as the result of one campaign, and return again to Sardis to recruit his army, the force of which had been considerably impaired by the battle, and so postpone the grand invasion till the next season. He accordingly set out on his return. He dispatched messengers, at the same

time, to Babylon, to Sparta, to Egypt, and to
other countries with which he was in alliance,
informing these various nations of the great
battle of Pteria and its results, and asking them
to send him, early in the following spring, all
the re-enforcements that they could command,
to join him in the grand campaign which he
was going to make the next season.

He continued his march homeward without
any interruption, sending off, from time to time,
as he was moving through his own dominions,
such portions of his troops as desired to return
to their homes, enjoining upon them to come
back to him in the spring. By this temporary
disbanding of a portion of his army, he saved
the expense of maintaining them through the
winter.

Very soon after Crœsus arrived at Sardis,
the whole country in the neighborhood of the
capital was thrown into a state of universal
alarm by the news that Cyrus was close at
hand. It seems that Cyrus had remained in
the vicinity of Pteria long enough to allow
Crœsus to return, and to give him time to dis-
miss his troops and establish himself securely
in the city. He then suddenly resumed his
march, and came on toward Sardis with the

B.C. 546.] CONQUEST OF LYDIA. 173

Confusion and alarm at Sardis.   The Lydian cavalry

utmost possible dispatch. Crœsus, in fact, had
no announcement of his approach until he heard
of his arrival.

All was now confusion and alarm, both within and without the city. Crœsus hastily collected all the forces that he could command.
He sent immediately to the neighboring cities,
summoning all the troops in them to hasten to
the capital. He enrolled all the inhabitants of
the city that were capable of bearing arms.
By these means he collected, in a very short
time, quite a formidable force, which he drew
up, in battle array, on a great plain not far
from the city, and there waited, with much
anxiety and solicitude, for Cyrus to come on.

The Lydian army was superior to that of
Cyrus in cavalry, and as the place where the
battle was to be fought was a plain, which was
the kind of ground most favorable for the operations of that species of force, Cyrus felt some
solicitude in respect to the impression which
might be made by it on his army. Nothing is
more terrible than the onset of a squadron of
horse when charging an enemy upon the field of
battle. They come in vast bodies, sometimes
consisting of many thousands, with the speed
of the wind, the men flourishing their sabers

12

and rending the air with the most unearthly
cries, those in advance being driven irresistibly
on by the weight and impetus of the masses behind.   The dreadful torrent bears down and
overwhelms every thing that attempts to resist its way.   They trample one another and
their enemies together promiscuously in the
dust; the foremost of the column press on with
the utmost fury, afraid quite as much of the
headlong torrent of friends coming on behind
them, as of the line of fixed and motionless
enemies who stand ready to receive them before.   These enemies, stationed to withstand
the charge, arrange themselves in triple or
quadruple rows, with the shafts of their spears
planted against the ground, and the points directed forward and upward to receive the advancing horsemen.   These spears transfix and
kill the foremost horses; but those that come
on behind, leaping and plunging over their fallen
companions, soon break through the lines and
put their enemies to flight, in a scene of indescribable havoc and confusion.

Crœsus had large bodies of horse, while Cyrus had no efficient troops to oppose them.   He
had a great number of camels in the rear of
his army, which had been employed as beasts

of burden to transport the baggage and stores
of the army on their march. Cyrus concluded
to make the experiment of opposing these camels
to the cavalry. It is frequently said by the
ancient historians that the horse has a natural
antipathy to the camel, and can not bear either
the smell or the sight of one, though this is not
found to be the case at the present day. However the fact might have been in this respect,
Cyrus determined to arrange the camels in his
front as he advanced into battle. He accordingly ordered the baggage to be removed, and,
releasing their ordinary drivers from the charge
of them, he assigned each one to the care of a
soldier, who was to mount him, armed with a
spear. Even if the supposed antipathy of the
horse for the camel did not take effect, Cyrus
thought that their large and heavy bodies, defended by the spears of their riders, would afford
the most effectual means of resistance against
the shock of the Lydian squadrons that he
was now able to command.

The battle commenced, and the squadrons
of horse came on. But, as soon as they came
near the camels, it happened that, either from
the influence of the antipathy above referred to,
or from alarm at the novelty of the spectacle

of such huge and misshapen beasts, or else because of the substantial resistance which the
camels and the spears of their riders made to
the shock of their charge, the horses were soon
thrown into confusion and put to flight. In
fact, a general panic seized them, and they became totally unmanageable. Some threw their
riders; others, seized with a sort of phrensy,
became entirely independent of control. They
turned, and trampled the foot soldiers of their
own army under foot, and threw the whole
body into disorder. The consequence was, that
the army of Crœsus was wholly defeated; they
fled in confusion, and crowded in vast throngs
through the gates into the city, and fortified
themselves there.

Cyrus advanced to the city, invested it closely
on all sides, and commenced a siege. But the
appearances were not very encouraging. The
walls were lofty, thick, and strong, and the
numbers within the city were amply sufficient
to guard them. Nor was the prospect much
more promising of being soon able to reduce
the city by famine. The wealth of Crœsus had
enabled him to lay up almost inexhaustible
stores of food and clothing, as well as treasures
of silver and gold. He hoped, therefore, to be

able to hold out against the besiegers until
help should come from some of his allies. He
had sent messengers to them, asking them to
come to his rescue without any delay, before
he was shut up in the city.

The city of Sardis was built in a position
naturally strong, and one part of the wall passed over rocky precipices which were considered
entirely impassable. There was a sort of glen
or rocky gorge in this quarter, outside of the
walls, down which dead bodies were thrown on
one occasion subsequently, at a time when the
city was besieged, and beasts and birds of prey
fed upon them there undisturbed, so lonely was
the place and so desolate. In fact, the walls
that crowned these precipices were considered
absolutely inaccessible, and were very slightly
built and very feebly guarded. There was an
ancient legend that, a long time before, when a
certain Males was king of Lydia, one of his
wives had a son in the form of a lion, whom
they called Leon, and an oracle declared that
if this Leon were carried around the walls of
the city, it would be rendered impregnable, and
should never be taken. They carried Leon,
therefore, around, so far as the regular walls
extended. When they came to this precipice

M

of rocks, they returned, considering that this
part of the city was impregnable without any
such ceremony. A spur or eminence from the
mountain of Tmolus, which was behind the
city, projected into it at this point, and there
was a strong citadel built upon its summit.

Cyrus continued the siege fourteen days, and
then he determined that he must, in some way
or other, find the means of carrying it by assault, and to do this he must find some place
to scale the walls. He accordingly sent a party
of horsemen around to explore every part, offering them a large reward if they would find any
place where an entrance could be effected. The
horsemen made the circuit, and reported that
their search had been in vain. At length a certain soldier, named Hyræades, after studying
for some time the precipices on the side which
had been deemed inaccessible, saw a sentinel,
who was stationed on the walls above, leave his
post and come climbing down the rocks for
some distance to get his helmet, which had accidentally dropped down. Hyræades watched
him both as he descended and as he returned.
He reflected on this discovery, communicated
it to others, and the practicability of scaling the
rock and the walls at that point was discussed.

THE SIEGE OF SARDIS.

In the end, the attempt was made and was successful. Hyræades went up first, followed by a few daring spirits who were ambitious of the glory of the exploit. They were not at first observed from above. The way being thus shown, great numbers followed on, and so large a force succeeded in thus gaining an entrance that the city was taken.

In the dreadful confusion and din of the storming of the city, Crœsus himself had a very narrow escape from death. He was saved by the miraculous speaking of his deaf and dumb son—at least such is the story. Cyrus had given positive orders to his soldiers, both before the great battle on the plain and during the siege, that, though they might slay whomever else they pleased, they must not harm Crœsus, but must take him alive. During the time of the storming of the town, when the streets were filled with infuriated soldiers, those on the one side wild with the excitement of triumph, and those on the other maddened with rage and despair, a party, rushing along, overtook Crœsus and his helpless son, whom the unhappy father, it seems, was making a desperate effort to save The Persian soldiers were about to transfix Crœsus with their spears. when the son, who

had never spoken before, called out, "It is Crœsus; do not kill him." The soldiers were ar-
rested by the words, and saved the monarch's
life. They made him prisoner, and bore him
away to Cyrus.

Crœsus had sent, a long time before, to inquire of the Delphic oracle by what means the
power of speech could be restored to his son.
The answer was, that that was a boon which he
had better not ask; for the day on which he
should hear his son speak for the first time,
would be the darkest and most unhappy day of
his life.

Cyrus had not ordered his soldiers to spare
the life of Crœsus in battle from any sentiment
of humanity toward him, but because he wished to have his case reserved for his own decision. When Crœsus was brought to him a
captive, he ordered him to be put in chains, and
carefully guarded. As soon as some degree of
order was restored in the city, a large funeral
pile was erected, by his directions, in a public
square, and Crœsus was brought to the spot.
Fourteen Lydian young men, the sons, probably, of the most prominent men in the state,
were with him. The pile was large enough
for them all, and they were placed upon it.

They were all laid upon the wood. Crœsus
raised himself and looked around, surveying
with extreme consternation and horror the preparations which were making for lighting the
pile. His heart sank within him as he thought
of the dreadful fate that was before him. The
spectators stood by in solemn silence, awaiting
the end. Crœsus broke this awful pause by
crying out, in a tone of anguish and despair,

"Oh Solon! Solon! Solon!"

The officers who had charge of the execution
asked him what he meant. Cyrus, too, who was
himself personally superintending the scene,
asked for an explanation. Crœsus was, for a
time, too much agitated and distracted to reply. There were difficulties in respect to language, too, which embarrassed the conversation,
as the two kings could speak to each other only
through an interpreter. At length Crœsus gave
an account of his interview with Solon, and of
the sentiment which the philosopher had expressed, that no one could decide whether a
man was truly prosperous and happy till it was
determined how his life was to end. Cyrus
was greatly interested in this narrative; but, in
the mean time, the interpreting of the conversation had been slow, a considerable period had

184　Cyrus the Great. [B.C. 546

Crœsus is saved. He becomes Cyrus's friend.

elapsed, and the officers had lighted the fire.
The pile had been made extremely combustible,
and the fire was rapidly making its way through
the whole mass. Cyrus eagerly ordered it to
be extinguished The efforts which the soldiers made for this purpose seemed, at first,
likely to be fruitless; but they were aided very
soon by a sudden shower of rain, which, coming down from the mountains, began, just at
this time, to fall; and thus the flames were extinguished, and Crœsus and the captives saved

Cyrus immediately, with a fickleness very
common among great monarchs in the treatment of both enemies and favorites, began to
consider Crœsus as his friend. He ordered him
to be unbound, brought him near his person,
and treated him with great consideration and
honor.

Crœsus remained after this for a long time
with Cyrus, and accompanied him in his subsequent campaigns. He was very much incensed at the oracle at Delphi for having deceived him by its false responses and predictions, and thus led him into the terrible snare
into which he had fallen. He procured the fet-
ters with which he had been chained when
placed upon the pile, and sent them to Delphi,

with orders that they should be thrown down upon the threshold of the temple—the visible symbol of his captivity and ruin—as a reproach to the oracle for having deluded him and caused his destruction. In doing this, the messengers were to ask the oracle whether imposition like that which had been practiced on Crœsus was the kind of gratitude it evinced to one who had enriched it by such a profusion of offerings and gifts.

To this the priests of the oracle said in reply, that the destruction of the Lydian dynasty had long been decreed by the Fates, in retribution for the guilt of Gyges, the founder of the line. He had murdered his master, and usurped the throne, without any title to it whatever. The judgments of Heaven had been denounced upon Gyges for this crime, to fall on himself or on some of his descendants. The Pythian Apollo at Delphi had done all in his power to postpone the falling of the blow until after the death of Crœsus, on account of the munificent benefactions which he had made to the oracle; but he had been unable to effect it: the decrees of Fate were inexorable. All that the oracle could do was to postpone—as it had done, it said, for three years—the execution of the sentence, and

to give Crœsus warning of the evil that was
impending. This had been done by announc-
ing to him that his crossing the Halys would
cause the destruction of a mighty empire,
meaning that of Lydia, and also by informing
him that when he should find a mule upon the
throne of Media he must expect to lose his own.
Cyrus, who was descended, on the father's side,
from the Persian stock, and on the mother's
from that of Media, was the hybrid sovereign
represented by the mule.

When this answer was reported to Crœsus,
it is said that he was satisfied with the expla-
nations, and admitted that the oracle was right,
and that he himself had been unreasonable and
wrong. However this may be, it is certain
that, among mankind at large, since Crœsus's
day, there has been a great disposition to over-
look whatever of criminality there may have
been in the falsehood and imposture of the oracle, through admiration of the adroitness and
dexterity which its ministers evinced in saving
themselves from exposure.

CHAPTER VIII.

THE CONQUEST OF BABYLON.

IN his advance toward the dominions of Crœsus in Asia Minor, Cyrus had passed to the
northward of the great and celebrated city of
Babylon. Babylon was on the Euphrates, toward the southern part of Asia. It was the
capital of a large and very fertile region, which
extended on both sides of the Euphrates toward
the Persian Gulf. The limits of the country,
however, which was subject to Babylon, varied
very much at different times, as they were extended or contracted by revolutions and wars.

The River Euphrates was the great source
of fertility for the whole region through which
it flowed. The country watered by this river
was very densely populated, and the inhabitants were industrious and peaceable, cultivating
their land, and living quietly and happily on its
fruits. The surface was intersected with canals, which the people had made for conveying
the water of the river over the land for the purpose of irrigating it. Some of these canals were

navigable. There was one great trunk which passed from the Euphrates to the Tigris, supplying many minor canals by the way, that was navigable for vessels of considerable burden.

The traffic of the country was, however, mainly conducted by means of boats of moderate size, the construction of which seemed to Herodotus very curious and remarkable. The city was enormously large, and required immense supplies of food, which were brought down in these boats from the agricultural country above. The boats were made in the following manner: first a frame was built, of the shape of the intended boat, broad and shallow and with the stem and stern of the same form This frame was made of willows, like a basket, and, when finished, was covered with a sheathing of skins. A layer of reeds was then spread over the bottom of the boat to protect the frame, and to distribute evenly the pressure of the cargo. The boat, thus finished, was laden with the produce of the country, and was then floated down the river to Babylon. In this navigation the boatmen were careful to protect the leather sheathing from injury by avoiding all contact with rocks, or even with the gravel of the shores. They kept their craft in the middle of the stream

by means of two oars, or, rather, an oar and a
paddle, which were worked, the first at the bows,
and the second at the stern. The advance of
the boat was in some measure accelerated by
these boatmen, though their main function was
to steer their vessel by keeping it out of eddies
and away from projecting points of land, and directing its course to those parts of the stream
where the current was swiftest, and where it
would consequently be borne forward most rapidly to its destination.

These boats were generally of very considerable size, and they carried, in addition to
their cargo and crew, one or more beasts of
burden—generally asses or mules. These animals were allowed the pleasure, if any pleasure
it was to them, of sailing thus idly down the
stream, for the sake of having them at hand at
the end of the voyage, to carry back again, up
the country, the skins, which constituted the
most valuable portion of the craft they sailed
in. It was found that these skins, if carefully
preserved, could be easily transported up the
river, and would answer the purpose of a second voyage. Accordingly, when the boats arrived at Babylon, the cargo was sold, the boats
were broken up, the skins were folded into
13

packs, and in this form the mules carried them
up the river again, the boatmen driving the
mules as they walked by their side.

Babylon was a city of immense extent and
magnitude. In fact, the accounts given of the
space which it covered have often been considered incredible. These accounts make the
space which was included within the walls four
or five times as large as London. A great deal
of this space was, however, occupied by parks
and gardens connected with the royal palaces,
and by open squares. Then, besides, the houses
occupied by the common people in the ancient
cities were of fewer stories in height, and consequently more extended on the ground, than
those built in modern times. In fact, it is probable that, in many instances, they were mere
ranges of huts and hovels, as is the case, indeed, to a considerable extent, in Oriental cities,
at the present day, so that it is not at all impossible that even so large an area as four or five
times the size of London may have been included within the fortifications of the city.

In respect to the walls of the city, very extraordinary and apparently contradictory accounts are given by the various ancient authors
who described them. Some make them seven

ty-five, and others two or three hundred feet
high There have been many discussions in
respect to the comparative credibility of these
several statements, and some ingenious attempts have been made to reconcile them. It
is not, however, at all surprising that there
should be such a diversity in the dimensions
given, for the walling of an ancient city was
seldom of the same height in all places. The
structure necessarily varied according to the
nature of the ground, being high wherever the
ground without was such as to give the enemy
an advantage in an attack, and lower in other
situations, where the conformation of the surface was such as to afford, of itself, a partial
protection. It is not, perhaps, impossible that,
at some particular points—as, for example,
across glens and ravines, or along steep declivities—the walls of Babylon may have been raised even to the very extraordinary height which
Herodotus ascribes to them.

The walls were made of bricks, and the
bricks were formed of clay and earth, which was
dug from a trench made outside of the lines.
This trench served the purpose of a ditch, to
strengthen the fortification when the wall was
completed. The water from the river, and

from streams flowing toward the river, was admitted to these ditches on every side, and kept them always full.

The sides of these ditches were lined with bricks too, which were made, like those of the walls, from the earth obtained from the excavations. They used for all this masonry a cement made from a species of bitumen, which was found in great quantities floating down one of the rivers which flowed into the Euphrates, in the neighborhood of Babylon.

The River Euphrates itself flowed through the city. There was a breast-work or low wall along the banks of it on either side, with openings at the terminations of the streets leading to the water, and flights of steps to go down. These openings were secured by gates of brass, which, when closed, would prevent an enemy from gaining access to the city from the river. The great streets, which terminated thus at the river on one side, extended to the walls of the city on the other, and they were crossed by other streets at right angles to them. In the outer walls of the city, at the extremities of all these streets, were massive gates of brass, with hinges and frames of the same metal. There were a hundred of these gates in all. They were

guarded by watch-towers on the walls above.
The watch-towers were built on both the inner
and outer faces of the wall, and the wall itself
was so broad that there was room between these
watch-towers for a chariot and four to drive
and turn.

The river, of course, divided the city into two
parts. The king's palace was in the center of
one of these divisions, within a vast circular in-
closure, which contained the palace buildings,
together with the spacious courts, and parks,
and gardens pertaining to them. In the center
of the other division was a corresponding inclos-
ure, which contained the great temple of Belus.
Here there was a very lofty tower, divided into
eight separate towers, one above another, with
a winding staircase to ascend to the summit.
In the upper story was a sort of chapel, with a
couch, and a table, and other furniture for use
in the sacred ceremonies, all of gold. Above
this, on the highest platform of all, was a grand
observatory, where the Babylonian astrologers
made their celestial observations.

There was a bridge across the river, connect-
ing one section of the city with the other, and
it is said that there was a subterranean passage
under the river also, which was used as a pri-

N

vate communication between two public edifices—palaces or citadels—which were situated
near the extremities of the bridge. All these
constructions were of the most grand and imposing character. In addition to the architectural magnificence of the buildings, the gates
and walls were embellished with a great variety of sculptures: images of animals, of every
form and in every attitude; and men, single
and in groups, models of great sovereigns, and
representations of hunting scenes, battle scenes,
and great events in the Babylonian history.

The most remarkable, however, of all the
wonders of Babylon—though perhaps not built
till after Cyrus's time—were what were called
the hanging gardens. Although called the
hanging gardens, they were not suspended in
any manner, as the name might denote, but
were supported upon arches and walls. The
arches and walls sustained a succession of terraces, rising one above another, with broad
flights of steps for ascending to them, and on
these terraces the gardens were made. The
upper terrace, or platform, was several hundred
feet from the ground; so high, that it was necessary to build arches upon arches within, in
order to attain the requisite elevation. The

lateral thrust of these arches was sustained by
a wall twenty-five feet in thickness, which surrounded the garden on all sides, and rose as
high as the lowermost tier of arches, upon which
would, of course, be concentrated the pressure
and weight of all the pile. The whole structure thus formed a sort of artificial hill, square
in form, and rising, in a succession of terraces,
to a broad and level area upon the top. The
extent of this grand square upon the summit
was four hundred feet upon each side.

The surface which served as the foundation
for the gardens that adorned these successive
terraces and the area above was formed in the
following manner : Over the masonry of the
arches there was laid a pavement of broad flat
stones, sixteen feet long and four feet wide.
Over these there was placed a stratum of reeds,
laid in bitumen, and above them another flooring of bricks, cemented closely together, so as
to be impervious to water. To make the security complete in this respect, the upper surface
of this brick flooring was covered with sheets
of lead, overlapping each other in such a manner as to convey all the water which might per-
colate through the mold away to the sides of
the garden. The earth and mold were placed

upon this surface, thus prepared, and the stratum was so deep as to allow large trees to take root and grow in it. There was an engine constructed in the middle of the upper terrace, by which water could be drawn up from the river, and distributed over every part of the vast pile.

The gardens, thus completed, were filled to profusion with every species of tree, and plant, and vine, which could produce fruit or flowers to enrich or adorn such a scene. Every country in communication with Babylon was made to contribute something to increase the endless variety of floral beauty which was here literally enthroned. Gardeners of great experience and skill were constantly employed in cultivating the parterres, pruning the fruit-trees and the vines, preserving the walks, and introducing new varieties of vegetation. In a word, the hanging gardens of Babylon became one of the wonders of the world.

The country in the neighborhood of Babylon extending from the river on either hand, was in general level and low, and subject to inundations. One of the sovereigns of the country, a queen named Nitocris, had formed the grand design of constructing an immense lake, to take off the superfluous water in case of a flood, and thus prevent an overflow. She also opened a great number of lateral and winding channels for the river, wherever the natural disposition of the surface afforded facilities for doing so, and the earth which was taken out in the course of these excavations was employed in raising the banks by artificial terraces, such as are made to confine the Mississippi at New Orleans, and are there called *levees.** The object of Nicotris in these measures was two-fold. She wished, in the first place, to open all practicable channels for the flow of the water, and then to confine the current within the channels thus made. She also wished to make the navigation of the stream as intricate and complicated as possible, so that, while the natives of the country might easily find their way, in boats, to the capital, a foreign enemy, if he should make the attempt, might be confused and lost. These were the rivers of Babylon on the banks of which the captive Jews sat down and wept when they remembered Zion.

This queen Nitocris seems to have been quite distinguished for her engineering and architectural plans. It was she that built the bridge across the Euphrates, within the city; and as

* From the French word *levée*. raised.

there was a feeling of jealousy and ill will, as usual in such a case, between the two divisions of the town which the river formed, she caused the bridge to be constructed with a movable platform or draw, by means of which the communication might be cut off at pleasure. This draw was generally up at night and down by day.

Herodotus relates a curious anecdote of this queen, which, if true, evinces in another way the peculiar originality of mind and the ingenuity which characterized all her operations. She caused her tomb to be built, before her death, over one of the principal gates of the city. Upon the façade of this monument was a very conspicuous inscription to this effect: " If any one of the sovereigns, my successors, shall be in extreme want of money, let him open my tomb and take what he may think proper ; but let him not resort to this resource unless the urgency is extreme."

The tomb remained for some time after the queen's death quite undisturbed. In fact, the people of the city avoided this gate altogether, on account of the dead body deposited above it, and the spot became well-nigh deserted. At length, in process of time, a subsequent sover

eign, being in want of money, ventured to open
the tomb. He found, however, no money within. The gloomy vault contained nothing but
the dead body of the queen, and a label with
this inscription: "If your avarice were not as
insatiable as it is base, you would not have in-
truded on the repose of the dead."

It was not surprising that Cyrus, having
been so successful in his enterprises thus far,
should now begin to turn his thoughts toward
this great Babylonian empire, and to feel a desire to bring it under his sway. The first thing,
however, was to confirm and secure his Lydian
conquests. He spent some time, therefore, in
organizing and arranging, at Sardis, the affairs
of the new government which he was to substitute for that of Crœsus there. He designated
certain portions of his army to be left for gar-
risons in the conquered cities. He appointed
Persian officers, of course, to command these
forces; but, as he wished to conciliate the Lydians, he appointed many of the municipal and
civil officers of the country from among them.
There would appear to be no danger in doing
this, as, by giving the command of the army to
Persians, he retained all the real power directly
in his own hands.

One of these civil officers, the most important, in fact, of all, was the grand treasurer.
To him Cyrus committed the charge of the
stores of gold and silver which came into his
possession at Sardis, and of the revenues which
were afterward to accrue. Cyrus appointed a
Lydian named Pactyas to this trust, hoping
by such measures to conciliate the people of
the country, and to make them more ready to
submit to his sway. Things being thus arranged, Cyrus, taking Crœsus with him, set
out with the main army to return toward the
East.

As soon as he had left Lydia, Pactyas excited the Lydians to revolt The name of the
commander-in-chief of the military forces which
Cyrus had left was Tabalus. Pactyas abandoned the city and retired toward the coast,
where he contrived to raise a large army,
formed partly of Lydians and partly of bodies
of foreign troops, which he was enabled to hire
by means of the treasures which Cyrus had put
under his charge. He then advanced to Sardis,
took possession of the town, and shut up Tabalus, with his Persian troops, in the citadel.

When the tidings of these events came to
Cyrus, he was very much incensed, and de-

termined to destroy the city. Crœsus, however, interceded very earnestly in its behalf.
He recommended that Cyrus, instead of burning Sardis, should send a sufficient force to dis-
arm the population, and that he should then
enact such laws and make such arrangements
as should turn the minds of the people to habits
of luxury and pleasure. "By doing this," said
Crœsus, "the people will, in a short time, become so enervated and so effeminate that you
will have nothing to fear from them."

Cyrus decided on adopting this plan. He
dispatched a Median named Mazares, an officer of his army, at the head of a strong force,
with orders to go back to Sardis, to deliver Tabalus from his danger, to seize and put to death
all the leaders in the Lydian rebellion excepting
Pactyas. Pactyas was to be saved alive, and
sent a prisoner to Cyrus in Persia.

Pactyas did not wait for the arrival of Mazares. As soon as he heard of his approach, he
abandoned the ground, and fled northwardly to
the city of Cyme, and sought refuge there.
When Mazares had reached Sardis and re-
established the government of Cyrus there, he
sent messengers to Cyme, demanding the surrender of the fugitive.

The people of Cyme were uncertain whether they ought to comply. They said that they must first consult an oracle. There was a very ancient and celebrated oracle near Mile-tus. They sent messengers to this oracle, de-manding to know whether it were according to the will of the gods or not that the fugitive should be surrendered. The answer brought back was, that they might surrender him.

They were accordingly making arrangements for doing this, when one of the citizens, a very prominent and influential man, named Aristod-icus, expressed himself not satisfied with the reply. He did not think it possible, he said, that the oracle could really counsel them to de-liver up a helpless fugitive to his enemies. The messengers must have misunderstood or misre-ported the answer which they had received. He finally persuaded his countrymen to send a sec-ond embassy: he himself was placed at the head of it. On their arrival, Aristodicus ad-dressed the oracle as follows:

"To avoid a cruel death from the Persians, Pactyas, a Lydian, fled to us for refuge. The Persians demanded that we should surrender him. Much as we are afraid of their power, we are still more afraid to deliver up a helpless suppliant for protection without clear and decided directions from you."

The embassy received to this demand the same reply as before.

Still Aristodicus was not satisfied; and, as if by way of bringing home to the oracle somewhat more forcibly a sense of the true character of such an action as it seemed to recommend, he began to make a circuit in the grove which was around the temple in which the oracle resided, and to rob and destroy the nests which the birds had built there, allured, apparently, by the sacred repose and quietude of the scene. This had the desired effect. A solemn voice was heard from the interior of the temple, saying, in a warning tone,

"Impious man! how dost thou dare to molest those who have placed themselves under my protection?"

To this Aristodicus replied by asking the oracle how it was that it watched over and guarded those who sought its own protection, while it directed the people of Cyme to abandon and betray suppliants for theirs. To this the oracle answered,

"I direct them to do it, in order that such impious men may the sooner bring down upon

their heads the judgments of heaven for having
dared to entertain even the thought of delivering up a helpless fugitive."

When this answer was reported to the people
of Cyme, they did not dare to give Pactyas up,
nor, on the other hand, did they dare to incur
the enmity of the Persians by retaining and
protecting him.   They accordingly sent him
secretly away.   The emissaries of Mazares,
however, followed him.   They kept constantly
on his track, demanding him successively of
every city where the hapless fugitive sought
refuge, until, at length, partly by threats and
partly by a reward, they induced a certain city
to surrender him.   Mazares sent him, a prisoner, to Cyrus.   Soon after this Mazares himself died, and Harpagus was appointed governor
of Lydia in his stead.

In the mean time, Cyrus went on with his
conquests in the heart of Asia, and at length,
in the course of a few years, he had completed
his arrangements and preparations for the at
tack on Babylon.   He advanced at the head
of a large force to the vicinity of the city.
The King of Babylon, whose name was Belshazzar, withdrew within the walls, shut the
gates, and felt perfectly secure.   A simple wall

was in those days a very effectual protection
against any armed force whatever, if it was only
high enough not to be scaled, and thick enough
to resist the blows of a battering ram.   The
artillery of modern times would have speedily
made a fatal breach in such structures; but
there was nothing but the simple force of man,
applied through brazen-headed beams of wood,
in those days, and Belshazzar knew well that
his walls would bid all such modes of demolition a complete defiance.   He stationed his
soldiers, therefore, on the walls, and his sentinels in the watch towers, while he himself, and
all the nobles of his court, feeling perfectly secure in their impregnable condition, and being
abundantly supplied with all the means that
the whole empire could furnish, both for sustenance and enjoyment, gave themselves up, in
their spacious palaces and gardens, to gayety,
festivity, and pleasure.

Cyrus advanced to the city.   He stationed
one large detachment of his troops at the open-
ing in the main walls where the river entered
into the city, and another one below, where it
issued from it.   These detachments were ordered to march into the city by the bed of the river, as soon as they should observe the water
14

subsiding.   He then employed a vast force of
laborers to open new channels, and to widen
and deepen those which had existed before, for
the purpose of drawing off the waters from
their usual bed.   When these passages were
thus prepared, the water was let into them one
night, at a time previously designated, and it
soon ceased to flow through the city.   The detachments of soldiers marched in over the bed
of the stream, carrying with them vast numbers of ladders.   With these they easily scaled
the low walls which lined the banks of the river, and Belshazzar was thunderstruck with the
announcement made to him in the midst of one
of his feasts that the Persians were in complete
and full possession of the city.

B.C.608.] RESTORATION OF THE JEWS. 207

The Jewish captivity.   Jeremiah and the book of Chronicles

CHAPTER IX.

THE RESTORATION OF THE JEWS.

THE period of the invasion of Babylonia by Cyrus, and the taking of the city, was during the time while the Jews were in captivity there. Cyrus was their deliverer. It results from this circumstance that the name of Cyrus is connected with sacred history more than that of any other great conqueror of ancient times

It was a common custom in the early ages of the world for powerful sovereigns to take the people of a conquered country captive, and make them slaves. They employed them, to some extent, as personal household servants, but more generally as agricultural laborers, to till the lands.

An account of the captivity of the Jews in Babylon is given briefly in the closing chapters of the second book of Chronicles, though many of the attendant circumstances are more fully detailed in the book of Jeremiah. Jeremiah was a prophet who lived in the time of the captivity. Nebuchadnezzar, the king of Babylon made repeated incursions into the land of Judea, sometimes carrying away the reigning monarch, sometimes deposing him and appointing another sovereign in his stead, sometimes assessing a tax or tribute upon the land, and sometimes plundering the city, and carrying away all the gold and silver that he could find. Thus the kings and the people were kept in a continual state of anxiety and terror for many years, exposed incessantly to the inroads of this nation of robbers and plunderers, that had, so unfortunately for them, found their way across their frontiers. King Zedekiah was the last of this oppressed and unhappy line of Jewish kings.

The prophet Jeremiah was accustomed to denounce the sins of the Jewish nation, by which these terrible calamities had been brought upon them, with great courage, and with an eloquence solemn and sublime. He declared that the miseries which the people suffered were the special judgments of Heaven, and he proclaimed repeatedly and openly, and in the most public places of the city, still heavier calamities which he said were impending. The people were troubled and distressed at these prophetic warnings, and some of them were deeply in-

censed against Jeremiah for uttering them.
Finally, on one occasion, he took his stand in
one of the public courts of the Temple, and, addressing the concourse of priests and people that
were there, he declared that, unless the nation
repented of their sins and turned to God, the
whole city should be overwhelmed. Even the
Temple itself, the sacred house of God, should
be destroyed, and the very site abandoned.

The priests and the people who heard this
denunciation were greatly exasperated. They
seized Jeremiah, and brought him before a great
judicial assembly for trial. The judges asked
him why he uttered such predictions, declaring
that by doing so he acted like an enemy to his
country and a traitor, and that he deserved to
die. The excitement was very great against
him, and the populace could hardly be restrained from open violence. In the midst of this
scene Jeremiah was calm and unmoved, and
replied to their accusations as follows:

"Every thing which I have said against this
city and this house, I have said by the direction of the Lord Jehovah. Instead of resenting
it, and being angry with me for delivering my
message, it becomes you to look at your sins,
and repent of them, and forsake them. It may

O

be that by so doing God will have mercy upon
you, and will avert the calamities which otherwise will most certainly come. As for myself,
here I am in your hands. You can deal with
me just as you think best. You can kill me
if you will, but you may be assured that if you
do so, you will bring the guilt and the consequences of shedding innocent blood upon yourselves and upon this city. I have said nothing
and foretold nothing but by commandment of
the Lord."*

The speech produced, as might have been
expected, a great division among the hearers.
Some were more angry than ever, and were
eager to put the prophet to death. Others defended him, and insisted that he should not die.
The latter, for the time, prevailed. Jeremiah
was set at liberty, and continued his earnest
expostulations with the people on account of
their sins, and his terrible annunciations of the
impending ruin of the city just as before.

These unwelcome truths being so painful for
the people to hear, other prophets soon began to
appear to utter contrary predictions, for the
sake, doubtless, of the popularity which they
should themselves acquire by their promises of

* Jeremiah, xxvi., 12-15.

B.C. 608.] RESTORATION OF THE JEWS. 211

Symbolic method of teaching.   The wooden yoke and the iron yoke

returning peace and prosperity. The name of
one of these false prophets was Hananiah. On
one occasion, Jeremiah, in order to present and
enforce what he had to say more effectually on
the minds of the people by means of a visible
symbol, made a small wooden yoke, by divine
direction, and placed it upon his neck, as a token of the bondage which his predictions were
threatening. Hananiah took this yoke from his
neck and broke it, saying that, as he had thus
broken Jeremiah's wooden yoke, so God would
break the yoke of Nebuchadnezzar from all nations within two years; and then, even those
of the Jews who had already been taken captive to Babylon should return again in peace.
Jeremiah replied that Hananiah's predictions
were false, and that, though the wooden yoke
was broken, God would make for Nebuchadnezzar a yoke of iron, with which he should
bend the Jewish nation in a bondage more cruel
than ever. Still, Jeremiah himself predicted
that after seventy years from the time when
the last great captivity should come, the Jews
should all be restored again to their native land.

He expressed this certain restoration of the
Jews, on one occasion, by a sort of symbol, by
means of which he made a much stronger im-

pression on the minds of the people than could
have been done by simple words. There was
a piece of land in the country of Benjamin, one
of the provinces of Judea, which belonged to
the family of Jeremiah, and it was held in such
a way that, by paying a certain sum of money,
Jeremiah himself might possess it, the right
of redemption being in him. Jeremiah was in
prison at this time. His uncle's son came into
the court of the prison, and proposed to him to
purchase the land. Jeremiah did so in the most
public and formal manner. The title deeds
were drawn up and subscribed, witnesses were
summoned, the money weighed and paid over,
the whole transaction being regularly completed according to the forms and usages then common for the conveyance of landed property.
When all was finished, Jeremiah gave the
papers into the hands of his scribe, directing
him to put them safely away and preserve them
with care, for after a certain period the country
of Judea would again be restored to the peaceable possession of the Jews, and such titles to
land would possess once more their full and
original value.

On one occasion, when Jeremiah's personal
liberty was restricted so that he could not utter

publicly, himself, his prophetical warnings, he
employed Baruch, his scribe, to write them from
his dictation, with a view of reading them to
the people from some public and frequented
part of the city.   The prophecy thus dictated
was inscribed upon a roll of parchment.   Baruch waited, when he had completed the writing, until a favorable opportunity occurred for
reading it, which was on the occasion of a great
festival that was held at Jerusalem, and which
brought the inhabitants of the land together
from all parts of Judea.   On the day of the
festival, Baruch took the roll in his hand, and
stationed himself at a very public place, at the
entrance of one of the great courts of the Temple; there, calling upon the people to hear him,
he began to read.   A great concourse gathered
around him, and all listened to him with profound attention.   One of the by-standers, however, went down immediately into the city, to
the king's palace, and reported to the king's
council, who were then assembled there, that a
great concourse was convened in one of the
courts of the Temple, and that Baruch was
there reading to them a discourse or prophecy
which had been written by Jeremiah.   The
members of the council sent a summons to Ba

214   CYRUS THE GREAT. [B.C. 608

Baruch summoned before the council.   The roll sent to the king.

ruch to come immediately to them, and to bring
his writing with him.

When Baruch arrived, they directed him to
read what he had written. Baruch accordingly
read it. They asked him when and how that
discourse was written. Baruch replied that he
had written it, word by word, from the dictation of Jeremiah. The officers informed him
that they should be obliged to report the circumstances to the king, and they counseled
Baruch to go to Jeremiah and recommend to
him to conceal himself, lest the king, in his anger, should do him some sudden and violent injury.*

The officers then, leaving the roll in one of
their own apartments, went to the king, and
reported the facts to him. He sent one of his
attendants, named Jehudi, to bring the roll.
When it came, the king directed Jehudi to
read it. Jehudi did so, standing by a fire which
had been made in the apartment, for it was
bitter cold.

After Jehudi had read a few pages from the
roll, finding that it contained a repetition of
the same denunciations and warnings by which

* See the account of these transactions in the 36th chapter
of Jeremiah.

the king had often been displeased before, he
took a knife and began to cut the parchment
into pieces, and to throw it on the fire. Some
other persons who were standing by interfered,
and earnestly begged the king not to allow the
roll to be burned. But the king did not interfere. He permitted Jehudi to destroy the parchment altogether, and then sent officers to take
Jeremiah and Baruch, and bring them to him;
but they were nowhere to be found.

The prophet, on one occasion, was reduced
to extreme distress by the persecutions which
his faithfulness, and the incessant urgency of
his warnings and expostulations had brought
upon him. It was at a time when the Chaldean armies had been driven away from Jerusalem for a short period by the Egyptians, as one
vulture drives away another from its prey. Jeremiah determined to avail himself of the opportunity to go to the province of Benjamin, to
visit his friends and family there. He was intercepted, however, at one of the gates, on his
way, and accused of a design to make his escape from the city, and go over to the Chaldeans. The prophet earnestly denied this charge.
They paid no regard to his declarations, but
sent him back to Jerusalem, to the officers of

216 CYRUS THE GREAT. [B.C 608.

The king sends for Jeremiah. He is imprisoned

the king's government, who confined him in a house which they used as a prison.

After he had remained in this place of confinement for several days, the king sent and took him from it, and brought him to the palace. The king inquired whether he had any prophecy to utter from the Lord. Jeremiah replied that the word of the Lord was, that the Chaldeans should certainly return again, and that Zedekiah himself should fall into their hands, and be carried captive to Babylon. While he thus persisted so strenuously in the declarations which he had made so often before, he demanded of the king that he should not be sent back again to the house of imprisonment from which he had been rescued. The king said he would not send him back, and he accordingly directed, instead, that he should be taken to the court of the public prison, where his confinement would be less rigorous, and there he was to be supplied daily with food, so long, as the king expressed it, as there should be any food remaining in the city.

But Jeremiah's enemies were not at rest. They came again, after a time, to the king, and represented to him that the prophet, by his gloomy and terrible predictions, discouraged and depressed the hearts of the people, and weakened their hands; that he ought, accordingly, to be regarded as a public enemy; and they begged the king to proceed decidedly against him. The king replied that he would give him into their hands, and they might do with him what they pleased.

There was a dungeon in the prison, the only access to which was from above. Prisoners were let down into it with ropes, and left there to die of hunger. The bottom of it was wet and miry, and the prophet, when let down into its gloomy depths, sank into the deep mire. Here he would soon have died of hunger and misery; but the king, feeling some misgivings in regard to what he had done, lest it might really be a true prophet of God that he had thus delivered into the hands of his enemies, inquired what the people had done with their prisoner; and when he learned that he had been thus, as it were, buried alive, he immediately sent officers with orders to take him out of the dungeon. The officers went to the dungeon. They opened the mouth of it. They had brought ropes with them, to be used for drawing the unhappy prisoner up, and cloths, also, which he was to fold together and place under his arms, where the ropes were to pass. These ropes and cloths they let down into the dungeon, and called upon Jeremiah to place them properly around his body. Thus they drew him safely up out of the dismal den.

These cruel persecutions of the faithful prophet were all unavailing either to silence his voice or to avert the calamities which his warnings portended. At the appointed time, the judgments which had been so long predicted came in all their terrible reality. The Babylonians invaded the land in great force, and encamped about the city. The siege continued for two years. At the end of that time the famine became insupportable. Zedekiah, the king, determined to make a sortie, with as strong a force as he could command, secretly, at night, in hopes to escape with his own life, and intending to leave the city to its fate. He succeeded in passing out through the city gates with his band of followers, and in actually passing the Babylonian lines; but he had not gone far before his escape was discovered. He was pursued and taken. The city was then stormed, and, as usual in such cases, it was given up to plunder and destruction. Vast numbers of the inhabitants were killed; many more were tak-

en captive; the principal buildings, both public
and private, were burned; the walls were broken down, and all the public treasures of the
Jews, the gold and silver vessels of the Temple,
and a vast quantity of private plunder, were
carried away to Babylon by the conquerors.
All this was seventy years before the conquest
of Babylon by Cyrus.

Of course, during the time of this captivity,
a very considerable portion of the inhabitants
of Judea remained in their native land. The
deportation of a whole people to a foreign land
is impossible. A vast number, however, of the
inhabitants of the country were carried away,
and they remained, for two generations, in a
miserable bondage. Some of them were employed as agricultural laborers in the rural districts of Babylon; others remained in the city,
and were engaged in servile labors there. The
prophet Daniel lived in the palaces of the king
He was summoned, as the reader will recollect,
to Belshazzar's feast, on the night when Cyrus
forced his way into the city, to interpret the
mysterious writing on the wall, by which the
fall of the Babylonian monarchy was announced
in so terrible a manner.

One year after Cyrus had conquered Baby-
15

lon, he issued an edict authorizing the Jews to return to Jerusalem, and to rebuild the city and the Temple. This event had been long before predicted by the prophets, as the result which God had determined upon for purposes of his own. We should not naturally have expected that such a conqueror as Cyrus would feel any real and honest interest in promoting the designs of God; but still, in the proclamation which he issued authorizing the Jews to return, he acknowledged the supreme divinity of Jehovah, and says that he was charged by him with the work of rebuilding his Temple, and restoring his worship at its ancient seat on Mount Zion. It has, however, been supposed by some scholars, who have examined attentively all the circumstances connected with these transactions, that so far as Cyrus was influenced by political considerations in ordering the return of the Jews, his design was to re-establish that nation as a barrier between his dominions and those of the Egyptians. The Egyptians and the Chaldeans had long been deadly enemies, and now that Cyrus had become master of the Chaldean realms, he would, of course, in assuming their territories and their power, be obliged to defend himself against their foes

B.C.536.] RESTORATION OF THE JEWS. 223

Assembling of the Jews.   The number that returned

Whatever may have been the motives of Cyrus, he decided to allow the Hebrew captives to return, and he issued a proclamation to that effect. As seventy years had elapsed since the captivity commenced, about two generations had passed away, and there could have been very few then living who had ever seen the land of their fathers. The Jews were, however, all eager to return. They collected in a vast assembly, with all the treasures which they were allowed to take, and the stores of provisions and baggage, and with horses, and mules, and other beasts of burden to transport them. When assembled for the march, it was found that the number, of which a very exact census was taken, was forty-nine thousand six hundred and ninety-seven.

They had also with them seven or eight hundred horses, about two hundred and fifty mules, and about five hundred camels. The chief part, however, of their baggage and stores was borne by asses, of which there were nearly seven thousand in the train. The march of this peaceful multitude of families—men, women, and children together—burdened as they went, not with arms and ammunition for conquest and destruction, but with tools and implements for honest

industry, and stores of provisions and utensils
for the peaceful purposes of social life, as it was,
in its bearings and results, one of the grandest
events of history, so it must have presented, in
its progress, one of the most extraordinary spectacles that the world has ever seen.

The grand caravan pursued its long and toilsome march from Babylon to Jerusalem without molestation.   All arrived safely, and the
people immediately commenced the work of
repairing the walls of the city and rebuilding
the Temple.   When, at length, the foundations
of the Temple were laid, a great celebration was
held to commemorate the event.   This celebration exhibited a remarkable scene of mingled
rejoicing and mourning.   The younger part of
the population, who had never seen Jerusalem
in its former grandeur, felt only exhilaration and
joy at their re-establishment in the city of their
fathers.   The work of raising the edifice, whose
foundations they had laid, was to them simply
a new enterprise, and they looked forward to
the work of carrying it on with pride and pleasure.   The old men, however, who remembered
the former Temple, were filled with mournful
recollections of days of prosperity and peace in
their childhood, and of the magnificence of the

former Temple, which they could now never
hope to see realized again.   It was customary
in those days, to express sorrow and grief by
exclamations and outcries, as gladness and joy
are expressed audibly now.   Accordingly, on
this occasion, the cries of grief and of bitter regret at the thought of losses which could now
never be retrieved, were mingled with the shouts
of rejoicing and triumph raised by the ardent
and young, who knew nothing of the past, but
looked forward with hope and happiness to the
future.

The Jews encountered various hinderances,
and met with much opposition in their attempts
to reconstruct their ancient city, and to re-establish the Mosaic ritual there.   We must, however, now return to the history of Cyrus, referring the reader for a narrative of the circumstances connected with the rebuilding of Jerusalem to the very minute account given in the
sacred books of Ezra and Nehemiah.

P

CHAPTER X.
THE STORY OF PANTHEA.

IN the preceding chapters of this work, we have followed mainly the authority of Herodotus, except, indeed, in the account of the visit of Cyrus to his grandfather in his childhood, which is taken from Xenophon. We shall, in this chapter, relate the story of Panthea, which is also one of Xenophon's tales. We give it as a specimen of the romantic narratives in which Xenophon's history abounds, and on account of the many illustrations of ancient manners and customs which it contains, leaving it for each reader to decide for himself what weight he will attach to its claims to be regarded as veritable history. We relate the story here in our own language, but as to the facts, we follow faithfully the course of Xenophon's narration.

Panthea was a Susian captive. She was taken, together with a great many other captives and much plunder, after one of the great battles which Cyrus fought with the Assyrians.

Her husband was an Assyrian general, though
he himself was not captured at this time with
his wife. The spoil which came into possession
of the army on the occasion of the battle in
which Panthea was taken was of great value.
There were beautiful and costly suits of arms,
rich tents made of splendid materials and highly
ornamented, large sums of money, vessels of
silver and gold, and slaves—some prized for their
beauty, and others for certain accomplishments
which were highly valued in those days. Cyrus appointed a sort of commission to divide this
spoil. He pursued always a very generous policy on all these occasions, showing no desire to
secure such treasures to himself, but distributing them with profuse liberality among his
officers and soldiers.

The commissioners whom he appointed in
this case divided the spoil among the various
generals of the army, and among the different
bodies of soldiery, with great impartiality.
Among the prizes assigned to Cyrus were two
singing women of great fame, and this Susian
lady. Cyrus thanked the distributors for the
share of booty which they had thus assigned to
him, but said that if any of his friends wished
for either of these captives, they could have

them. An officer asked for one of the singers.
Cyrus gave her to him immediately, saying, "I
consider myself more obliged to you for asking
her, than you are to me for giving her to you."
As for the Susian lady, Cyrus had not yet seen
her, but he called one of his most intimate and
confidential friends to him, and requested him
to take her under his charge.

The name of this officer was Araspes. He
was a Mede, and he had been Cyrus's particular friend and playmate when he was a boy,
visiting his grandfather in Media. The reader
will perhaps recollect that he is mentioned toward the close of our account of that visit, as
the special favorite to whom Cyrus presented
his robe or mantle when he took leave of his
friends in returning to his native land.

Araspes, when he received this charge, asked
Cyrus whether he had himself seen the 'ady.
Cyrus replied that he had not. Araspes then
proceeded to give an account of her. The name
of her husband was Abradates, and he was the
king of Susa, as they termed him. The reason
why he was not taken prisoner at the same
time with his wife was, that when the battle
was fought and the Assyrian camp captured,
he was absent, having gone away on an em-

bassage to another nation. This circumstance shows that Abradates, though called a king, could hardly have been a sovereign and inde pendent prince, but rather a governor or vice roy—those words expressing to our minds more truly the station of such a sort of king as could be sent on an embassy.

Araspes went on to say that, at the time of their making the capture, he, with some others, went into Panthea's tent, where they found her and her attendant ladies sitting on the ground, with veils over their faces, patiently awaiting their doom. Notwithstanding the concealment produced by the attitudes and dress of these la dies, there was something about the air and figure of Panthea which showed at once that she was the queen. The leader of Araspes's party asked them all to rise. They did so, and then the superiority of Panthea was still more apparent than before. There was an extraor dinary grace and beauty in her attitude and in all her motions. She stood in a dejected pos ture, and her countenance was sad, though in expressibly lovely. She endeavored to appear calm and composed, though the tears had evi dently been falling from her eyes.

The soldiers pitied her in her distress, and

the leader of the party attempted to console her,
as Araspes said, by telling her that she had
nothing to fear; that they were aware that her
husband was a most worthy and excellent man;
and although, by this capture, she was lost to
him, she would have no cause to regret the
event, for she would be reserved for a new husband not at all inferior to her former one either
in person, in understanding, in rank, or in power.

These well-meant attempts at consolation did
not appear to have the good effect desired.
They only awakened Panthea's grief and suffering anew. The tears began to fall again
faster than before. Her grief soon became more
and more uncontrollable. She sobbed and cried
aloud, and began to wring her hands and tear her
mantle—the customary Oriental expression of
inconsolable sorrow and despair. Araspes said
that in these gesticulations her neck, and hands,
and a part of her face appeared, and that she
was the most beautiful woman that he had ever
beheld. He wished Cyrus to see her.

Cyrus said, "No; he would not see her by
any means." Araspes asked him why. He
said that there would be danger that he should
forget his duty to the army, and lose his interest in the great military enterprise in which he

was engaged, if he should allow himself to become captivated by the charms of such a lady, as he very probably would be if he were now to visit her. Araspes said in reply that Cyrus might at least see her; as to becoming captivated with her, and devoting himself to her to such a degree as to neglect his other duties, he could certainly control himself in respect to that danger. Cyrus said that it was not certain that he could so control himself; and then there followed a long discussion between Cyrus and Araspes, in which Araspes maintained that every man had the command of his own heart and affections, and that, with proper determination and energy, he could direct the channels in which they should run, and confine them within such limits and bounds as he pleased. Cyrus, on the other hand, maintained that human passions were stronger than the human will; that no one could rely on the strength of his resolutions to control the impulses of the heart once strongly excited, and that a man's only safety was in controlling the circumstances which tended to excite them. This was specially true, he said, in respect to the passion of love. The experience of mankind, he said, had shown that no strength of moral principle, no

firmness of purpose, no fixedness of resolution,
no degree of suffering, no fear of shame, was
sufficient to control, in the hearts of men, the
impetuosity of the passion of love, when it was
once fairly awakened. In a word, Araspes ad-
vocated, on the subject of love, a sort of new
school philosophy, while that of Cyrus leaned
very seriously toward the old.

In conclusion, Cyrus jocosely counseled Araspes to beware lest he should prove that love was
stronger than the will by becoming himself
enamored of the beautiful Susian queen. Araspes said that Cyrus need not fear; there was
no danger. He must be a miserable wretch
indeed, he said, who could not summon within
him sufficient resolution and energy to control
his own passions and desires. As for himself,
he was sure that he was safe.

As usual with those who are self-confident
and boastful, Araspes failed when the time of
trial came. He took charge of the royal captive whom Cyrus committed to him with a very
firm resolution to be faithful to his trust. He
pitied the unhappy queen's misfortunes, and
admired the heroic patience and gentleness of
spirit with which she bore them. The beauty
of her countenance, and her thousand personal

charms, which were all heightened by the expression of sadness and sorrow which they bore, touched his heart. It gave him pleasure to grant her every indulgence consistent with her condition of captivity, and to do every thing in his power to promote her welfare. She was very grateful for these favors, and the few brief words and looks of kindness with which she returned them repaid him for his efforts to please her a thousand-fold. He saw her, too, in her tent, in the presence of her maidens, at all times; and as she looked upon him as only her custodian and guard, and as, too, her mind was wholly occupied by the thoughts of her absent husband and her hopeless grief, her actions were entirely free and unconstrained in his presence. This made her only the more attractive; every attitude and movement seemed to possess, in Araspes's mind, an inexpressible charm. In a word, the result was what Cyrus had predicted. Araspes became wholly absorbed in the interest which was awakened in him by the charms of the beautiful captive. He made many resolutions, but they were of no avail. While he was away from her, he felt strong in his determination to yield to these feelings no more; but as soon as he came into her presence, all these resolutions melted who.ly away, and he yielded his heart entirely to the control of emotions which, however vincible they might appear at a distance, were found, when the time of trial came, to possess a certain mysterious and magic power, which made it most delightful for the heart to yield before them in the contest, and utterly impossible to stand firm and resist. In a word, when seen at a distance, love appeared to him an enemy which he was ready to brave, and was sure that he could overcome; but when near, it transformed itself into the guise of a friend, and he accordingly threw down the arms with which he had intended to combat it, and gave himself up to it in a delirium of pleasure.

Things continued in this state for some time. The army advanced from post to post, and from encampment to encampment, taking the captives in their train. New cities were taken, new provinces overrun, and new plans for future conquests were formed. At last a case occurred in which Cyrus wished to send some one as a spy into a distant enemy's country. The circumstances were such that it was necessary that a person of considerable intelligence and rank should go, as Cyrus wished the messenger

whom he should send to make his way to the
court of the sovereign, and become personally
acquainted with the leading men of the state,
and to examine the general resources of the
kingdom. It was a very different case from
that of an ordinary spy, who was to go into a
neighboring camp merely to report the numbers and disposition of an organized army. Cyrus was uncertain whom he should send on such
an embassy.

In the mean time, Araspes had ventured to
express to Panthea his love for her. She was
offended. In the first place, she was faithful to
her husband, and did not wish to receive such
addresses from any person. Then, besides,
she considered Araspes, having been placed in
charge of her by Cyrus, his master, only for the
purpose of keeping her safely, as guilty of a
betrayal of his trust in having dared to cherish
and express sentiments of affection for her himself. She, however, forbore to reproach him,
or to complain of him to Cyrus. She simply
repelled the advances that he made, supposing
that, if she did this with firmness and decision,
Araspes would feel rebuked and would say no
more. It did not, however, produce this effect.
Araspes continued to importune her with dec-

larations of love, and at length she felt compelled to appeal to Cyrus.

Cyrus, instead of being incensed at what
might have been considered a betrayal of trust
on the part of Araspes, only laughed at the failure and fall in which all his favorite's promises
and boastings had ended. He sent a messenger to Araspes to caution him in regard to his
conduct, telling him that he ought to respect
the feelings of such a woman as Panthea had
proved herself to be. The messenger whom
Cyrus sent was not content with delivering his
message as Cyrus had dictated it. He made it
much more stern and severe. In fact, he reproached the lover, in a very harsh and bitter
manner, for indulging such a passion. He told
him that he had betrayed a sacred trust reposed
in him, and acted in a manner at once impious
and unjust. Araspes was overwhelmed with
remorse and anguish, and with fear of the consequences which might ensue, as men are when
the time arrives for being called to account for
transgressions which, while they were committing them, gave them little concern.

When Cyrus heard how much Araspes had
been distressed by the message of reproof which
he had received, and by his fears of punishment,

he sent for him. Araspes came. Cyrus told
him that he had no occasion to be alarmed. "I
do not wonder," said he, "at the result which
has happened. We all know how difficult it is
to resist the influence which is exerted upon our
minds by the charms of a beautiful woman,
when we are thrown into circumstances of
familiar intercourse with her. Whatever of
wrong there has been ought to be considered
as more my fault than yours. I was wrong in
placing you in such circumstances of temptation, by giving you so beautiful a woman in
charge."

Araspes was very much struck with the generosity of Cyrus, in thus endeavoring to soothe
his anxiety and remorse, and taking upon himself the responsibility and the blame. He
thanked Cyrus very earnestly for his kindness;
but he said that, notwithstanding his sovereign's
willingness to forgive him, he felt still oppressed
with grief and concern, for the knowledge of
his fault had been spread abroad in the army;
his enemies were rejoicing over him, and were
predicting his disgrace and ruin; and some persons had even advised him to make his escape,
by absconding before any worse calamity should
befall him.

16

"If this is so," said Cyrus, "it puts it in your power to render me a very essential service." Cyrus then explained to Araspes the necessity that he was under of finding some confidential agent to go on a secret mission into the enemy's country, and the importance that the messenger should go under such circumstances as not to be suspected of being Cyrus's friend in disguise. "You can pretend to abscond," said he; "it will be immediately said that you fled for fear of my displeasure. I will pretend to send in pursuit of you. The news of your evasion will spread rapidly, and will be carried, doubtless, into the enemy's country; so that, when you arrive there, they will be prepared to welcome you as a deserter from my cause, and a refugee."

This plan was agreed upon, and Araspes prepared for his departure. Cyrus gave him his instructions, and they concerted together the information—fictitious, of course—which he was to communicate to the enemy in respect to Cyrus's situation and designs. When all was ready for his departure, Cyrus asked him how it was that he was so willing to separate himself thus from the beautiful Panthea. He said in reply, that when he was absent from Panthea,

he was capable of easily forming any determination, and of pursuing any line of conduct that
his duty required, while yet, in her presence, he
found his love for her, and the impetuous feelings to which it gave rise, wholly and absolutely uncontrollable.

As soon as Araspes was gone, Panthea, who
supposed that he had really fled for fear of the
indignation of the king, in consequence of his
unfaithfulness to his trust, sent to Cyrus a message, expressing her regret at the unworthy conduct and the flight of Araspes, and saying that
she could, and gladly would, if he consented,
repair the loss which the desertion of Araspes
occasioned by sending for her own husband.
He was, she said, dissatisfied with the government under which he lived, having been cruelly
and tyrannically treated by the prince. "If
you will allow me to send for him," she added,
"I am sure he will come and join your army;
and I assure you that you will find him a much
more faithful and devoted servant than Araspes
has been."

Cyrus consented to this proposal, and Panthea sent for Abradates. Abradates came at
the head of two thousand horse, which formed
a very important addition to the forces under

Cyrus's command. The meeting between Pan
thea and her husband was joyful in the extreme
When Abradates learned from his wife how honorable and kind had been the treatment which
Cyrus had rendered to her, he was overwhelmed
with a sense of gratitude, and he declared that
he would do the utmost in his power to requite
the obligations he was under.

Abradates entered at once, with great ardor
and zeal, into plans for making the force which
he had brought as efficient as possible in the
service of Cyrus. He observed that Cyrus was
interested, at that time, in attempting to build
and equip a corps of armed chariots, such as
were often used in fields of battle in those days.
This was a very expensive sort of force, corre-
ponding, in that respect, with the artillery used
in modern times. The carriages were heavy
and strong, and were drawn generally by two
horses. They had short, scythe-like blades of
steel projecting from the axle-trees on each side,
by which the ranks of the enemy were mowed
down when the carriages were driven among
them. The chariots were made to contain, besides the driver of the horses, one or more warriors, each armed in the completest manner
These warriors stood on the floor of the vehicle.

The War Chariot of Abradates.

and fought with javelins and spears. The great
plains which abound in the interior countries
of Asia were very favorable for this species of
warfare.

Abradates immediately fitted up for Cyrus a
hundred such chariots at his own expense, and
provided horses to draw them from his own
troop. He made one chariot much larger than
the rest, for himself, as he intended to take
command of this corps of chariots in person.
His own chariot was to be drawn by eight
horses. His wife Panthea was very much interested in these preparations. She wished to
do something herself toward the outfit. She
accordingly furnished, from her own private
treasures, a helmet, a corslet, and arm-pieces
of gold. These articles formed a suit of armor
sufficient to cover all that part of the body
which would be exposed in standing in the
chariot. She also provided breast-pieces and
side-pieces of brass for the horses. The whole
chariot, thus equipped, with its eight horses in
their gay trappings and resplendent armor, and
with Abradates standing within it, clothed in
his panoply of gold, presented, as it drove, in the
sight of the whole army, around the plain of
the encampment, a most imposing spectacle

It was a worthy leader, as the spectators thought, to head the formidable column of a hundred similar engines which were to follow in its train. If we imagine the havoc which a hundred scythe-armed carriages would produce when driven, with headlong fury, into dense masses of men, on a vast open plain, we shall have some idea of one item of the horrors of ancient war.

The full splendor of Abradates's equipments were not, however, displayed at first, for Panthea kept what she had done a secret for a time, intending to reserve her contribution for a parting present to her husband when the period should arrive for going into battle. She had accordingly taken the measure for her work by stealth, from the armor which Abradates was accustomed to wear, and had caused the artificers to make the golden pieces with the utmost secrecy. Besides the substantial defenses of gold which she provided, she added various other articles for ornament and decoration There was a purple robe, a crest for the helmet, which was of a violet color, plumes and likewise bracelets for the wrists. Panthea kept all these things herself until the day arrived when her husband was going into battle for the first time with his train, and then, when

he went into his tent to prepare himself to ascend his chariot, she brought them to him.

Abradates was astonished when he saw them
He soon understood how they had been provided, and he exclaimed, with a heart full of surprise and pleasure, " And so, to provide me
with this splendid armor and dress, you have
been depriving yourself of all your finest and
most beautiful ornaments!"

" No," said Panthea, " you are yourself my
finest ornament, if you appear in other people's
eyes as you do in mine, and I have not depriv-
ed myself of you."

The appearance which Abradates made in
other people's eyes was certainly very splendid
on this occasion. There were many spectators
present to see him mount his chariot and drive
away; but so great was their admiration of
Panthea's affection and regard for her husband,
and so much impressed were they with her
beauty, that the great chariot, the resplendent
horses, and the grand warrior with his armor of
gold, which the magnificent equipage was intended to convey, were, all together, scarcely
able to draw away the eyes of the spectators
from her. She stood, for a while, by the side
of the chariot, addressing her husband in an un-

der tone, reminding him of the obligations which
they were under to Cyrus for his generous and
noble treatment of her, and urging him, now
that he was going to be put to the test, to re-
deem the promise which she had made in his
name, that Cyrus would find him faithful,
brave, and true.

The driver then closed the door by which Abradates had mounted, so that Panthea was separated from her husband, though she could still
see him as he stood in his place. She gazed
upon him with a countenance full of affection
and solicitude. She kissed the margin of the
chariot as it began to move away. She walked
along after it as it went, as if, after all, she
could not bear the separation. Abradates turned, and when he saw her coming on after the
carriage, he said, waving his hand for a parting
salutation, "Farewell, Panthea ; go back now
to your tent, and do not be anxious about me.
Farewell." Panthea turned—her attendants
came and took her away—the spectators all
turned, too, to follow her with their eyes, and
no one paid any regard to the chariot or to Abradates until she was gone.

On the field of battle, before the engagement
commenced, Cyrus, in passing along the lines,

paused, when he came to the chariots of Abra
dates, to examine the arrangements which had
been made for them, and to converse a moment
with the chief. He saw that the chariots were
drawn up in a part of the field where there was
opposed to them a very formidable array of
Egyptian soldiers. The Egyptians in this war
were allies of the enemy. Abradates, leaving
his chariot in the charge of his driver, descended and came to Cyrus, and remained in conversation with him for a few moments, to receive
his last orders. Cyrus directed him to remain
where he was, and not to attack the enemy
until he received a certain signal. At length
the two chieftains separated; Abradates returned to his chariot, and Cyrus moved on. Abradates then moved slowly along his lines, to
encourage and animate his men, and to give
them the last directions in respect to the charge
which they were about to make on the enemy
when the signal should be given. All eyes were
turned to the magnificent spectacle which his
equipage presented as it advanced toward them;
the chariot, moving slowly along the line, the
tall and highly-decorated form of its commander
rising in the center of it, while the eight horses,
animated by the sound of the trumpets, and by

the various excitements of the scene, stepped proudly, their brazen armor clanking as they came.

When, at length, the signal was given, Abradates, calling on the other chariots to follow, put his horses to their speed, and the whole line rushed impetuously on to the attack of the Egyptians. War horses, properly trained to their work, will fight with their hoofs with almost as much reckless determination as men will with spears. They rush madly on to encounter whatever opposition there may be before them, and strike down and leap over whatever comes in their way, as if they fully understood the nature of the work that their riders or drivers were wishing them to do. Cyrus, as he passed along from one part of the battle field to another, saw the horses of Abradates's line dashing thus impetuously into the thickest ranks of the enemy. The men, on every side, were beaten down by the horses' hoofs, or overturned by the wheels, or cut down by the scythes; and they who here and there escaped these dangers, became the aim of the soldiers who stood in the chariots, and were transfixed with their spears. The heavy wheels rolled and jolted mercilessly over the bodies of the

wounded and the fallen, while the scythes
caught hold of and cut through every thing
that came in their way—whether the shafts of
javelins and spears, or the limbs and bodies of
men—and tore every thing to pieces in their terrible career. As Cyrus rode rapidly by, he saw
Abradates in the midst of this scene, driving on
in his chariot, and shouting to his men in a
phrensy of excitement and triumph.

The battle in which these events occurred
was one of the greatest and most important
which Cyrus fought. He gained the victory.
His enemies were every where routed and driv-
en from the field. When the contest was at
length decided, the army desisted from the
slaughter and encamped for the night. On
the following day, the generals assembled at
the tent of Cyrus to discuss the arrangements
which were to be made in respect to the disposition of the captives and of the spoil, and to
the future movements of the army. Abradates
was not there. For a time, Cyrus, in the excitement and confusion of the scene, did not observe his absence. At length he inquired for
him. A soldier present told him that he had
been killed from his chariot in the midst of the
Egyptians, and that his wife was at that mo-

ment attending to the interment of the body,
on the banks of a river which flowed near the
field of battle.   Cyrus, on hearing this, uttered
a loud exclamation of astonishment and sorrow.
He dropped the business in which he had been
engaged with his council, mounted his horse,
commanded attendants to follow him with every
thing that could be necessary on such an occasion, and then, asking those who knew to lead
the way, he drove off to find Panthea.

When he arrived at the spot, the dead body
of Abradates was lying upon the ground, while
Panthea sat by its side, holding the head in her
lap, overwhelmed herself with unutterable sorrow.   Cyrus leaped from his horse, knelt down
by the side of the corpse, saying, at the same
time, " Alas ! thou brave and faithful soul, and
art thou gone ?"

At the same time, he took hold of the hand
of Abradates ; but, as he attempted to raise it,
the arm came away from the body.   It had
been cut off by an Egyptian sword.   Cyrus was
himself shocked at the spectacle, and Panthea's
grief broke forth anew.   She cried out with bitter anguish, replaced the arm in the position in
which she had arranged it before, and told
Cyrus that the rest of the body was in the

same condition. Whenever she attempted to speak, her sobs and tears almost prevented her utterance. She bitterly reproached herself for having been, perhaps, the cause of her husband's death, by urging him, as she had done, to fidelity and courage when he went into battle. "And now," she said, "he is dead, while I, who urged him forward into the danger, am still alive."

Cyrus said what he could to console Panthea's grief; but he found it utterly inconsolable. He gave directions for furnishing her with every thing which she could need, and promised her that he would make ample arrangements for providing for her in future. "You shall be treated," he said, "while you remain with me, in the most honorable manner ; or if you have any friends whom you wish to join, you shall be sent to them safely whenever you please."

Panthea thanked him for his kindness. She had a friend, she said, whom she wished to join, and she would let him know in due time who it was. In the mean time, she wished that Cyrus would leave her alone, for a while, with her servants, and her waiting-maid, and the dead body of her husband. Cyrus accordingly withdrew. As soon as he had gone, Panthea

Panthea kills herself on the dead body of her husband.

sent away the servants also, retaining the waiting-maid alone. The waiting-maid began to be anxious and concerned at witnessing these mysterious arrangements, as if they portended some new calamity. She wondered what her mistress was going to do. Her doubts were dispelled by seeing Panthea produce a sword, which she had kept concealed hitherto beneath her robe. Her maid begged her, with much earnestness and many tears, not to destroy herself; but Panthea was immovable. She said she could not live any longer. She directed the maid to envelop her body, as soon as she was dead, in the same mantle with her husband, and to have them both deposited together in the same grave; and before her stupefied attendant could do any thing to save her, she sat down by the side of her husband's body, laid her head upon his breast, and in that position gave herself the fatal wound. In a few minutes she ceased to breathe.

Cyrus expressed his respect for the memory of Abradates and Panthea by erecting a lofty monument over their common grave.

CONVERSATIONS.   253

General character of Xenophon's history.   Dialogues and conversations

CHAPTER XI.
CONVERSATIONS.

WE have given the story of Panthea, as contained in the preceding chapter, in our own language, it is true, but without any intentional addition or embellishment whatever. Each reader will judge for himself whether such a narrative, written for the entertainment of vast assemblies at public games and cele- brations, is most properly to be regarded as an invention of romance, or as a simple record of veritable history.

A great many extraordinary and dramatic incidents and adventures, similar in general character to the story of Panthea, are inter woven with the narrative in Xenophon's his- tory.   There are also, besides these, many long and minute details of dialogues and conversa- tions, which, if they had really occurred, would have required a very high degree of skill in ste- nography to produce such reports of them as Xenophon has given.   The incidents, too, out of which these conversations grew, are worthy of

17

attention, as we can often judge, by the nature
and character of an incident described, whether
it is one which it is probable might actually occur in real life, or only an invention intended to
furnish an opportunity and a pretext for the in-
culcation of the sentiments, or the expression of
the views of the different speakers.   It was the
custom in ancient days, much more than it is
now, to attempt to add to the point and spirit of
a discussion, by presenting the various views
which the subject naturally elicited in the form
of a conversation arising out of circumstances
invented to sustain it.   The incident in such
cases was, of course, a fiction, contrived to furnish points of attachment for the dialogue—a
sort of trellis, constructed artificially to support
the vine.

We shall present in this chapter some specimens of these conversations, which will give the
reader a much more distinct idea of the nature
of them than any general description can convey.

At one time in the course of Cyrus's career,
just after he had obtained some great victory,
and was celebrating his triumphs, in the midst
of his armies, with spectacles and games, he
instituted a series of races, in which the various

nations that were represented in his army furnished their several champions as competitors The army marched out from the city which Cyrus had captured, and where he was then residing, in a procession of the most imposing magnificence. Animals intended to be offered in sacrifice, caparisoned in trappings of gold, horsemen most sumptuously equipped, chariots of war splendidly built and adorned, and banners and trophies of every kind, were conspicuous in the train. When the vast procession reached the race-ground, the immense concourse was formed in ranks around it, and the racing went on.

When it came to the turn of the Sacian nation to enter the course, a private man, of no apparent importance in respect to his rank or standing, came forward as the champion; though the man appeared insignificant, his horse was as fleet as the wind. He flew around the arena with astonishing speed, and came in at the goal while his competitor was still midway of the course. Every body was astonished at this performance. Cyrus asked the Sacian whether he would be willing to sell that horse, if he could receive a kingdom in exchange for it—kingdoms being the coin with which such sovereigns as Cyrus made their purchases. The Sacian replied that he would not sell his horse for any kingdom, but that he would readily give him away to oblige a worthy man.

"Come with me," said Cyrus, "and I will show you where you may throw blindfold, and not miss a worthy man."

So saying, Cyrus conducted the Sacian to a part of the field where a number of his officers and attendants were moving to and fro, mounted upon their horses, or seated in their chariots of war. The Sacian took up a hard clod of earth from a bank as he walked along. At length they were in the midst of the group.

"Throw!" said Cyrus.

The Sacian shut his eyes and threw.

It happened that, just at that instant, an of· ficer named Pheraulas was riding by. He was conveying some orders which Cyrus had given him to another part of the field. Pheraulas had been originally a man of humble life, but he had been advanced by Cyrus to a high position on account of the great fidelity and zeal which he had evinced in the performance of his duty. The clod which the Sacian threw struck Pheraulas in the mouth, and wounded him severely. Now it is the part of a good soldier to stand at

his post or to press on, in obedience to his orders, as long as any physical capacity remains;
and Pheraulas, true to his military obligation,
rode on without even turning to see whence and
from what cause so unexpected and violent an
assault had proceeded.

The Sacian opened his eyes, looked around,
and coolly asked who it was that he had hit.
Cyrus pointed to the horseman who was riding
rapidly away, saying, "That is the man, who is
riding so fast past those chariots yonder. You
hit *him*."

"Why did he not turn back, then?" asked
the Sacian.

"It is strange that he did not," said Cyrus;
"he must be some madman."

The Sacian went in pursuit of him. He
found Pheraulas with his face covered with blood
and dirt, and asked him if he had received a
blow. "I have," said Pheraulas, "as you see."
"Then," said the Sacian, "I make you a present of my horse." Pheraulas asked an explanation. The Sacian accordingly gave him an account of what had taken place between himself
and Cyrus, and said, in the end, that he gladly
gave him his horse, as he, Pheraulas, had so de-
cisively proved himself to be a most worthy man

R

Pheraulas accepted the present, with many thanks, and he and the Sacian became there-after very strong friends.

Some time after this, Pheraulas invited the Sacian to an entertainment, and when the hour arrived, he set before his friend and the other guests a most sumptuous feast, which was serv-ed in vessels of gold and silver, and in an apart-ment furnished with carpets, and canopies, and couches of the most gorgeous and splendid de-scription. The Sacian was much impressed with this magnificence, and he asked Pheraulas whether he had been a rich man at home, that is, before he had joined Cyrus's army. Phe-raulas replied that he was not then rich. His father, he said, was a farmer, and he himself had been accustomed in early life to till the ground with the other laborers on his father's farm. All the wealth and luxury which he now enjoyed had been bestowed upon him, he said, by Cyrus.

"How fortunate you are!" said the Sacian; "and it must be that you enjoy your present riches all the more highly on account of having experienced in early life the inconveniences and ills of poverty. The pleasure must be more intense in having desires which have long been

felt gratified at last than if the objects which
they rested upon had been always in one's possession."

"You imagine, I suppose," replied Pheraul-
ias, "that I am a great deal happier in consequence of all this wealth and splendor; but it is
not so. As to the real enjoyments of which our
natures are capable, I can not receive more now
than I could before. I can not eat any more,
drink any more, or sleep any more, or do any
of these things with any more pleasure than
when I was poor. All that I gain by this
abundance is, that I have more to watch, more
to guard, more to take care of. I have many
servants, for whose wants I have to provide, and
who are a constant source of solicitude to me
One calls for food, another for clothes, and a
third is sick, and I must see that he has a physician. My other possessions, too, are a constant care. A man comes in, one day, and
brings me sheep that have been torn by the
wolves; and, on another day, tells me of oxen
that have fallen from a precipice, or of a dis-
temper which has broken out among the flocks
or herds. My wealth, therefore, brings me only
an increase of anxiety and trouble, without any
addition to my joys."

"But those things," said the Sacian, "which you name, must be unusual and extraordinary occurrences. When all things are going on prosperously and well with you, and you can look around on all your possessions and feel that they are yours, then certainly you must be happier than I am."

"It is true," said Pheraulas, "that there is a pleasure in the possession of wealth, but that pleasure is not great enough to balance the suffering which the calamities and losses inevitably connected with it occasion. That the suffering occasioned by losing our possessions is greater than the pleasure of retaining them, is proved by the fact that the pain of a loss is so exciting to the mind that it often deprives men of sleep, while they enjoy the most calm and quiet repose so long as their possessions are retained, which proves that the pleasure does not move them so deeply. They are kept awake by the vexation and chagrin on the one hand, but they are never kept awake by the satisfaction on the other."

"That is true," replied the Sacian. "Men are not kept awake by the mere continuing to possess their wealth, but they very often are by the original acquisition of it."

"Yes, indeed," replied Pheraulas; "and if the enjoyment of *being* rich could always continue as great as that of first becoming so, the rich would, I admit, be very happy men; but it is not, and can not be so. They who possess much, must lose, and expend, and give much; and this necessity brings more of pain than the possessions themselves can give of pleasure."

The Sacian was not convinced. The giving and expending, he maintained, would be to him, in itself, a source of pleasure. He should like to have much, for the very purpose of being able to expend much. Finally, Pheraulas proposed to the Sacian, since he seemed to think that riches would afford him so much pleasure, and as he himself, Pheraulas, found the possession of them only a source of trouble and care, that he would convey all his wealth to the Sacian, he himself to receive only an ordinary maintenance from it.

"You are in jest," said the Sacian.

"No," said Pheraulas, "I am in earnest." And he renewed his proposition, and pressed the Sacian urgently to accept of it.

The Sacian then said that nothing could give him greater pleasure than such an arrangement. He expressed great gratitude for so gen-

erous an offer, and promised that, if he received
the property, he would furnish Pheraulas with
most ample and abundant supplies for all his
wants, and would relieve him entirely of all responsibility and care. He promised, moreover,
to obtain from Cyrus permission that Pheraulas
should thereafter be excused from the duties of
military service, and from all the toils, privations, and hardships of war, so that he might
thenceforth lead a life of quiet, luxury, and
ease, and thus live in the enjoyment of all the
benefits which wealth could procure, without
its anxieties and cares.

The plan, thus arranged, was carried into effect. Pheraulas divested himself of his possessions, conveying them all to the Sacian. Both
parties were extremely pleased with the operation of the scheme, and they lived thus together
for a long time. Whatever Pheraulas acquired
in any way, he always brought to the Sacian,
and the Sacian, by accepting it, relieved Pheraulas of all responsibility and care. The Sacian loved Pheraulas, as Xenophon says, in
closing this narrative, because he was thus continually bringing him gifts; and Pheraulas loved the Sacian, because he was always willing to
take the gifts which were thus brought to him

Among the other conversations, whether real
or imaginary, which Xenophon records, he gives
some specimens of those which took place at
festive entertainments in Cyrus's tent, on occasions when he invited his officers to dine with
him.   He commenced the conversation, on one
of these occasions, by inquiring of some of the
officers present whether they did not think that
the common soldiers were equal to the officers
themselves in intelligence, courage, and military skill, and in all the other substantial qualities of a good soldier.

"I know not how that may be," replied one
of the officers.   "How they will prove when
they come into action with the enemy, I can
not tell; but a more perverse and churlish set
of fellows in camp, than those I have got in my
regiment, I never knew. The other day, for
example, when there had been a sacrifice, the
meat of the victims was sent around to be distributed to the soldiers. In our regiment, when
the steward came in with the first distribution,
he began by me, and so went round, as far as
what he had brought would go. The next time
he came, he began at the other end. The supply failed before he had got to the place where
he had left off before, so that there was a man

in the middle that did not get any thing. This man immediately broke out in loud and angry complaints, and declared that there was no equality or fairness whatever in such a mode of division, unless they began sometimes in the center of the line.

"Upon this," continued the officer, "I called to the discontented man, and invited him to come and sit by me, where he would have a better chance for a good share. He did so. It happened that, at the next distribution that was made, we were the last, and he fancied that only the smallest pieces were left, so he began to complain more than before. 'Oh, misery!' said he, 'that I should have to sit here!' 'Be patient,' said I; 'pretty soon they will begin the distribution with us, and then you will have the best chance of all.' And so it proved; for, at the next distribution, they began at us, and the man took his share first; but when the second and third men took theirs, he fancied that their pieces looked larger than his, and he reached forward and put his piece back into the basket, intending to change it; but the steward moved rapidly on, and he did not get another, so that he lost his distribution altogether. He was then quite furious with rage and vexation."

Cyrus and all the company laughed very heartily at these mischances of greediness and discontent ; and then other stories, of a somewhat similar character, were told by other guests. One officer said that a few days previous he was drilling a part of his troops, and he had before him on the plain what is called, in military language, a *squad* of men, whom he was teaching to march. When he gave the order to advance, one, who was at the head of the file, marched forward with great alacrity, but all the rest stood still. "I asked him," continued the officer, "what he was doing. 'Marching,' said he, 'as you ordered me to do.' 'It was not you alone that I ordered to march,' said I, 'but all.' So I sent him back to his place, and then gave the command again. Upon this they all advanced promiscuously and in disorder toward me, each one acting for himself, without regard to the others, and leaving the file-leader, who ought to have been at the head, altogether behind. The file-leader said, 'Keep back! keep back!' Upon this the men were offended, and asked what they were to do about such contradictory orders. 'One commands us to advance, and another to keep back!' said they; 'how are we to know which to obey?' "

Cyrus and his guests were so much amused at the awkwardness of these recruits, and the ridiculous predicament in which the officer was placed by it, that the narrative of the speaker was here interrupted by universal and long-continued laughter.

"Finally," continued the officer, "I sent the men all back to their places, and explained to them that, when a command was given, they were not to obey it in confusion and unseemly haste, but regularly and in order, each one following the man who stood before him. 'You must regulate your proceeding,' said I, 'by the action of the file-leader; when he advances, you must advance, following him in a line, and governing your movements in all respects by his.'"

"Just at this moment," continued the officer, "a man came to me for a letter which was to go to Persia, and which I had left in my tent. I directed the file-leader to run to my tent and bring the letter to me. He immediately set off, and the rest, obeying literally the directions which I had just been giving them, all followed, running behind him in a line like a troop of savages, so that I had the whole squad of twenty men running in a body off the field to fetch a letter!"

When the general hilarity which these recitals occasioned had a little subsided, Cyrus said he thought that they could not complain of the character of the soldiers whom they had to command, for they were certainly, according to these accounts, sufficiently ready to obey the orders they received. Upon this, a certain one of the guests who was present, named Aglaitadas, a gloomy and austere-looking man, who had not joined at all in the merriment which the conversation had caused, asked Cyrus if he believed those stories to be true.

"Why?" asked Cyrus; "what do *you* think of them?"

"*I* think," said Aglaitadas, "that these officers invented them to make the company laugh. It is evident that they were not telling the truth, since they related the stories in such a vain and arrogant way."

"Arrogant!" said Cyrus; "you ought not to call them arrogant; for, even if they invented their narrations, it was not to gain any selfish ends of their own, but only to amuse us and promote our enjoyment. Such persons should be called polite and agreeable rather than arrogant."

"If, Aglaitadas," said one of the officers who

had related the anecdotes, " we had told you melancholy stories to make you gloomy and wretched, you might have been justly displeased ; but you certainly ought not to complain of us for making you merry."

"Yes," said Aglaitadas, "I think I may. To make a man laugh is a very insignificant and useless thing.   It is far better to make him weep.   Such thoughts and such conversation as makes us serious, thoughtful, and sad, and even moves us to tears, are the most salutary and the best."

"Well," replied the officer, " if you will take my advice, you will lay out all your powers of inspiring gloom, and melancholy, and of bringing tears, upon our enemies, and bestow the mirth and laughter upon us.   There must be a prodigious deal of laughter in you, for none ever comes out.   You neither use nor expend it yourself, nor do you afford it to your friends."

"Then," said Aglaitadas, "why do you attempt to draw it from me ?"

"It *is* preposterous !" said another of the company ; "for one could more easily strike fire out of Aglaitadas than get a laugh from him !"

Aglaitadas could not help smiling at this comparison ; upon which Cyrus, with an air

of counterfeited gravity, reproved the person
who had spoken, saying that he had corrupted
the most sober man in the company by making
him smile, and that to disturb such gravity as
that of Aglaitadas was carrying the spirit of
mirth and merriment altogether too far.

These specimens will suffice. They serve to
give a more distinct idea of the Cyropædia of
Xenophon than any general description could
afford. The book is a drama, of which the principal elements are such narratives as the story
of Panthea, and such conversations as those contained in this chapter, intermingled with long
discussions on the principles of government, and
on the discipline and management of armies.
The principles and the sentiments which the
work inculcates and explains are now of little
value, being no longer applicable to the affairs
of mankind in the altered circumstances of the
present day. The book, however, retains its
rank among men on account of a certain beautiful and simple magnificence characterizing the
style and language in which it is written, which,
however, can not be appreciated except by those
who read the narrative in the original tongue.

18

270   CYRUS THE GREAT. [B.C. 530

Progress of Cyrus's conquests.   The northern countries

CHAPTER XII.

THE DEATH OF CYRUS.

AFTER having made the conquest of the Babylonian empire, Cyrus found himself the sovereign of nearly all of Asia, so far as it was then known. Beyond his dominions there lay, on every side, according to the opinions which then prevailed, vast tracts of uninhabitable territory, desolate and impassable. These wildernesses were rendered unfit for man, sometimes by excessive heat, sometimes by excessive cold, sometimes from being parched by perpetual drought, which produced bare and desolate deserts, and sometimes by incessant rains, which drenched the country and filled it with morasses and fens. On the north was the great Caspian Sea, then almost wholly unexplored, and extending, as the ancients believed, to the Polar Ocean.

On the west side of the Caspian Sea were the Caucasian Mountains, which were supposed, in those days, to be the highest on the globe. In the neighborhood of these mountains there was a country, inhabited by a wild and half-savage people, who were called Scythians. This was, in fact, a sort of generic term, which was applied, in those days, to almost all the aboriginal tribes beyond the confines of civilization. The Scythians, however, if such they can properly be called, who lived on the borders of the Caspian Sea, were not wholly uncivilized. They possessed many of those mechanical arts which are the first to be matured among warlike nations. They had no iron or steel, but they were accustomed to work other metals, particularly gold and brass. They tipped their spears and javelins with brass, and made brazen plates for defensive armor, both for themselves and for their horses. They made, also, many ornaments and decorations of gold. These they attached to their helmets, their belts, and their banners. They were very formidable in war, being, like all other northern nations, perfectly desperate and reckless in battle. They were excellent horsemen, and had an abundance of horses with which to exercise their skill; so that their armies consisted, like those of the Cossacks of modern times, of great bodies of cavalry.

The various campaigns and conquests by

which Cyrus obtained possession of his extended dominions occupied an interval of about thirty years. It was near the close of this interval, when he was, in fact, advancing toward a late period of life, that he formed the plan of penetrating into these northern regions, with a view of adding them also to his domains.

He had two sons, Cambyses and Smerdis. His wife is said to have been a daughter of Astyages, and that he married her soon after his conquest of the kingdom of Media, in order to reconcile the Medians more easily to his sway, by making a Median princess their queen. Among the western nations of Europe such a marriage would be abhorred, Astyages having been Cyrus's grandfather; but among the Orientals, in those days, alliances of this nature were not uncommon. It would seem that this queen was not living at the time that the events occurred which are to be related in this chapter. Her sons had grown up to maturity and were now princes of great distinction.

One of the Scythian or northern nations to which we have referred were called the Massagetæ. They formed a very extensive and powerful realm. They were governed, at this time, by a queen named Tomyris. She was a

widow, past middle life. She had a son named Spargapizes, who had, like the sons of Cyrus, attained maturity, and was the heir to the
throne. Spargapizes was, moreover, the com
mander-in-chief of the armies of the queen.

The first plan which Cyrus formed for the
annexation of the realm of the Massagetæ to
his own dominions was by a matrimonial alliance. He accordingly raised an army and commenced a movement toward the north, sending,
at the same time, embassadors before him into
the country of the Massagetæ, with offers of
marriage to the queen. The queen knew very
well that it was her dominions, and not herself,
that constituted the great attraction for Cyrus,
and, besides, she was of an age when ambition
is a stronger passion than love. She refused
the offers, and sent back word to Cyrus forbid-
ding his approach.

Cyrus, however, continued to move on. The
boundary between his dominions and those of
the queen was at the River Araxes, a stream
flowing from west to east, through the central
parts of Asia, toward the Caspian Sea. As
Cyrus advanced, he found the country growing
more and more wild and desolate. It was inhabited by savage tribes, who lived on roots and

S

274   CYRUS THE GREAT.   [B.C. 530

Customs of the savages.   Cyrus arrives at the Araxes

herbs, and who were elevated very little, in any respect, above the wild beasts that roamed in the forests around them. They had one very singular custom, according to Herodotus. It seems that there was a plant which grew among them, that bore a fruit, whose fumes, when it was roasting on a fire, had an exhilarating effect, like that produced by wine. These savages, therefore, Herodotus says, were accustomed to assemble around a fire, in their convivial festivities, and to throw some of this fruit in the midst of it. The fumes emitted by the fruit would soon begin to intoxicate the whole circle, when they would throw on more fruit, and become more and more excited, until, at length, they would jump up, and dance about, and sing, in a state of complete inebriation.

Among such savages as these, and through the forests and wildernesses in which they lived, Cyrus advanced till he reached the Araxes. Here, after considering, for some time, by what means he could best pass the river, he determined to build a floating bridge, by means of boats and rafts obtained from the natives on the banks, or built for the purpose. It would be obviously much easier to transport the army by using these boats and rafts to *float* the men across, instead of constructing a bridge with them; but this would not have been safe, for the transportation of the army by such a means would be gradual and slow; and if the enemy were lurking in the neighborhood, and should make an attack upon them in the midst of the operation, while a part of the army were upon one bank and a part upon the other, and another portion still, perhaps, in boats upon the stream the defeat and destruction of the whole would be almost inevitable. Cyrus planned the formation of the bridge, therefore, as a means of transporting his army in a body, and of landing them on the opposite bank in solid columns, which could be formed into order of battle without any delay.

While Cyrus was engaged in the work of constructing the bridge, embassadors appeared, who said that they had been sent from Tomyris. She had commissioned them, they said, to warn Cyrus to desist entirely from his designs upon her kingdom, and to return to his own. This would be the wisest course, too, Tomyris said, for himself, and she counseled him, for his own welfare, to follow it. He could not foresee the result, if he should invade her dominions and encounter her armies. Fortune had favored

276   CYRUS THE GREAT.   [B.C. 530.

Warning of Tomyris.   Cyrus calls a council of war

him thus far, it was true, but fortune might change, and he might find himself, before he was aware, at the end of his victories. Still, she said, she had no expectation that he would be disposed to listen to this warning and advice, and, on her part, she had no objection to his persevering in his invasion. She did not fear him. He need not put himself to the expense and trouble of building a bridge across the Araxes. She would agree to withdraw all her forces three days' march into her own country, so that he might cross the river safely and at his leisure, and she would await him at the place where she should have encamped; or, if he preferred it, she would cross the river and meet him on his own side. In that case, he must retire three days' march from the river, so as to afford her the same opportunity to make the passage undisturbed which she had offered him. She would then come over and march on to attack him. She gave Cyrus his option which branch of this alternative to choose.

Cyrus called a council of war to consider the question. He laid the case before his officers and generals, and asked for their opinion. They were unanimously agreed that it would be best for him to accede to the last of the two proposals made to him, viz., to draw back three days' journey toward his own dominions, and wait for Tomyris to come and attack him there.

There was, however, one person present at this consultation, though not regularly a member of the council, who gave Cyrus different advice. This was Crœsus, the fallen king of Lydia. Ever since the time of his captivity, he had been retained in the camp and in the household of Cyrus, and had often accompanied him in his expeditions and campaigns. Though a captive, he seems to have been a friend; at least, the most friendly relations appeared to subsist between him and his conqueror; and he often figures in history as a wise and honest counselor to Cyrus, in the various emergencies in which he was placed. He was present on this occasion, and he dissented from the opinion which was expressed by the officers of the army.

"I ought to apologize, perhaps," said he, "for presuming to offer any counsel, captive as I am; but I have derived, in the school of calamity and misfortune in which I have been taught, some advantages for learning wisdom which you have never enjoyed. It seems to me that it will be much better for you not to

fall back, but to advance and attack Tomyris
in her own dominions; for, if you retire in this
manner, in the first place, the act itself is dis-
creditable to you: it is a retreat. Then, if, in
the battle that follows, Tomyris conquers you,
she is already advanced three days' march into
your dominions, and she may go on, and, before
you can take measures for raising another army,
make herself mistress of your empire. On the
other hand, if, in the battle, you conquer her, you
will be then six days' march back of the position which you would occupy if you were to
advance now.

"I will propose," continued Crœsus, "the
following plan: Cross the river according to
Tomyris's offer, and advance the three days'
journey into her country. Leave a small part
of your force there, with a great abundance of
your most valuable baggage and supplies—luxuries of all kinds, and rich wines, and such articles as the enemy will most value as plunder.
Then fall back with the main body of your army
toward the river again, in a secret manner, and
encamp in an ambuscade. The enemy will attack your advanced detachment. They will
conquer them. They will seize the stores and
supplies, and will suppose that your whole army

is vanquished.   They will fall upon the plunder
in disorder, and the discipline of their army will
be overthrown.   They will go to feasting upon
the provisions and to drinking the wines, and
then, when they are in the midst of their festivities and revelry, you can come back suddenly with the real strength of your army, and
wholly overwhelm them."

Cyrus determined to adopt the plan which
Crœsus thus recommended.   He accordingly
gave answer to the embassadors of Tomyris that
he would accede to the first of her proposals
If she would draw back from the river three
days' march, he would cross it with his army
as soon as practicable, and then come forward
and attack her.   The embassadors received
this message, and departed to deliver it to their
queen.   She was faithful to her agreement, and
drew her forces back to the place proposed, and
left them there, encamped under the command
of her son.

Cyrus seems to have felt some forebodings
in respect to the manner in which this expedition was to end.   He was advanced in life, and
not now as well able as he once was to endure
the privations and hardships of such campaigns.
Then, the incursion which he was to make was

into a remote, and wild, and dangerous country
and he could not but be aware that he might
never return.   Perhaps he may have had some
compunctions of conscience, too, at thus wan-
tonly disturbing the peace and invading the territories of an innocent neighbor, and his mind
may have been the less at ease on that account.
At any rate, he resolved to settle the affairs of
his government before he set out, in order to secure both the tranquillity of the country while
he should be absent, and the regular transmission of his power to his descendants in case he
should never return.

Accordingly, in a very formal manner, and
in the presence of all his army, he delegated
his power to Cambyses, his son, constituting
him regent of the realm during his absence.
He committed Crœsus to his son's special care,
charging him to pay him every attention and
honor.   It was arranged that these persons, as
well as a considerable portion of the army, and
a large number of attendants that had followed
the camp thus far, were not to accompany the
expedition across the river, but were to remain
behind and return to the capital.   These arrangements being all thus finally made, Cyrus
took leave of his son and of Crœsus, crossed the

river with that part of the army which was to
proceed, and commenced his march.

The uneasiness and anxiety which Cyrus
seems to have felt in respect to his future fate
on this memorable march affected even his
dreams It seems that there was among the
officers of his army a certain general named
Hystaspes. He had a son named Darius, then
a youth of about twenty years of age, who had
been left at home, in Persia, when the army
marched, not being old enough to accompany
them. Cyrus dreamed, one night, immediately
after crossing the river, that he saw this young
Darius with wings on his shoulders, that extended, the one over Asia and the other over
Europe, thus overshadowing the world. When
Cyrus awoke and reflected upon his dream, it
seemed to him to portend that Darius might
be aspiring to the government of his empire
He considered it a warning intended to put him
on his guard.

When he awoke in the morning, he sent for
Hystaspes, and related to him his dream. "I
am satisfied," said he, "that it denotes that
your son is forming ambitious and treasonable
designs Do you, therefore, return home, and
arrest him in this fatal course. Secure him,

282   CYRUS THE GREAT. [B.C. 530

Hystaspes's commission.   Cyrus marches into the queen's country

and let him be ready to give me an account of his conduct when I shall return."

Hystaspes, having received this commission, left the army and returned. The name of this Hystaspes acquired a historical immortality in a very singular way, that is, by being always used as a part of the appellation by which to designate his distinguished son. In after years Darius did attain to a very extended power. He became Darius the Great. As, however, there were several other Persian monarchs called Darius, some of whom were nearly as great as this the first of the name, the usage was gradually established of calling him Darius Hystaspes; and thus the name of the father has become familiar to all mankind, simply as a consequence and pendant to the celebrity of the son

After sending off Hystaspes, Cyrus went on. He followed, in all respects, the plan of Crœsus He marched his army into the country of Tomyris, and advanced until he reached the point agreed upon. Here he stationed a feeble portion of his army, with great stores of provisions and wines, and abundance of such articles as would be prized by the barbarians as booty. He then drew back with the main body of his army toward the Araxes, and concealed his forces in a hidden encampment. The result was as Crœsus had anticipated. The body which he had left was attacked by the troops of Tomyris, and effectually routed. The provisions and stores fell into the hands of the victors. They gave themselves up to the most unbounded joy, and their whole camp was soon a universal scene of rioting and excess. Even the commander, Spargapizes, Tomyris's son, became intoxicated with the wine.

While things were in this state, the main body of the army of Cyrus returned suddenly and unexpectedly, and fell upon their now helpless enemies with a force which entirely overwhelmed them. The booty was recovered, large numbers of the enemy were slain, and others were taken prisoners. Spargapizes himself was captured; his hands were bound; he was taken into Cyrus's camp, and closely guarded.

The result of this stratagem, triumphantly successful as it was, would have settled the contest, and made Cyrus master of the whole realm, if, as he, at the time, supposed was the case, the main body of Tomyris's forces had been engaged in this battle; but it seems that Tomyris had learned, by reconnoiterers and spies, how large a force there was in Cyrus's

284 CYRUS THE GREAT. [B.C. 530.

Tomyris's concern for her son's safety.   Her conciliatory message.

camp, and had only sent a detachment of her
own troops to attack them, not judging it necessary to call out the whole. Two thirds of her
army remained still uninjured. With this large
force she would undoubtedly have advanced
without any delay to attack Cyrus again, were
it not for her maternal concern for the safety of
her son. He was in Cyrus's power, a helpless
captive, and she did not know to what cruelties
he would be exposed if Cyrus were to be exasperated against her. While her heart, therefore, was burning with resentment and anger,
and with an almost uncontrollable thirst for revenge, her hand was restrained. She kept back
her army, and sent to Cyrus a conciliatory
message.

She said to Cyrus that he had no cause to be
specially elated at his victory; that it was only
one third of her forces that had been engaged,
and that with the remainder she held him completely in her power. She urged him, therefore, to be satisfied with the injury which he
had already inflicted upon her by destroying
one third of her army, and to liberate her son,
retire from her dominions, and leave her in
peace. If he would do so, she would not molest
him in his departure; but if he would not, she

swore by the sun, the great god which she and
her countrymen adored, that, insatiable as he
was for blood, she would give it to him till he
had his fill.

Of course Cyrus was not to be frightened by
such threats as these. He refused to deliver
up the captive prince, or to withdraw from the
country, and both parties began to prepare
again for war.

Spargapizes was intoxicated when he was
taken, and was unconscious of the calamity
which had befallen him. When at length he
awoke from his stupor, and learned the full extent of his misfortune, and of the indelible disgrace which he had incurred, he was overwhelmed with astonishment, disappointment,
and shame. The more he reflected upon his
condition, the more hopeless it seemed. Even
if his life were to be spared, and if he were to
recover his liberty, he never could recover his
honor. The ignominy of such a defeat and such
a captivity, he knew well, must be indelible.

He begged Cyrus to loosen his bonds and allow him personal liberty within the camp. Cyrus, pitying perhaps, his misfortunes, and the
deep dejection and distress which they occasioned, acceded to this request. Spargapizes watch-

19

ed an opportunity to seize a weapon when he was not observed by his guards, and killed himself.

His mother Tomyris, when she heard of his fate, was frantic with grief and rage. She considered Cyrus as the wanton destroyer of the peace of her kingdom and the murderer of her son, and she had now no longer any reason for restraining her thirst for revenge. She immediately began to concentrate her forces, and to summon all the additional troops that she could obtain from every part of her kingdom. Cyrus, too, began in earnest to strengthen his lines, and to prepare for the great final struggle.

At length the armies approached each other, and the battle began. The attack was commenced by the archers on either side, who shot showers of arrows at their opponents as they were advancing. When the arrows were spent, the men fought hand to hand, with spears, and javelins, and swords. The Persians fought desperately, for they fought for their lives They were in the heart of an enemy's country, with a broad river behind them to cut off their retreat, and they were contending with a wild and savage foe, whose natural barbarity was rendered still more ferocious and terrible than

ever by the exasperation which they felt, in
sympathy with their injured queen. For a long
time it was wholly uncertain which side would
win the day. The advantage, here and there
along the lines, was in some places on one side,
and in some places on the other; but, though
overpowered and beaten, the several bands,
whether of Persians or Scythians, would neither retreat nor surrender, but the survivors,
when their comrades had fallen, continued to
fight on till they were all slain. It was evident,
at last, that the Scythians were gaining the
day. When night came on, the Persian army
was found to be almost wholly destroyed; the
remnant dispersed. When all was over, the
Scythians, in exploring the field, found the dead
body of Cyrus among the other ghastly and
mutilated remains which covered the ground.
They took it up with a ferocious and exulting
joy, and carried it to Tomyris.

Tomyris treated it with every possible indignity. She cut and mutilated the lifeless
form, as if it could still feel the injuries inflicted by her insane revenge. "Miserable wretch!"
said she; "though I am in the end your con
queror, you have ruined my peace and happiness forever. You have murdered my son

But I promised you your fill of blood, and you shall have it." So saying, she filled a can with Persian blood, obtained, probably, by the execution of her captives, and, cutting off the head of her victim from the body, she plunged it in, exclaiming, "Drink there, insatiable monster, till your murderous thirst is satisfied."

This was the end of Cyrus. Cambyses, his son, whom he had appointed regent during his absence, succeeded quietly to the government of his vast dominions.

In reflecting on this melancholy termination of this great conqueror's history, our minds naturally revert to the scenes of his childhood, and we wonder that so amiable, and gentle, and generous a boy should become so selfish, and unfeeling, and overbearing as a man. But such are the natural and inevitable effects of ambition and an inordinate love of power. The history of a conqueror is always a tragical and melancholy tale. He begins life with an exhibition of great and noble qualities, which awaken in us, who read his history, the same admiration that was felt for him, personally, by his friends and countrymen while he lived, and on which the vast ascendency which he acquired over the minds of his fellow-men, and which led

to his power and fame, was, in a great measure,
founded.   On the other hand, he ends life neglected, hated, and abhorred.   His ambition has
been gratified, but the gratification has brought
with it no substantial peace or happiness; on
the contrary, it has filled his soul with uneasiness, discontent, suspiciousness, and misery.
The histories of heroes would be far less painful in the perusal if we could reverse this moral
change of character, so as to have the cruelty, the selfishness, and the oppression exhaust
themselves in the comparatively unimportant
transactions of early life, and the spirit of kindness, generosity, and beneficence blessing and
beautifying its close.   To be generous, disinterested, and noble, seems to be necessary as
the precursor of great military success; and to
be hard-hearted, selfish, and cruel is the almost
inevitable consequence of it.   The exceptions
to this rule, though some of them are very
splendid, are yet very few.

THE END.

HISTORY

OF

ALEXANDER THE GREAT

BY JACOB ABBOTT.

𝔚𝔦𝔱𝔥 𝔈𝔫𝔤𝔯𝔞𝔟𝔦𝔫𝔤𝔰.

NEW YORK.

HARPER & BROTHERS, PUBLISHERS,

PREFACE.

THE history of the life of every individual who has, for any reason, attracted extensively the attention of mankind, has been written in a great variety of ways by a multitude of authors, and persons sometimes wonder why we should have so many different accounts of the same thing. The reason is, that each one of these accounts is intended for a different set of readers, who read with ideas and purposes widely dissimilar from each other. Among the twenty millions of people in the United States, there are perhaps two millions, between the ages of fifteen and twenty-five, who wish to become acquainted, in general, with the leading events in the history of the Old World, and of ancient times, but who, coming upon the stage in this land and at this period, have ideas and conceptions so widely different from those of other nations and of other times, that a mere republica-

tion of existing accounts is not what they require. The story must be told expressly for
them. The things that are to be explained,
the points that are to be brought out, the comparative degree of prominence to be given to
the various particulars, will all be different, on
account of the difference in the situation, the
ideas, and the objects of these new readers,
compared with those of the various other classes
of readers which former authors have had in
view. It is for this reason, and with this view,
that the present series of historical narratives is
presented to the public. The author, having
had some opportunity to become acquainted
with the position, the ideas, and the intellectual wants of those whom he addresses, presents
the result of his labors to them, with the hope
that it may be found successful in accomplishing its design.

CONTENTS.

Chapter		Page
I.	HIS CHILDHOOD AND YOUTH	13
II.	BEGINNING OF HIS REIGN	36
III.	THE REACTION	57
IV.	CROSSING THE HELLESPONT	78
V.	CAMPAIGN IN ASIA MINOR	103
VI.	DEFEAT OF DARIUS	128
VII.	THE SIEGE OF TYRE	147
VIII.	ALEXANDER IN EGYPT	169
IX.	THE GREAT VICTORY	189
X.	THE DEATH OF DARIUS	213
XI.	DETERIORATION OF CHARACTER	234
XII.	ALEXANDER'S END	251

ENGRAVINGS

	Page
MAP. EXPEDITION OF ALEXANDER...... *Frontispiece.*	
ALEXANDER AND BUCEPHALUS...................	27
MAP OF MACEDON AND GREECE.................	48
MAP OF MACEDON AND GREECE.................	58
MAP OF THE PLAIN OF TROY	88
PARIS AND HELEN	94
ACHILLES	97
MAP OF THE GRANICUS......................	104
THE BATHING IN THE RIVER CYDNUS	124
MAP OF THE PLAIN OF ISSUS	134
THE SIEGE OF TYRE	157
THE FOCUS................................	185
THE CALTROP	197
ALEXANDER AT THE PASS OF SUSA	211
PROPOSED IMPROVEMENT OF MOUNT ATHOS.....	261

ALEXANDER THE GREAT.

CHAPTER I.

HIS CHILDHOOD AND YOUTH.

ALEXANDER THE GREAT died when he was quite young. He was but thirty-two years of age when he ended his career, and as he was about twenty when he commenced it, it was only for a period of twelve years that he was actually engaged in performing the work of his life. Napoleon was nearly three times as long on the great field of human action.

Notwithstanding the briefness of Alexander's career, he ran through, during that short period, a very brilliant series of exploits, which were so bold, so romantic, and which led him into such adventures in scenes of the greatest magnificence and splendor, that all the world looked on with astonishment then, and mankind have continued to read the story since, from age to age, with the greatest interest and attention.

The secret of Alexander's success was his character. He possessed a certain combination of mental and personal attractions, which in every age gives to those who exhibit it a mysterious and almost unbounded ascendency over all within their influence. Alexander was characterized by these qualities in a very remarkable degree. He was finely formed in person, and very prepossessing in his manners. He was active, athletic, and full of ardor and enthusiasm in all that he did. At the same time, he was calm, collected, and considerate in emergencies requiring caution, and thoughtful and far-seeing in respect to the bearings and consequences of his acts. He formed strong attachments, was grateful for kindnesses shown to him, considerate in respect to the feelings of all who were connected with him in any way, faithful to his friends, and generous toward his foes In a word, he had a noble character, though he devoted its energies unfortunately to conquest and war. He lived, in fact, in an age when great personal and mental powers had scarcely any other field for their exercise than this. He entered upon his career with great ardor, and the position in which he was placed gave him the opportunity to act in it with prodigious effect.

There were several circumstances combined,
in the situation in which Alexander was placed,
to afford him a great opportunity for the exercise of his vast powers. His native country
was on the confines of Europe and Asia. Now
Europe and Asia were, in those days, as now,
marked and distinguished by two vast masses
of social and civilized life, widely dissimilar from
each other. The Asiatic side was occupied by
the Persians, the Medes, and the Assyrians.
The European side by the Greeks and Romans.
They were separated from each other by the
waters of the Hellespont, the Ægean Sea, and
the Mediterranean, as will be seen by the map
These waters constituted a sort of natural barrier, which kept the two races apart. The
races formed, accordingly, two vast organizations, distinct and widely different from each
other, and of course rivals and enemies.

It is hard to say whether the Asiatic or European civilization was the highest. The two
were so different that it is difficult to compare
them. On the Asiatic side there was wealth,
luxury, and splendor ; on the European, energy, genius, and force. On the one hand were
vast cities, splendid palaces, and gardens which
were the wonder of the world ; on the other,

20

strong citadels, military roads and bridges, and compact and well-defended towns. The Persians had enormous armies, perfectly provided for, with beautiful tents, horses elegantly caparisoned, arms and munitions of war of the finest workmanship, and officers magnificently dressed, and accustomed to a life of luxury and splendor. The Greeks and Romans, on the other hand, prided themselves on their compact bodies of troops, inured to hardship and thoroughly disciplined. Their officers gloried not in luxury and parade, but in the courage, the steadiness, and implicit obedience of their troops, and in their own science, skill, and powers of military calculation. Thus there was a great difference in the whole system of social and military organization in these two quarters of the globe.

Now Alexander was born the heir to the throne of one of the Grecian kingdoms. He possessed, in a very remarkable degree, the energy, and enterprise, and military skill so characteristic of the Greeks and Romans. He organized armies, crossed the boundary between Europe and Asia, and spent the twelve years of his career in a most triumphant military incursion into the very center and seat of Asiatic power, destroying the Asiatic armies, conquering the most splendid cities, defeating or taking captive the kings, and princes, and generals that opposed his progress. The whole world looked on with wonder to see such a course of conquest, pursued so successfully by so young a man, and with so small an army, gaining continual victories, as it did, over such vast numbers of foes, and making conquests of such accumulated treasures of wealth and splendor.

The name of Alexander's father was Philip. The kingdom over which he reigned was called Macedon. Macedon was in the northern part of Greece. It was a kingdom about twice as large as the State of Massachusetts, and one third as large as the State of New York. The name of Alexander's mother was Olympias. She was the daughter of the King of Epirus, which was a kingdom somewhat smaller than Macedon, and lying westward of it. Both Macedon and Epirus will be found upon the map at the commencement of this volume. Olympias was a woman of very strong and determined character. Alexander seemed to inherit her energy, though in his case it was combined with other qualities of a more attractive character, which his mother did not possess.

B

He was, of course, as the young prince, a very important personage in his father's court. Every one knew that at his father's death he would become King of Macedon, and he was consequently the object of a great deal of care and attention. As he gradually advanced in the years of his boyhood, it was observed by all who knew him that he was endued with extraordinary qualities of mind and of character, which seemed to indicate, at a very early age, his future greatness.

Although he was a prince, he was not brought up in habits of luxury and effeminacy. This would have been contrary to all the ideas which were entertained by the Greeks in those days. They had then no fire-arms, so that in battle the combatants could not stand quietly, as they can now, at a distance from the enemy, coolly discharging musketry or cannon. In ancient battles the soldiers rushed toward each other, and fought hand to hand, in close combat, with swords, or spears, or other weapons requiring great personal strength, so that headlong bravery and muscular force were the qualities which generally carried the day.

The duties of officers, too, on the field of battle, were very different then from what they are

B.C. 356.] CHILDHOOD AND YOUTH. 19

Ancient and modern military officers.   Alexander's nurse.

now. An officer *now* must be calm, collected,
and quiet. His business is to plan, to calculate,
to direct, and arrange. He has to do this sometimes, it is true, in circumstances of the most
imminent danger, so that he must be a man
of great self-possession and of undaunted courage. But there is very little occasion for him
to exert any great physical force.

In ancient times, however, the great business of the officers, certainly in all the subordinate grades, was to lead on the men, and set
them an example by performing themselves
deeds in which their own great personal prowess was displayed. Of course it was considered extremely important that the child destined
to be a general should become robust and powerful in constitution from his earliest years, and
that he should be inured to hardship and fatigue. In the early part of Alexander's life this
was the main object of attention.

The name of the nurse who had charge of
our hero in his infancy was Lannice. She did
all in her power to give strength and hardihood
to his constitution, while, at the same time, she
treated him with kindness and gentleness
Alexander acquired a strong affection for her,
and he treated her with great consideration as

long as he lived.   He had a governor, also, in
his early years, named Leonnatus, who had the
general charge of his education.   As soon as he
was old enough to learn, they appointed him a
preceptor also, to teach him such branches as
were generally taught to young princes in those
days.   The name of this preceptor was Lysimachus.

They had then no printed books, but there
were a few writings on parchment rolls which
young scholars were taught to read.   Some of
these writings were treatises on philosophy, others were romantic histories, narrating the exploits of the heroes of those days—of course, with
much exaggeration and embellishment.   There
were also some poems, still more romantic than
the histories, though generally on the same
themes.   The greatest productions of this kind
were the writings of Homer, an ancient poet
who lived and wrote four or five hundred years
before Alexander's day.   The young Alexander
was greatly delighted with Homer's tales.   These
tales are narrations of the exploits and adventures of certain great warriors at the siege of
Troy—a siege which lasted ten years—and they
are written with so much beauty and force, they
contain such admirable delineations of charac

ter, and such graphic and vivid descriptions of romantic adventures, and picturesque and striking scenes, that they have been admired in every age by all who have learned to understand the language in which they are written.

Alexander could understand them very easily, as they were written in his mother tongue. He was greatly excited by the narrations themselves, and pleased with the flowing smoothness of the verse in which the tales were told. In the latter part of his course of education he was placed under the charge of Aristotle, who was one of the most eminent philosophers of ancient times. Aristotle had a beautiful copy of Homer's poems prepared expressly for Alexander, taking great pains to have it transcribed with perfect correctness, and in the most elegant manner. Alexander carried this copy with him in all his campaigns. Some years afterward, when he was obtaining conquests over the Persians, he took, among the spoils of one of his victories, a very beautiful and costly casket, which King Darius had used for his jewelry or for some other rich treasures. Alexander determined to make use of this box as a depository for his beautiful copy of Homer, and he always carried it with him, thus protected, in all his subsequent campaigns.

Alexander was full of energy and spirit, but he was, at the same time, like all who ever become truly great, of a reflective and considerate turn of mind. He was very fond of the studies which Aristotle led him to pursue, although they were of a very abstruse and difficult character. He made great progress in metaphysical philosophy and mathematics, by which means his powers of calculation and his judgment were greatly improved.

He early evinced a great degree of ambition. His father Philip was a powerful warrior, and made many conquests in various parts of Greece, though he did not cross into Asia. When news of Philip's victories came into Macedon, all the rest of the court would be filled with rejoicing and delight; but Alexander, on such occasions, looked thoughtful and disappointed, and complained that his father would conquer every country, and leave him nothing to do.

At one time some embassadors from the Persian court arrived in Macedon when Philip was away. These embassadors saw Alexander, of course, and had opportunities to converse with him. They expected that he would be interested in hearing about the splendors, and pomp, and parade of the Persian monarchy. They

B.C. 340.] CHILDHOOD AND YOUTH. 2⁵

Stories of the embassadors.   Maturity of Alexander's mind

had stories to tell him about the famous hanging gardens, which were artificially constructed
in the most magnificent manner, on arches raised high in the air; and about a vine made of
gold, with all sorts of precious stones upon it instead of fruit, which was wrought as an ornament over the throne on which the King of Persia often gave audience; of the splendid palaces
and vast cities of the Persians; and the banquets, and fêtes, and magnificent entertainments and celebrations which they used to have
there. They found, however, to their surprise,
that Alexander was not interested in hearing
about any of these things. He would always
turn the conversation from them to inquire
about the geographical position of the different
Persian countries, the various routes leading
into the interior, the organization of the Asiatic armies, their system of military tactics, and,
especially, the character and habits of Artaxerxes, the Persian king.

The embassadors were very much surprised
at such evidences of maturity of mind, and of
far-seeing and reflective powers on the part of
the young prince. They could not help com-
paring him with Artaxerxes. "Alexander,"
said they, "is *great*, while our king is only

rich." The truth of the judgment which these embassadors thus formed in respect to the qualities of the young Macedonian, compared with those held in highest estimation on the Asiatic side, was fully confirmed in the subsequent stages of Alexander's career.

In fact, this combination of a calm and calculating thoughtfulness, with the ardor and energy which formed the basis of his character, was one great secret of Alexander's success. The story of Bucephalus, his famous horse, illustrates this in a very striking manner. This animal was a war-horse of very spirited character, which had been sent as a present to Philip while Alexander was young. They took the horse out into one of the parks connected with the palace, and the king, together with many of his courtiers, went out to view him. The horse pranced about in a very furious manner, and seemed entirely unmanageable. No one dared to mount him. Philip, instead of being gratified at the present, was rather disposed to be displeased that they had sent him an animal of so fiery and apparently vicious a nature that nobody dared to attempt to subdue him.

In the mean time, while all the other bystanders were joining in the general condemnation of the horse, Alexander stood quietly by, watching his motions, and attentively studying his character. He perceived that a part of the difficulty was caused by the agitations which the horse experienced in so strange and new a scene, and that he appeared, also, to be somewhat frightened by his own shadow, which happened at that time to be thrown very strongly and distinctly upon the ground. He saw other indications, also, that the high excitement which the horse felt was not viciousness, but the excess of noble and generous impulses. It was courage, ardor, and the consciousness of great nervous and muscular power.

Philip had decided that the horse was useless, and had given orders to have him sent back to Thessaly, whence he came. Alexander was very much concerned at the prospect of losing so fine an animal. He begged his father to allow him to make the experiment of mounting him. Philip at first refused, thinking it very presumptuous for such a youth to attempt to subdue an animal so vicious that all his experienced horsemen and grooms condemned him; however, he at length consented. Alexander went up to the horse and took hold of his bridle. He patted him upon the neck, and soothed him

with his voice, showing, at the same time, by
his easy and unconcerned manner, that he was
not in the least afraid of him. A spirited horse
knows immediately when any one approaches
him in a timid or cautious manner. He appears
to look with contempt on such a master, and to
determine not to submit to him. On the contrary, horses seem to love to yield obedience to
man, when the individual who exacts the obedience possesses those qualities of coolness and
courage which their instincts enable them to appreciate.

At any rate, Bucephalus was calmed and subdued by the presence of Alexander. He allowed himself to be caressed. Alexander turned
his head in such a direction as to prevent his
seeing his shadow. He quietly and gently laid
off a sort of cloak which he wore, and sprang
upon the horse's back. Then, instead of attempting to restrain him, and worrying and checking
him by useless efforts to hold him in, he gave
him the rein freely, and animated and encouraged him with his voice, so that the horse flew
across the plains at the top of his speed, the king
and the courtiers looking on, at first with fear
and trembling, but soon afterward with feelings
of the greatest admiration and pleasure. After

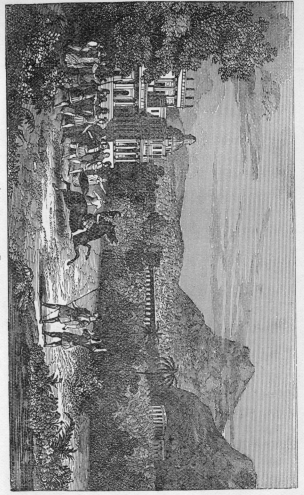

ALEXANDER AND BUCEPHALUS.

the horse had satisfied himself with his run it
was easy to rein him in, and Alexander returned with him in safety to the king. The courtiers
overwhelmed him with their praises and congratulations. Philip commended him very highly :
he told him that he deserved a larger kingdom
than Macedon to govern.

Alexander's judgment of the true character
of the horse proved to be correct. He became
very tractable and docile, yielding a ready submission to his master in every thing. He would
kneel upon his fore legs at Alexander's command, in order that he might mount more easily. Alexander retained him for a long time,
and made him his favorite war horse. A great
many stories are related by the historians of
those days of his sagacity and his feats of war.
Whenever he was equipped for the field with
his military trappings, he seemed to be highly
elated with pride and pleasure, and at such
times he would not allow any one but Alexander to mount him.

What became of him at last is not certainly
known. There are two accounts of his end.
One is, that on a certain occasion Alexander
got carried too far into the midst of his enemies,
on a battle field, and that, after fighting desper

ately for some time, Bucephalus made the most
extreme exertions to carry him away. He was
severely wounded again and again, and though
his strength was nearly gone, he would not stop,
but pressed forward till he had carried his master away to a place of safety, and that then he
dropped down exhausted, and died. It may be,
however, that he did not actually die at this
time, but slowly recovered; for some historians
relate that he lived to be thirty years old—
which is quite an old age for a horse—and that
he then died. Alexander caused him to be
buried with great ceremony, and built a small
city upon the spot in honor of his memory. The
name of this city was Bucephalia.

Alexander's character matured rapidly, and
he began very early to act the part of a man.
When he was only sixteen years of age, his father, Philip, made him regent of Macedon
while he was absent on a great military campaign among the other states of Greece. Without doubt Alexander had, in this regency, the
counsel and aid of high officers of state of great
experience and ability. He acted, however,
himself, in this high position, with great energy
and with complete success; and, at the same
time, with all that modesty of deportment, and

that delicate consideration for the officers under him—who, though inferior in rank, were yet his superiors in age and experience—which his position rendered proper, but which few persons so young as he would have manifested in circumstances so well calculated to awaken the feelings of vanity and elation.

Afterward, when Alexander was about eighteen years old, his father took him with him on a campaign toward the south, during which Philip fought one of his great battles at Chæronea, in Bœotia. In the arrangements for this battle, Philip gave the command of one of the wings of the army to Alexander, while he reserved the other for himself. He felt some solicitude in giving his young son so important a charge, but he endeavored to guard against the danger of an unfortunate result by putting the ablest generals on Alexander's side, while he reserved those on whom he could place less reliance for his own. Thus organized, the army went into battle.

Philip soon ceased to feel any solicitude for Alexander's part of the duty. Boy as he was, the young prince acted with the utmost bravery, coolness, and discretion. The wing which he commanded was victorious, and Philip was oblig-

ed to urge himself and the officers with him to
greater exertions, to avoid being outdone by his
son   In the end Philip was completely victorious, and the result of this great battle was to
make his power paramount and supreme over
all the states of Greece.

Notwithstanding, however, the extraordinary discretion and wisdom which characterized
the mind of Alexander in his early years, he
was often haughty and headstrong, and in
cases where his pride or his resentment were
aroused, he was sometimes found very impetuous and uncontrollable.   His mother Olympias
was of a haughty and imperious temper, and
she quarreled with her husband, King Philip;
or, perhaps, it ought rather to be said that he
quarreled with her.   Each is said to have been
unfaithful to the other, and, after a bitter con-
tention, Philip repudiated his wife and married
another lady.   Among the festivities held on
the occasion of this marriage, there was a great
banquet, at which Alexander was present, and
an incident occurred which strikingly illustrates
the impetuosity of his character.

One of the guests at this banquet, in saying
something complimentary to the new queen,
made use of expressions which Alexander con

sidered as in disparagement of the character of his mother and of his own birth. His anger was immediately aroused. He threw the cup from which he had been drinking at the offenders' head. Attalus, for this was his name, threw his cup at Alexander in return; the guests at the table where they were sitting rose, and a scene of uproar and confusion ensued.

Philip, incensed at such an interruption of the order and harmony of the wedding feast, drew his sword and rushed toward Alexander, but by some accident he stumbled and fell upon the floor. Alexander looked upon his fallen father with contempt and scorn, and exclaimed, "What a fine hero the states of Greece have to lead their armies—a man that can not get across the floor without tumbling down." He then turned away and left the palace. Immediately afterward he joined his mother Olympias, and went away with her to her native country, Epirus, where the mother and son remained for a time in a state of open quarrel with the husband and father.

In the mean time Philip had been planning a great expedition into Asia. He had arranged the affairs of his own kingdom, and had formed a strong combination among the states of Greece

C

by which powerful armies had been raised, and
he had been designated to command them. His
mind was very intently engaged in this vast
enterprise. He was in the flower of his years,
and at the height of his power. His own kingdom was in a very prosperous and thriving condition, and his ascendency over the other kingdoms and states on the European side had been
fully established. He was excited with ambition, and full of hope. He was proud of his
son Alexander, and was relying upon his efficient aid in his schemes of conquest and aggrandizement. He had married a youthful and
beautiful bride, and was surrounded by scenes
of festivity, congratulation, and rejoicing. He
was looking forward to a very brilliant career,
considering all the deeds that he had done and
all the glory which he had acquired as only the
introduction and prelude to the far more distinguished and conspicuous part which he was intending to perform.

Alexander, in the mean time, ardent and impetuous, and eager for glory as he was, looked
upon the position and prospects of his father
with some envy and jealousy. He was impa-
tient to be monarch himself. His taking sides
so promptly with his mother in the domestic

quarrel was partly owing to the feeling that his
father was a hinderance and an obstacle in the
way of his own greatness and fame. He felt
within himself powers and capacities qualifying
him to take his father's place, and reap for himself the harvest of glory and power which seemed to await the Grecian armies in the coming
campaign. While his father lived, however, he
could be only a prince; influential, accomplished, and popular, it is true, but still without any
substantial and independent power. He was
restless and uneasy at the thought that, as his
father was in the prime and vigor of manhood,
many long years must elapse before he could
emerge from this confined and subordinate condition. His restlessness and uneasiness were,
however, suddenly ended by a very extraordinary occurrence, which called him, with scarce-
.y an hour's notice, to take his father's place
upon the throne.

CHAPTER II.
BEGINNING OF HIS REIGN.

ALEXANDER was suddenly called upon to succeed his father on the Macedonian throne, in the most unexpected manner, and in the midst of scenes of the greatest excitement and agitation. The circumstances were these:

Philip had felt very desirous, before setting out upon his great expedition into Asia, to become reconciled to Alexander and Olympias. He wished for Alexander's co-operation in his plans; and then, besides, it would be dangerous to go away from his own dominions with such a son left behind, in a state of resentment and hostility.

So Philip sent kind and conciliatory messages to Olympias and Alexander, who had gone, it will be recollected, to Epirus, where *her* friends resided. The brother of Olympias was King of Epirus. He had been at first incensed at the indignity which had been put upon his sister by Philip's treatment of her; but Philip now tried to appease his anger, also, by friendly negotiations and messages. At last he arranged a marriage between this King of Epirus and one of his own daughters, and this completed the reconciliation. Olympias and Alexander returned to Macedon, and great preparations were made for a very splendid wedding.

Philip wished to make this wedding not merely the means of confirming his reconciliation with his former wife and son, and establishing friendly relations with the King of Epirus: he also prized it as an occasion for paying marked and honorable attention to the princes and great generals of the other states of Greece. He consequently made his preparations on a very extended and sumptuous scale, and sent invitations to the influential and prominent men far and near.

These great men, on the other hand, and all the other public authorities in the various Grecian states, sent compliments, congratulations, and presents to Philip, each seeming ambitious to contribute his share to the splendor of the celebration. They were not wholly disinterested in this, it is true. As Philip had been made commander-in-chief of the Grecian armies which were about to undertake the conquest of Asia, and as, of course, his influence and power in

all that related to that vast enterprise would be
paramount and supreme ; and as all were ambitious to have a large share in the glory of that
expedition, and to participate, as much as possible, in the power and in the renown which
seemed to be at Philip's disposal, all were, of
course, very anxious to secure his favor. A
short time before, they were contending against
him ; but now, since he had established his ascendency, they all eagerly joined in the work
of magnifying it and making it illustrious.

Nor could Philip justly complain of the hol-
lowness and falseness of these professions of
friendship. The compliments and favors which
he offered to them were equally hollow and
heartless. He wished to secure *their* favor as
a means of aiding him up the steep path to
fame and power which he was attempting to
climb They wished for his, in order that he
might, as he ascended himself, help them up
with him. There was, however, the greatest
appearance of cordial and devoted friendship
Some cities sent him presents of golden crowns,
beautifully wrought, and of high cost. Others
dispatched embassies, expressing their good
wishes for him, and their confidence in the success of his plans. Athens, the city which was

the great seat of literature and science in Greece,
sent a *poem*, in which the history of the expedition into Persia was given by anticipation. In
this poem Philip was, of course, triumphantly
successful in his enterprise. He conducted his
armies in safety through the most dangerous
passes and defiles ; he fought glorious battles,
gained magnificent victories, and possessed himself of all the treasures of Asiatic wealth and
power. It ought to be stated, however, in justice to the poet, that, in narrating these imaginary exploits, he had sufficient delicacy to rep-
resent Philip and the Persian monarch by fictitious names.

The wedding was at length celebrated, in one
of the cities of Macedon, with great pomp and
splendor. There were games, and shows, and
military and civic spectacles of all kinds to
amuse the thousands of spectators that assembled to witness them. In one of these specta
cles they had a procession of statues of the gods.
There were twelve of these statues, sculptured
with great art, and they were borne along on
elevated pedestals, with censers, and incense,
and various ceremonies of homage, while vast
multitudes of spectators lined the way. There
was a thirteenth statue, more magnificent than

the other twelve, which represented Philip himself in the character of a god.

This was not, however, so impious as it would at first view seem, for the gods whom the ancients worshiped were, in fact, only deifications of old heroes and kings who had lived in early times, and had acquired a reputation for supernatural powers by the fame of their exploits, exaggerated in descending by tradition in superstitious times. The ignorant multitude accordingly, in those days, looked up to a living king with almost the same reverence and homage which they felt for their deified heroes; and these deified heroes furnished them with all the ideas they had of God. Making a monarch a god, therefore, was no very extravagant flattery

After the procession of the statues passed along, there came bodies of troops, with trumpets sounding and banners flying. The officers rode on horses elegantly caparisoned, and prancing proudly. These troops escorted princes, ambassadors, generals, and great officers of state, all gorgeously decked in their robes, and wearing their badges and insignia.

At length King Philip himself appeared in the procession. He had arranged to have a large space left, in the middle of which he was to walk. This was done in order to make his position the more conspicuous, and to mark more strongly his own high distinction above all the other potentates present on the occasion. Guards preceded and followed him, though at considerable distance, as has been already said He was himself clothed with white robes, and his head was adorned with a splendid crown

The procession was moving toward a great theater, where certain games and spectacles were to be exhibited. The statues of the gods were to be taken into the theater, and placed in conspicuous positions there, in the view of the assembly, and then the procession itself was to follow. All the statues had entered except that of Philip, which was just at the door, and Philip himself was advancing in the midst of the space left for him, up the avenue by which the theater was approached, when an occurrence took place by which the whole character of the scene, the destiny of Alexander, and the fate of fifty nations, was suddenly and totally changed. It was this. An officer of the guards, who had his position in the procession near the king, was seen advancing impetuously toward him, through the space which separated him from the rest, and, before the specta-

tors had time even to wonder what he was going to do, he stabbed him to the heart. Philip
fell down in the street and died.

A scene of indescribable tumult and confusion ensued. The murderer was immediately
cut to pieces by the other guards. They found,
however, before he was dead, that it was Pausanias, a man of high standing and influence, a
general officer of the guards. He had had horses
provided, and other assistance ready, to enable
him to make his escape, but he was cut down
by the guards before he could avail himself of
them.

An officer of state immediately hastened to
Alexander, and announced to him his father's
death and his own accession to the throne. An
assembly of the leading counselors and statesmen was called, in a hasty and tumultuous
manner, and Alexander was proclaimed king
with prolonged and general acclamations. Alexander made a speech in reply. The great assembly looked upon his youthful form and face
as he arose, and listened with intense interest
to hear what he had to say. He was between
nineteen and twenty years of age; but, though
thus really a boy, he spoke with all the decision
and confidence of an energetic man. He said

that he should at once assume his father's position, and carry forward his plans. He hoped to
do this so efficiently that every thing would go
directly onward, just as if his father had continued to live, and that the nation would find
that the only change which had taken place was
in the *name* of the king.

The motive which induced Pausanias to murder Philip in this manner was never fully ascertained. There were various opinions about
it. One was, that it was an act of private revenge, occasioned by some neglect or injury
which Pausanias had received from Philip.
Others thought that the murder was instigated
by a party in the states of Greece, who were
hostile to Philip, and unwilling that he should
command the allied armies that were about to
penetrate into Asia. Demosthenes, the celebrated orator, was Philip's great enemy among
the Greeks. Many of his most powerful orations were made for the purpose of arousing his
countrymen to resist his ambitious plans and
to curtail his power. These orations were called his Philippics, and from this origin has aris-
en the practice, which has prevailed ever since
that day, of applying the term philippics to denote, in general, any strongly denunciatory ha-
rangues.

Now Demosthenes, it is said, who was at this time in Athens, announced the death of Philip in an Athenian assembly before it was possible that the news could have been conveyed there. He accounted for his early possession of the intelligence by saying it was communicated to him by some of the gods. Many persons have accordingly supposed that the plan of assassinating Philip was devised in Greece; that Demosthenes was a party to it; that Pausanias was the agent for carrying it into execution; and that Demosthenes was so confident of the success of the plot, and exulted so much in this certainty, that he could not resist the temptation of thus anticipating its announcement.

There were other persons who thought that the *Persians* had plotted and accomplished this murder, having induced Pausanias to execute the deed by the promise of great rewards. As Pausanias himself, however, had been instantly killed, there was no opportunity of gaining any information from him on the motives of his conduct, even if he would have been disposed to impart any.

At all events, Alexander found himself suddenly elevated to one of the most conspicuous positions in the whole political world. It was

not simply that he succeeded to the throne of
Macedon; even this would have been a lofty position for so young a man; but Macedon was
a very small part of the realm over which Philip
had extended his power. The ascendency which
he had acquired over the whole Grecian empire,
and the vast arrangements he had made for an
incursion into Asia, made Alexander the object
of universal interest and attention. The ques
tion was, whether Alexander should attempt to
take his father's place in respect to all this general power, and undertake to sustain and carry
on his vast projects, or whether he should content himself with ruling, in quiet, over his native country of Macedon.

Most prudent persons would have advised a
young prince, under such circumstances, to
have decided upon the latter course. But Alexander had no idea of bounding his ambition by
any such limits. He resolved to spring at once
completely into his father's seat, and not only to
possess himself of the whole of the power which
his father had acquired, but to commence, immediately, the most energetic and vigorous efforts for a great extension of it.

His first plan was to punish his father's mur
derers. He caused the circumstances of the

case to be investigated, and the persons suspected of having been connected with Pausanias in
the plot to be tried. Although the designs and
motives of the murderers could never be fully
ascertained, still several persons were found
guilty of participating in it, and were condemned to death and publicly executed.

Alexander next decided not to make any
change in his father's appointments to the great
offices of state, but to let all the departments of
public affairs go on in the same hands as before. How sagacious a line of conduct was
this! Most ardent and enthusiastic young
men, in the circumstances in which he was
placed, would have been elated and vain at their
elevation, and would have replaced the old and
well-tried servants of the father with personal
favorites of their own age, inexperienced and
incompetent, and as conceited as themselves.
Alexander, however, made no such changes
He continued the old officers in command, endeavoring to have every thing go on just as if
his father had not died.

There were two officers in particular who
were the ministers on whom Philip had mainly
relied. Their names were Antipater and Parmenio. Antipater had charge of the civil, and

Parmenio of military affairs. Parmenio was a very distinguished general. He was at this time nearly sixty years of age. Alexander had great confidence in his military powers, and felt a strong personal attachment for him. Parmenio entered into the young king's service with great readiness, and accompanied him through almost the whole of his career. It seemed strange to see men of such age, standing, and experience, obeying the orders of such a boy; but there was something in the genius, the power, and the enthusiasm of Alexander's character which inspired ardor in all around him, and made every one eager to join his standard and to aid in the execution of his plans.

Macedon, as will be seen on the following map, was in the northern part of the country occupied by the Greeks, and the most powerful states of the confederacy and all the great and influential cities were south of it. There was Athens, which was magnificently built, its splendid citadel crowning a rocky hill in the center of it. It was the great seat of literature, philosophy, and the arts, and was thus a center of attraction for all the civilized world. There was Corinth, which was distinguished for the gayety and pleasure which reigned there. All possible

48 ALEXANDER THE GREAT. [B.C. 336.

Map of Macedon and Greece.   Athens and Corinth

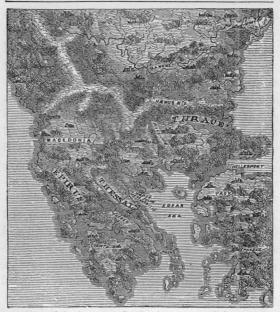

means of luxury and amusement were concentrated within its walls. The lovers of knowledge and of art, from all parts of the earth,
flocked to Athens, while those in pursuit of
pleasure, dissipation, and indulgence chose
Corinth for their home. Corinth was beautifully situated on the isthmus, with prospects
of the sea on either hand. It had been a fa

mous city for a thousand years in Alexander's
day.

There was also Thebes. Thebes was farther
north than Athens and Corinth. It was situated on an elevated plain, and had, like other
ancient cities, a strong citadel, where there was
at this time a Macedonian garrison, which Philip had placed there. Thebes was very wealthy
and powerful. It had also been celebrated as
the birth-place of many poets and philosophers
and other eminent men. Among these was
Pindar, a very celebrated poet who had flourished one or two centuries before the time of Alexander. His descendants still lived in Thebes,
and Alexander, some time after this, had occasion
to confer upon them a very distinguished honor.

There was Sparta also, called sometimes
Lacedæmon. The inhabitants of this city were
famed for their courage, hardihood, and physical strength, and for the energy with which they
devoted themselves to the work of war. They
were nearly all soldiers, and all the arrangements of the state and of society, and all the
plans of education, were designed to promote
military ambition and pride among the officers,
and fierce and indomitable courage and endurance in the men.

D

These cities and many others, with the states which were attached to them, formed a large, and flourishing, and very powerful community, extending over all that part of Greece which lay south of Macedon. Philip, as has been already said, had established his own ascendency over all this region, though it had cost him many perplexing negotiations and some hard-fought battles to do it. Alexander considered it somewhat uncertain whether the people of all these states and cities would be disposed to transfer readily, to so youthful a prince as he, the high commission which his father, a very powerful monarch and soldier, had extorted from them with so much difficulty. What should he do in the case? Should he give up the expectation of it? Should he send embassadors to them, presenting his claims to occupy his father's place? Or should he not act at all, but wait quietly at home in Macedon until they should decide the question?

Instead of doing either of these things, Alexander decided on the very bold step of setting out himself, at the head of an army, to march into southern Greece, for the purpose of presenting in person, and, if necessary, of enforcing his claim to the same post of honor and

power which had been conferred upon his father
Considering all the circumstances of the case,
this was perhaps one of the boldest and most decided steps of Alexander's whole career. Many
of his Macedonian advisers counseled him not
to make such an attempt; but Alexander would
not listen to any such cautions. He collected
his forces, and set forth at the head of them.

Between Macedon and the southern states of
Greece was a range of lofty and almost impassable mountains. These mountains extended
through the whole interior of the country, and
the main route leading into southern Greece
passed around to the eastward of them, where
they terminated in cliffs, leaving a narrow passage between the cliffs and the sea. This pass
was called the Pass of Thermopylæ, and it was
considered the key to Greece. There was a
town named Anthela near the pass, on the outward side.

There was in those days a sort of general con-
gress or assembly of the states of Greece, which
was held from time to time, to decide questions
and disputes in which the different states were
continually getting involved with each other.
This assembly was called the Amphictyonic
Council, on account, as is said, of its having been

52 ALEXANDER THE GREAT. [B.C. 336

March through Thessaly.   Alexander's traits of character

established by a certain king named Amphicty-
on. A meeting of this council was appointed to
receive Alexander. It was to be held at Thermopylæ, or, rather, at Anthela, which was just
without the pass, and was the usual place at
which the council assembled. This was because the pass was in an intermediate position
between the northern and southern portions of
Greece, and thus equally accessible from either.

In proceeding to the southward, Alexander
had first to pass through Thessaly, which was
a very powerful state immediately south of
Macedon. He met with some show of resistance at first, but not much. The country was
impressed with the boldness and decision of
character manifested in the taking of such a
course by so young a man. Then, too, Alexander, so far as he became personally known,
made a very favorable impression upon every
one. His manly and athletic form, his frank
and open manners, his spirit, his generosity,
and a certain air of confidence, independence,
and conscious superiority, which were com
bined, as they always are in the case of true
greatness, with an unaffected and unassuming
modesty—these and other traits, which were
obvious to all who saw him, in the person and

character of Alexander, made every one his friend. Common men take pleasure in yielding to the influence and ascendency of one whose spirit they see and feel stands on a higher eminence and wields higher powers than their own. They like a leader. It is true, they must feel confident of his superiority; but when this superiority stands out so clearly and distinctly marked, combined, too, with all the graces and attractions of youth and manly beauty, as it was in the case of Alexander, the minds of men are brought very easily and rapidly under its sway.

The Thessalians gave Alexander a very favorable reception. They expressed a cordial readiness to instate him in the position which his father had occupied. They joined their forces to his, and proceeded southward toward the Pass of Thermopylæ.

Here the great council was held. Alexander took his place in it as a member. Of course, he must have been an object of universal interest and attention. The impression which he made here seems to have been very favorable. After this assembly separated, Alexander proceeded southward, accompanied by his own forces, and tended by the various princes and potentates

of Greece, with their attendants and followers
The feelings of exultation and pleasure with
which the young king defiled through the Pass
of Thermopylæ, thus attended, must have been
exciting in the extreme.

The Pass of Thermopylæ was a scene strongly associated with ideas of military glory and
renown.   It was here that, about a hundred and
fifty years before, Leonidas, a Spartan general,
with only three hundred soldiers, had attempted
to withstand the pressure of an immense Persian force which was at that time invading
Greece.   He was one of the kings of Sparta,
and he had the command, not only of his three
hundred Spartans, but also of all the allied forces of the Greeks that had been assembled to
repel the Persian invasion.   With the help of
these allies he withstood the Persian forces for
some time, and as the pass was so narrow between the cliffs and the sea, he was enabled to
resist them successfully.   At length, however,
a strong detachment from the immense Persian
army contrived to find their way over the mountains and around the pass, so as to establish themselves in a position from which they could come
down upon the small Greek army in their rear.
Leonidas, perceiving this, ordered all his allies

from the other states of Greece to withdraw, leaving himself and his three hundred countrymen alone in the defile.

He did not expect to repel his enemies or to defend the pass. He knew that he must die, and all his brave followers with him, and that the torrent of invaders would pour down through the pass over their bodies. But he considered himself stationed there to defend the passage, and he would not desert his post. When the battle came on he was the first to fall. The soldiers gathered around him and defended his dead body as long as they could. At length, overpowered by the immense numbers of their foes, they were all killed but one man. He made his escape and returned to Sparta. A monument was erected on the spot with this inscription: "Go, traveler, to Sparta, and say that we lie here, on the spot at which we were stationed to defend our country."

Alexander passed through the defile. He advanced to the great cities south of it—to Athens to Thebes, and to Corinth. Another great assembly of all the monarchs and potentates of Greece was convened in Corinth; and here Alexander attained the object of his ambition, in having the command of the great expedition into

Asia conferred upon him. The impression which
he made upon those with whom he came into
connection by his personal qualities must have
been favorable in the extreme. That such a
youthful prince should be selected by so powerful a confederation of nations as their leader in
such an enterprise as they were about to engage in, indicates a most extraordinary power
on his part of acquiring an ascendency over the
minds of men, and of impressing all with a sense
of his commanding superiority. Alexander returned to Macedon from his expedition to the
southward in triumph, and began at once to
arrange the affairs of his kingdom, so as to be
ready to enter, unembarrassed, upon the great
career of conquest which he imagined was before him.

CHAPTER III.
THE REACTION.

THE country which was formerly occupied by Macedon and the other states of Greece is now Turkey in Europe.   In the northern part of it is a vast chain of mountains called now the Balkan.   In Alexander's day it was Mount Hæmus.   This chain forms a broad belt of lofty and uninhabitable land, and extends from the Black Sea to the Adriatic.

A branch of this mountain range, called Rhodope, extends southwardly from about the middle of its length, as may be seen by the map. Rhodope separated Macedonia from a large and powerful country, which was occupied by a somewhat rude but warlike race of men.   This country was Thrace.   Thrace was one great fertile basin or valley, sloping toward the center in every direction, so that all the streams from the mountains, increased by the rains which fell over the whole surface of the ground, flowed together into one river, which meandered through the center of the valley, and flowed out at last into the Ægean Sea.   The name of this river

was the Hebrus.   All this may be seen distinct
ly upon the map

The Balkan, or Mount Hæmus, as it was
then called, formed the great northern frontier
of Macedon and Thrace.   From the summits of
the range, looking northward, the eye surveyed
a vast extent of land, constituting one of the
most extensive and fertile valleys on the globe.

It was the valley of the Danube.   It was inhabited, in those days, by rude tribes whom the
Greeks and Romans always designated as barbarians.   They were, at any rate, wild and warlike, and, as they had not the art of writing,
they have left us no records of their institutions
or their history.   We know nothing of them, or
of the other half-civilized nations that occupied
the central parts of Europe in those days, except what their inveterate and perpetual enemies have thought fit to tell us.   According to
their story, these countries were filled with nations and tribes of a wild and half-savage character, who could be kept in check only by the
most vigorous exertion of military power.

Soon after Alexander's return into Macedon,
he learned that there were symptoms of revolt
among these nations.   Philip had subdued them,
and established the kind of peace which the
Greeks and Romans were accustomed to enforce upon their neighbors.   But now, as they
had heard that Philip, who had been so terrible
a warrior, was no more, and that his son, scarcely out of his teens, had succeeded to the throne,
they thought a suitable occasion had arrived to
try their strength.   Alexander made immediate
arrangements for moving northward with his
army to settle this question.

He conducted his forces through a part of Thrace without meeting with any serious resistance, and approached the mountains. The soldiers looked upon the rugged precipices and lofty summits before them with awe. These northern mountains were the seat and throne, in the imaginations of the Greeks and Romans, of old Boreas, the hoary god of the north wind. They conceived of him as dwelling among those cold and stormy summits, and making excursions in winter, carrying with him his vast stores of frost and snow, over the southern valleys and plains. He had wings, a long beard, and white locks, all powdered with flakes of snow. Instead of feet, his body terminated in tails of serpents, which, as he flew along, lashed the air, writhing from under his robes. He was violent and impetuous in temper, rejoicing in the devastation of winter, and in all the sublime phenomena of tempests, cold, and snow. The Greek conception of Boreas made an impression upon the human mind that twenty centuries have not been able to efface. The north wind of winter is personified as Boreas to the present day in the literature of every nation of the Western world.

The Thracian forces had assembled in the defiles, with other troops from the northern countries, to arrest Alexander's march, and he had some difficulty in repelling them. They had got, it is said, some sort of loaded wagons upon the summit of an ascent, in the pass of the mountains, up which Alexander's forces would have to march. These wagons were to be run down upon them as they ascended. Alexander ordered his men to advance, notwithstanding this danger. He directed them, where it was practicable, to open to one side and the other, and allow the descending wagon to pass through. When this could not be done, they were to fall down upon the ground when they saw this strange military engine coming, and locking their shields together over their heads, allow the wagon to roll on over them, bracing up energetically against its weight. Notwithstanding these precautions, and the prodigious muscular power with which they were carried into effect, some of the men were crushed. The great body of the army was, however, unharmed; as soon as the force of the wagons was spent, they rushed up the ascent, and attacked their enemies with their pikes. The barbarians fled in all directions, terrified at the force and invulnerability of men whom loaded wagons, rolling

over their bodies down a steep descent, could
not kill.

Alexander advanced from one conquest like
this to another, moving toward the northward
and eastward after he had crossed the mountains, until at length he approached the mouths
of the Danube.   Here one of the great chieftains
of the barbarian tribes had taken up his position, with his family and court, and a principal
part of his army, upon an island called Peucé,
which may be seen upon the map at the beginning of this chapter.   This island divided the
current of the stream, and Alexander, in attempting to attack it, found that it would be
best to endeavor to effect a landing upon the
upper point of it

To make this attempt, he collected all the
boats and vessels which he could obtain, and
embarked his troops in them above, directing
them to fall down with the current, and to land
upon the island.   This plan, however, did not
succeed very well; the current was too rapid
for the proper management of the boats.   The
shores, too, were lined with the forces of the
enemy, who discharged showers of spears and
arrows at the men, and pushed off the boats
when they attempted to land.   Alexander at

ength gave up the attempt, and concluded to leave the island, and to cross the river itself further above, and thus carry the war into the very heart of the country.

It is a serious undertaking to get a great body of men and horses across a broad and rapid river, when the people of the country have done all in their power to remove or destroy all possible means of transit, and when hostile bands are on the opposite bank, to embarrass and impede the operations by every mode in their power. Alexander, however, advanced to the undertaking with great resolution. To cross the Danube especially, with a military force, was, in those days, in the estimation of the Greeks and Romans, a very great exploit. The river was so distant, so broad and rapid, and its banks were bordered and defended by such ferocious foes, that to cross its eddying tide, and penetrate into the unknown and unexplored regions beyond, leaving the broad, and deep, and rapid stream to cut off the hopes of retreat, implied the possession of extreme self-reliance, courage, and decision.

Alexander collected all the canoes and boats which he could obtain up and down the river. He built large rafts, attaching to them the skins

23

of beasts sewed together and inflated, to give
them buoyancy.   When all was ready, they began the transportation of the army in the night,
in a place where the enemy had not expected
that the attempt would have been made.   There
were a thousand horses, with their riders, and
four thousand foot soldiers, to be conveyed across.
It is customary, in such cases, to swim the horses
over, leading them by lines, the ends of which
are held by men in boats.   The men themselves,
with all the arms, ammunition, and baggage, had
to be carried over in the boats or upon the rafts.
Before morning the whole was accomplished.

The army landed in a field of grain.   This
circumstance, which is casually mentioned by
historians, and also the story of the wagons in
the passes of Mount Hæmus, proves that these
northern nations were not absolute barbarians
in the sense in which that term is used at the
present day.   The arts of cultivation and of construction must have made some progress among
them, at any rate; and they proved, by some of
their conflicts with Alexander, that they were
well-trained and well-disciplined soldiers.

The Macedonians swept down the waving
grain with their pikes, to open a way for the
advance of the cavalry, and early in the morn-

ing Alexander found and attacked the army of
his enemies, who were utterly astonished at
finding him on their side of the river.   As may
be easily anticipated, the barbarian army was
beaten in the battle that ensued.   Their city
was taken.   The booty was taken back across
the Danube to be distributed among the soldiers
of the army.   The neighboring nations and tribes
were overawed and subdued by this exhibition
of Alexander's courage and energy.   He made
satisfactory treaties with them all; took hosta-
ges, where necessary, to secure the observance
of the treaties, and then recrossed the Danube
and set out on his return to Macedon.

He found that it was *time* for him to return.
The southern cities and states of Greece had
not been unanimous in raising him to the office
which his father had held.   The Spartans and
some others were opposed to him.   The party
thus opposed were inactive and silent while Alexander was in their country, on his first visit
to southern Greece; but after his return they
began to contemplate more decisive action, an l
afterward, when they heard of his having un-
dertaken so desperate an enterprise as going
northward with his forces, and actually crossing the Danube, they considered him as so com-

E

pletely out of the way that they grew very cour
ageous, and meditated open rebellion.

The city of Thebes did at length rebel. Philip
had conquered this city in former struggles, and
had left a Macedonian garrison there in the cit
adel. The name of the citadel was Cadmeia.
The officers of the garrison, supposing that all
was secure, left the soldiers in the citadel, and
came, themselves, down to the city to reside.
Things were in this condition when the rebellion
against Alexander's authority broke out. They
killed the officers who were in the city, and summoned the garrison to surrender. The garrison
refused, and the Thebans besieged it.

This outbreak against Alexander's authority
was in a great measure the work of the great
orator Demosthenes, who spared no exertions
to arouse the southern states of Greece to resist Alexander's dominion. He especially exerted all the powers of his eloquence in Athens
in the endeavor to bring over the Athenians to
take sides against Alexander.

While things were in this state—the Thebans having understood that Alexander had
been killed at the north, and supposing that, at
all events, if this report should not be true, he
was, without doubt, still far away, involved in

contentions with the barbarian nations, from
which it was not to be expected that he could
be very speedily extricated—the whole city was
suddenly thrown into consternation by the report that a large Macedonian army was approaching from the north, with Alexander at its
head, and that it was, in fact, close upon them.

It was now, however, too late for the Thebans to repent of what they had done. They
were far too deeply impressed with a conviction
of the decision and energy of Alexander's character, as manifested in the whole course of his
proceedings since he began to reign, and especially by his sudden reappearance among them
so soon after this outbreak against his authority, to imagine that there was now any hope for
them except in determined and successful resistance. They shut themselves up, therefore,
in their city, and prepared to defend themselves
to the last extremity.

Alexander advanced, and, passing round the
city toward the southern side, established his
head-quarters there, so as to cut off effectually
all communication with Athens and the southern
cities. He then extended his posts all around
the place so as to invest it entirely. These preparations made, he paused before he commenced

the work of subduing the city, to give the inhabitants an opportunity to submit, if they
would, without compelling him to resort to
force. The conditions, however, which he imposed were such that the Thebans thought it
best to take their chance of resistance. They
refused to surrender, and Alexander began to
prepare for the onset.

He was very soon ready, and with his characteristic ardor and energy he determined on
attempting to carry the city at once by assault.
Fortified cities generally require a siege, and
sometimes a very long siege, before they can be
subdued. The army within, sheltered behind
the parapets of the walls, and standing there in
a position above that of their assailants, have
such great advantages in the contest that a long
time often elapses before they can be compelled
to surrender. The besiegers have to invest the
city on all sides to cut off all supplies of provisions, and then, in those days, they had to con-
struct engines to make a breach somewhere in
the walls, through which an assaulting party
could attempt to force their way in.

The time for making an assault upon a besieged city depends upon the comparative
strength of those within and without, and also,

still more, on the ardor and resolution of the
besiegers. In warfare, an army, in investing
a fortified place, spends ordinarily a considerable time in burrowing their way along in
trenches, half under ground, until they get near
enough to plant their cannon where the balls
can take effect upon some part of the wall.
Then some time usually elapses before a breach
is made, and the garrison is sufficiently weakened to render an assault advisable. When,
however, the time at length arrives, the most
bold and desperate portion of the army are designated to lead the attack. Bundles of small
branches of trees are provided to fill up ditches
with, and ladders for mounting embankments
and walls. The city, sometimes, seeing these
preparations going on, and convinced that the
assault will be successful, surrenders before it is
made. When the besieged do thus surrender,
they save themselves a vast amount of suffering, for the carrying of a city by assault is perhaps the most horrible scene which the passions
and crimes of men ever offer to the view of
heaven.

It is horrible, because the soldiers, exasperated
to fury by the resistance which they meet with,
and by the awful malignity of the passions al-

ways excited in the hour of battle, if they succeed, burst suddenly into the precincts of domestic life, and find sometimes thousands of
families—mothers, and children, and defenseless maidens—at the mercy of passions excited
to phrensy. Soldiers, under such circumstances, can not be restrained, and no imagination
can conceive the horrors of the sacking of a city,
carried by assault, after a protracted siege. Tigers do not spring upon their prey with greater
ferocity than man springs, under such circumstances, to the perpetration of every possible
cruelty upon his fellow man. After an ordinary battle upon an open field, the conquerors have
only men, armed like themselves, to wreak their
vengeance upon. The scene is awful enough,
however, here. But in carrying a city by storm,
which takes place usually at an unexpected time,
and often in the night, the maddened and victorious assaulters suddenly burst into the sacred
scenes of domestic peace, and seclusion, and love
—the very worst of men, filled with the worst
of passions, stimulated by the resistance they
have encountered, and licensed by their victory
to give all these passions the fullest and most
unrestricted gratification. To plunder, burn,
destroy, and kill, are the lighter and more harmless of the crimes they perpetrate.

Thebes was carried by assault. Alexander did not wait for the slow operations of a siege. He watched a favorable opportunity, and burst over and through the outer line of fortifications which defended the city. The attempt to do this was very desperate, and the loss of life great; but it was triumphantly successful. The Thebans were driven back toward the inner wall, and began to crowd in, through the gates, into the city, in terrible confusion. The Macedonians were close upon them, and pursuers and pursued, struggling together, and trampling upon and killing each other as they went, flowed in, like a boiling and raging torrent which nothing could resist, through the open arch-way.

It was impossible to close the gates. The whole Macedonian force were soon in full possession of the now defenseless houses, and for many hours screams, and wailings, and cries of horror and despair testified to the awful atrocity of the crimes attendant on the sacking of a city. At length the soldiery were restrained. Order was restored. The army retired to the posts assigned them, and Alexander began to deliberate what he should do with the conquered town.

He determined to destroy it—to offer, once for

all, a terrible example of the consequences of
rebellion against him. The case was not one,
he considered, of the ordinary conquest of a *foe*.
The states of Greece—Thebes with the rest—
had once solemnly conferred upon him the authority against which the Thebans had now re-
belled. They were *traitors*, therefore, in his
judgment, not mere enemies, and he determined
that the penalty should be utter destruction.

But, in carrying this terrible decision into effect, he acted in a manner so deliberate, discriminating, and cautious, as to diminish very
much the irritation and resentment which it
would otherwise have caused, and to give it its
full moral effect as a measure, not of angry resentment, but of calm and deliberate retribution
—just and proper, according to the ideas of the
time. In the first place, he released all the
priests. Then, in respect to the rest of the population, he discriminated carefully between those
who had favored the rebellion and those who
had been true to their allegiance to him. The
latter were allowed to depart in safety And if,
in the case of any family, it could be shown that
one individual had been on the Macedonian side,
the single instance of fidelity outweighed the
treason of the other members, and the whole
family was saved

And the officers appointed to carry out these provisions were liberal in the interpretation and application of them, so as to save as many as there could be any possible pretext for saving. The descendants and family connections of Pindar, the celebrated poet, who has been already mentioned as having been born in Thebes, were all pardoned also, whichever side they may have taken in the contest. The truth was, that Alexander, though he had the sagacity to see that he was placed in circumstances where prodigious moral effect in strengthening his position would be produced by an act of great severity, was swayed by so many generous impulses, which raised him above the ordinary excitements of irritation and revenge, that he had every desire to make the suffering as light, and to limit it by as narrow bounds, as the nature of the case would allow. He doubtless also had an instinctive feeling that the moral effect itself of so dreadful a retribution as he was about to inflict upon the devoted city would be very much increased by forbearance and generosity, and by extreme regard for the security and protection of those who had shown themselves his friends.

After all these exceptions had been made,

and the persons to whom they applied had been dismissed, the rest of the population were sold into slavery, and then the city was utterly and entirely destroyed. The number thus sold was about thirty thousand, and six thousand had been killed in the assault and storming of the city. Thus Thebes was made a ruin and a desolation, and it remained so, a monument of Alexander's terrible energy and decision, for twenty years.

The effect of the destruction of Thebes upon the other cities and states of Greece was what might have been expected. It came upon them like a thunder-bolt. Although Thebes was the only city which had openly revolted, there had been strong symptoms of disaffection in many other places. Demosthenes, who had been silent while Alexander was present in Greece, during his first visit there, had again been endeavoring to arouse opposition to Macedonian ascendency, and to concentrate and bring out into action the influences which were hostile to Alexander. He said in his speeches that Alexander was a mere boy, and that it was disgraceful for such cities as Athens, Sparta, and Thebes to submit to his sway. Alexander had heard of these things, and, as he was coming

down into Greece, through the Straits of Thermopylæ, before the destruction of Thebes, he
said, "They say I am a boy. I am coming to
teach them that I am a man."

He did teach them that he was a man. His
unexpected appearance, when they imagined
him entangled among the mountains and wilds
of unknown regions in the north; his sudden
investiture of Thebes; the assault; the calm
deliberations in respect to the destiny of the
city, and the slow, cautious, discriminating, but
inexorable energy with which the decision was
carried into effect, all coming in such rapid succession, impressed the Grecian commonwealth
with the conviction that the personage they had
to deal with was no boy in character, whatever
might be his years. All symptoms of disaffection against the rule of Alexander instantly disappeared, and did not soon revive again.

Nor was this effect due entirely to the terror
inspired by the retribution which had been visited upon Thebes. All Greece was impressed with a new admiration for Alexander's character as they witnessed these events, in which
his impetuous energy, his cool and calm decision, his forbearance, his magnanimity, and his
faithfulness to his friends, were all so conspicu

ous. His pardoning the priests, whether they had been for him or against him, made every friend of religion incline to his favor. The same interposition in behalf of the poet's family and descendants spoke directly to the heart of every poet, orator, historian, and philosopher throughout the country, and tended to make all the lovers of literature his friends. His magnanimity, also, in deciding that one single friend of his in a family should save that family, instead of ordaining, as a more short-sighted conqueror would have done, that a single enemy should condemn it, must have awakened a strong feeling of gratitude and regard in the hearts of all who could appreciate fidelity to friends and generosity of spirit. Thus, as the news of the destruction of Thebes, and the selling of so large a portion of the inhabitants into slavery, spread over the land, its effect was to turn over so great a part of the population to a feeling of admiration of Alexander's character, and confidence in his extraordinary powers, as to leave only a small minority disposed to take sides with the punished rebels, or resent the destruction of the city.

From Thebes Alexander proceeded to the southward. Deputations from the cities were sent to him, congratulating him on his victories, and offering their adhesion to his cause.   His influence and ascendency seemed firmly established now in the country of the Greeks, and in due time he returned to Macedon, and cele brated at Ægæ, which was at this time his capital, the establishment and confirmation of his power, by games, shows, spectacles, illuminations, and sacrifices to the gods, offered on a scale of the greatest pomp and magnificence He was now ready to turn his thoughts toward the long-projected plan of the expedition into Asia.

CHAPTER IV.
CROSSING THE HELLESPONT.

ON Alexander's arrival in Macedon, he immediately began to turn his attention to the subject of the invasion of Asia. He was full of ardor and enthusiasm to carry this project into effect. Considering his extreme youth, and the captivating character of the enterprise, it is strange that he should have exercised so much deliberation and caution as his conduct did really evince. He had now settled every thing in the most thorough manner, both within his dominions and among the nations on his borders, and, as it seemed to him, the time had come when he was to commence active preparations for the great Asiatic campaign.

He brought the subject before his ministers and counselors. They, in general, concurred with him in opinion. There were, however, two who were in doubt, or rather who were, in fact, opposed to the plan, though they expressed their non-concurrence in the form of doubts. These two persons were Antipater and Par-

menio, the venerable officers who have been already mentioned as having served Philip so
faithfully, and as transferring, on the death of
the father, their attachment and allegiance at
once to the son.

Antipater and Parmenio represented to Alexander that if he were to go to Asia at that
time, he would put to extreme hazard all the interests of Macedon. As he had no family, there
was, of course, no direct heir to the crown, and,
in case of any misfortune happening by which
his life should be lost, Macedon would become
at once the prey of contending factions, which
would immediately arise, each presenting its
own candidate for the vacant throne. The sagacity and foresight which these statesmen
evinced in these suggestions were abundantly
confirmed in the end. Alexander did die in
Asia, his vast kingdom at once fell into pieces,
and it was desolated with internal commotions
and civil wars for a long period after his death

Parmenio and Antipater accordingly advised
the king to postpone his expedition. They advised him to seek a wife among the princesses
of Greece, and then to settle down quietly to
the duties of domestic life, and to the government of his kingdom for a few years; then,

24

when every thing should have become settled
and consolidated in Greece, and his family was
established in the hearts of his countrymen, he
could leave Macedon more safely. Public affairs would go on more steadily while he lived,
and, in case of his death, the crown would descend, with comparatively little danger of civil
commotion, to his heir.

But Alexander was fully decided against any
such policy as this. He resolved to embark in
the great expedition at once. He concluded to
make Antipater his vicegerent in Macedon during his absence, and to take Parmenio with him
into Asia. It will be remembered that Antipater was the statesman and Parmenio the general; that is, Antipater had been employed more
by Philip in civil, and Parmenio in military af
fairs, though in those days every body who was
in public life was more or less a soldier.

Alexander left an army of ten or twelve thou
sand men with Antipater for the protection of
Macedon. He organized another army of about
thirty-five thousand to go with him. This was
considered a very small army for such a vast
undertaking. One or two hundred years before
this time, Darius, a king of Persia, had invaded
Greece with an army of five hundred thousand

men, and yet he had been defeated and driven
back, and now Alexander was undertaking to
retaliate with a great deal less than one tenth
part of the force.

Of Alexander's army of thirty-five thousand,
thirty thousand were foot soldiers, and about
five thousand were horse. More than half the
whole army was from Macedon. The remainder was from the southern states of Greece. A
large body of the horse was from Thessaly, which,
as will be seen on the map,* was a country south
of Macedon. It was, in fact, one broad expand-
ed valley, with mountains all around. Tor-
rents descended from these mountains, forming
streams which flowed in currents more and more
deep and slow as they descended into the plains,
and combining at last into one central river,
which flowed to the eastward, and escaped from
the environage of mountains through a most
celebrated dell called the Vale of Tempe. On
the north of this valley is Olympus, and on the
south the two twin mountains Pelion and Ossa
There was an ancient story of a war in Thes
aly between the giants who were imagined to
have lived there in very early days, and the
gods The giants piled Pelion upon Ossa to

* At the commencement of Chapter iii.

enable them to get up to heaven in their assault
upon their celestial enemies. The fable has
led to a proverb which prevails in every lan‧
guage in Europe, by which all extravagant and
unheard-of exertions to accomplish an end is
said to be a piling of Pelion upon Ossa.

Thessaly was famous for its horses and its
horsemen. The slopes of the mountains furnished the best of pasturage for the rearing of
the animals, and the plains below afforded broad
and open fields for training and exercising the
bodies of cavalry formed by means of them.
The Thessalian horse were famous throughout
all Greece. Bucephalus was reared in Thessaly.

Alexander, as king of Macedon, possessed extensive estates and revenues, which were his
own personal property, and were independent
of the revenues of the state. Before setting
out on his expedition, he apportioned these
among his great officers and generals, both
those who were to go and those who were to
remain. He evinced great generosity in this
but it was, after all, the spirit of ambition, more
than that of generosity, which led him to do it.
The two great impulses which animated him
were the pleasure of doing great deeds, and the
fame and glory of having done them. These

two principles are very distinct in their nature,
though often conjoined.   They were paramount
and supreme in Alexander's character, and every other human principle was subordinate to
them.   Money was to him, accordingly, only a
means to enable him to accomplish these ends.
His distributing his estates and revenues in the
manner above described was only a judicious ap-
propriation of the money to the promotion of the
great ends he wished to attain; it was expendi-
ture, not gift.   It answered admirably the end
he had in view.   His friends all looked upon
him as extremely generous and self-sacrificing.
They asked him what he had reserved for himself.   "Hope," said Alexander.

At length all things were ready, and Alexander began to celebrate the religious sacrifices,
spectacles, and shows which, in those days, always preceded great undertakings of this kind
There was a great ceremony in honor of Jupiter and the nine Muses, which had long been
celebrated in Macedon as a sort of annual national festival.   Alexander now caused great
preparations for this festival.

In the days of the Greeks, public worship and
public amusement were combined in one and
the same series of spectacles and ceremonies

All worship was a theatrical show, and almost
all shows were forms of worship. The religious
instincts of the human heart demand some sort
of sympathy and aid, real or imaginary, from
the invisible world, in great and solemn undertakings, and in every momentous crisis in its
history. It is true that Alexander's soldiers,
about to leave their homes to go to another
quarter of the globe, and into scenes of danger
and death from which it was very improbable
that many of them would ever return, had no
other celestial protection to look up to than the
spirits of ancient heroes, who, they imagined,
had, somehow or other, found their final home
in a sort of heaven among the summits of the
mountains, where they reigned, in some sense,
over human affairs; but this, small as it seems
to us, was a great deal to them. They felt,
when sacrificing to these gods, that they were
invoking their presence and sympathy. These
deities having been engaged in the same enterprises themselves, and animated with the same
hopes and fears, the soldiers imagined that the
semi-human divinities invoked by them would
take an interest in their dangers, and rejoice in
their success.

The Muses, in honor of whom, as well as Jupiter, this great Macedonian festival was held, were nine singing and dancing maidens, beautiful in countenance and form, and enchantingly graceful in all their movements. They came, the ancients imagined, from Thrace, in the north, and went first to Jupiter upon Mount Olympus, who made them goddesses. Afterward they went southward, and spread over Greece, making their residence, at last, in a palace upon Mount Parnassus, which will be found upon the map just north of the Gulf of Corinth and west of Bœotia. They were worshiped all over Greece and Italy as the goddesses of music and dancing. In later times particular sciences and arts were assigned to them respectively, as history, astronomy, tragedy, &c., though there was no distinction of this kind in early days.

The festivities in honor of Jupiter and the Muses were continued in Macedon nine days, a number corresponding with that of the dancing goddesses. Alexander made very magnificent preparations for the celebration on this occasion. He had a tent made, under which, it is said, a hundred tables could be spread; and here he entertained, day after day, an enormous company of princes, potentates, and generals

He offered sacrifices to such of the gods as he supposed it would please the soldiers to imagine that they had propitiated. Connected with these sacrifices and feastings, there were athletic and military spectacles and shows—races and wrestlings—and mock contests, with blunted spears. All these things encouraged and quickened the ardor and animation of the soldiers. It aroused their ambition to distinguish themselves by their exploits, and gave them an increased and stimulated desire for honor and fame. Thus inspirited by new desires for human praise, and trusting in the sympathy and protection of powers which were all that they conceived of as divine, the army prepared to set forth from their native land, bidding it a long, and, as it proved to most of them, a final farewell.

By following the course of Alexander's expedition upon the map at the commencement of chapter iii., it will be seen that his route lay first along the northern coasts of the Ægean Sea. He was to pass from Europe into Asia by crossing the Hellespont between Sestos and Abydos. He sent a fleet of a hundred and fifty galleys, of three banks of oars each, over the Ægean Sea, to land at Sestos, and be ready to transport his army across the straits. The army, in the mean time, marched by land. They had to cross the rivers which flow into the Ægean Sea on the northern side; but as these rivers were in Macedon, and no opposition was encountered upon the banks of them, there was no serious difficulty in effecting the passage. When they reached Sestos, they found the fleet ready there, awaiting their arrival.

It is very strikingly characteristic of the mingling of poetic sentiment and enthusiasm with calm and calculating business efficiency, which shone conspicuously so often in Alexander's career, that when he arrived at Sestos, and found that the ships were there, and the army safe, and that there was no enemy to oppose his landing on the Asiatic shore, he left Parmenio to conduct the transportation of the troops across the water, while he himself went away in a single galley on an excursion of sentiment and romantic adventure. A little south of the place where his army was to cross, there lay, on the Asiatic shore, an extended plain, on which were the ruins of Troy. Now Troy was the city which was the scene of Homer's poems—those poems which had excited so much interest in the mind of Alexander in his early years; and he determined, instead of crossing the Helles-

The plain of Troy   Tenedos   Moun· Ida   The Scamander.

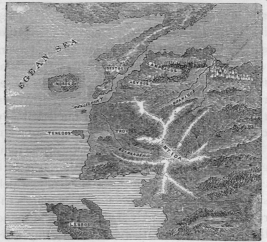

THE PLAIN OF TROY.

pont with the main body of his army, to pro
ceed southward in a single galley, and land,
himself, on the Asiatic shore, on the very spot
which the romantic imagination of his youth
had dwelt upon so often and so long.

Troy was situated upon a plain. Homer describes an island off the coast, named Tenedos,
and a mountain near called Mount Ida. There
was also a river called the Scamander. The
island, the mountain, and the river remain, preserving their original names to the present day,

except that the river is now called the Mender: but, although various vestiges of ancient ruins are found scattered about the plain, no spot can be identified as the site of the city. Some scholars have maintained that there probably never was such a city; that Homer invented the whole, there being nothing real in all that he describes except the river, the mountain, and the island. His story is, however, that there was a great and powerful city there, with a kingdom attached to it, and that this city was besieged by the Greeks for ten years, at the end of which time it was taken and destroyed.

The story of the origin of this war is substan tially this. Priam was king of Troy. His wife, a short time before her son was born, dreamed that at his birth the child turned into a torch and set the palace on fire. She told this dream to the soothsayers, and asked them what it meant. They said it must mean that her son would be the means of bringing some terrible calamities and disasters upon the family. The mother was terrified, and, to avert these calamities, gave the child to a slave as soon as it was born, and ordered him to destroy it. The slave pitied the helpless babe, and, not liking to destroy it with his own hand, carried it to Mount Ida, and left it there in the forests to die.

A she bear, roaming through the woods, found
the child, and, experiencing a feeling of maternal tenderness for it, she took care of it, and
reared it as if it had been her own offspring
The child was found, at last, by some shepherds
who lived upon the mountain, and they adopted
it as their own, robbing the brute mother of her
charge. They named the boy Paris. He grew
in strength and beauty, and gave early and extraordinary proofs of courage and energy, as if
he had imbibed some of the qualities of his fierce
foster mother with the milk she gave him. He
was so remarkable for athletic beauty and manly courage, that he not only easily won the heart
of a nymph of Mount Ida, named Œnone, whom
he married, but he also attracted the attention
of the goddesses in the heavens.

At length these goddesses had a dispute which
they agreed to refer to him. The origin of the
dispute was this. There was a wedding among
them, and one of them, irritated at not having
been invited, had a golden apple made, on which
were engraved the words, "To BE GIVEN TO THE
MOST BEAUTIFUL." She threw this apple into
the assembly : her object was to make them
quarrel for it. In fact, she was herself the god-
dess of discord, and, independently of her cause

of pique in this case, she loved to promote disputes. It is in allusion to this ancient tale that
any subject of dispute, brought up unnecessari-
ly among friends, is called to this day an *apple*
of discord.

Three of the goddesses claimed the apple,
each insisting that she was more beautiful than
the others, and this was the dispute which they
agreed to refer to Paris. They accordingly exhibited themselves before him in the mountains,
that he might look at them and decide. They
did not, however, seem willing, either of them,
to trust to an impartial decision of the question,
but each offered the judge a bribe to induce him
to decide in her favor. One promised him a
kingdom, another great fame, and the third,
Venus, promised him the most beautiful woman in the world for his wife. He decided in favor of Venus; whether because she was justly
entitled to the decision, or through the influence
of the bribe, the story does not say

All this time Paris remained on the mountain, a simple shepherd and herdsman, not knowing his relationship to the monarch who reigned
over the city and kingdom on the plain below.
King Priam, however, about this time, in some
games which he was celebrating, offered, as a

prize to the victor, the finest bull which could
be obtained on Mount Ida. On making examination, Paris was found to have the finest bull,
and the king, exercising the despotic power
which kings in those days made no scruple of
assuming in respect to helpless peasants, took
it away. Paris was very indignant. It happened, however, that a short time afterward
there was another opportunity to contend for
the same bull, and Paris, disguising himself as
a prince, appeared in the lists, conquered every
competitor, and bore away the bull again to his
nome in the fastnesses of the mountain.

In consequence of this his appearance at
court, the daughter of Priam, whose name was
Cassandra, became acquainted with him, and,
inquiring into his story, succeeded in ascertaining that he was her brother, the long-lost child,
that had been supposed to be put to death. King
Priam was convinced by the evidence which she
brought forward, and Paris was brought home
to his father's house. After becoming established in his new position, he remembered the
promise of Venus that he should have the most
beautiful woman in the world for his wife, and
he began, accordingly, to inquire where he could
find her.

PARIS AND HELEN

There was in Sparta, one of the cities of
Southern Greece, a certain king Menelaus, who
had a youthful bride named Helen, who was
famed far and near for her beauty. Paris came
to the conclusion that she was the most lovely
woman in the world, and that he was entitled,
in virtue of Venus's promise, to obtain possession of her, if he could do so by any means
whatever. He accordingly made a journey into
Greece, visited Sparta, formed an acquaintance
with Helen, persuaded her to abandon her husband and her duty, and elope with him to Troy.

Menelaus was indignant at this outrage. He
called on all Greece to take up arms and join
him in the attempt to recover his bride. They
responded to this demand. They first sent to
Priam, demanding that he should restore Helen
to her husband. Priam refused to do so, taking part with his son. The Greeks then raised
a fleet and an army, and came to the plains of
Troy, encamped before the city, and persevered
for ten long years in besieging it, when at length
it was taken and destroyed.

These stories relating to the origin of the war,
however, marvelous and entertaining as they
are, were not the points which chiefly interested the mind of Alexander. The portions of Ho-
25

mer's narratives which most excited his enthu
siasm were those relating to the characters of
the heroes who fought, on one side and on the
other, at the siege, their various adventures,
and the delineations of their motives and principles of conduct, and the emotions and excitements they experienced in the various circumstances in which they were placed.   Homer described with great beauty and force the work-
ings of ambition, of resentment, of pride, of ri-
valry, and all those other impulses of the human heart which would excite and control the
action of impetuous men in the circumstances
in which his heroes were placed.

Each one of the heroes whose history and adventures he gives, possessed a well-marked and
striking character, and differed in temperament
and action from the rest.   Achilles was one.
He was fiery, impetuous, and implacable in
character, fierce and merciless; and, though
perfectly undaunted and fearless, entirely destitute of magnanimity.   There was a river called the Styx, the waters of which were said to
have the property of making any one invulnerable.   The mother of Achilles dipped him into
it in his infancy, holding him by the heel.   The
heel, not having been immersed, was the only

KOINTOΣ
ΛΛΟΣΑ
ΕΗΘΙΕΙ

ACHILLES.

part which could be wounded. Thus he was safe in battle, and was a terrible warrior. He, however, quarreled with his comrades and withdrew from their cause on slight pretexts, and then became reconciled again, influenced by equally frivolous reasons.

Agamemnon was the commander-in-chief of the Greek army. After a certain victory, by which some captives were taken, and were to be divided among the victors, Agamemnon was obliged to restore one, a noble lady, who had fallen to his share, and he took away the one that had been assigned to Achilles to replace her. This incensed Achilles, and he withdrew

G

for a long time from the contest; and, in consequence of his absence, the Trojans gained great
and continued victories against the Greeks
For a long time nothing could induce Achilles
to return.

At length, however, though he would not go
himself, he allowed his intimate friend, whose
name was Patroclus, to take his armor and go
into battle.   Patroclus was at first successful,
but was soon killed by Hector, the brother of
Paris.   This aroused anger and a spirit of revenge in the mind of Achilles.   He gave up his
quarrel with Agamemnon and returned to the
combat.   He did not remit his exertions till he
had slain Hector, and then he expressed his bru-
tal exultation, and satisfied his revenge, by drag-
ging the dead body at the wheels of his chariot
around the walls of the city.   He then sold the
body to the distracted father for a ransom.

It was such stories as these, which are related in the poems of Homer with great beauty
and power, that had chiefly interested the mind
of Alexander.   The subjects interested him;
the accounts of the contentions, the rivalries,
the exploits of these warriors, the delineations
of their character and springs of action, and the
narrations of the various incidents and events to

which such a war gave rise, were all calculated to captivate the imagination of a young martial hero.

Alexander accordingly resolved that his first landing in Asia should be at Troy. He left his army under the charge of Parmenio, to cross from Sestos to Abydos, while he himself set forth in a single galley to proceed to the southward. There was a port on the Trojan shore where the Greeks had been accustomed to disembark, and he steered his course for it. He had a bull on board his galley which he was going to offer as a sacrifice to Neptune when half way from shore to shore.

Neptune was the god of the sea. It is true that the Hellespont is not the open ocean, but it is an arm of the sea, and thus belonged properly to the dominions which the ancients assigned to the divinity of the waters. Neptune was conceived of by the ancients as a monarch dwelling on the seas or upon the coasts, and riding over the waves seated in a great shell, or sometimes in a chariot, drawn by dolphins or sea-horses. In these excursions he was attended by a train of sea-gods and nymphs, who, half floating, half swimming, followed him over the billows. Instead of a scepter Neptune carried a trident. A trident was a sort of three-pronged harpoon, such as was used in those days by the fishermen of the Mediterranean. It was from this circumstance, probably, that it was chosen as the badge of authority for the god of the sea.

Alexander took the helm, and steered the galley with his own hands toward the Asiatic shore. Just before he reached the land, he took his place upon the prow, and threw a javelin at the shore as he approached it, a symbol of the spirit of defiance and hostility with which he advanced to the frontiers of the eastern world. He was also the first to land. After disembarking his company, he offered sacrifices to the gods, and then proceeded to visit the places which had been the scenes of the events which Homer had described.

Homer had written five hundred years before the time of Alexander, and there is some doubt whether the ruins and the remains of cities which our hero found there were really the scenes of the narratives which had interested him so deeply. He, however, at any rate, believed them to be so, and he was filled with enthusiasm and pride as he wandered among them. He seems to have been most interested in the character of Achilles, and he said that he envied him his happy lot in having such a friend as Patroclus to help him perform his exploits, and such a poet as Homer to celebrate them.

After completing his visit upon the plain of Troy, Alexander moved toward the northeast with the few men who had accompanied him in his single galley. In the mean time Parmenio had crossed safely, with the main body of the army, from Sestos to Abydos. Alexander overtook them on their march, not far from the place of their landing. To the northward of this place, on the left of the line of march which Alexander was taking, was the city of Lampsacus.

Now a large portion of Asia Minor, although for the most part under the dominion of Persia, had been in a great measure settled by Greeks, and, in previous wars between the two nations, the various cities had been in possession, sometimes of one power and sometimes of the other. In these contests the city of Lampsacus had incurred the high displeasure of the Greeks by rebelling, as they said, on one occasion, against them. Alexander determined to destroy it as he passed. The inhabitants were aware of this intention, and sent an embassador to Alexander to implore his mercy. When the embassador approached, Alexander, knowing his errand, uttered a declaration in which he bound himself by a solemn oath not to grant the request he was about to make. "I have come," said the embassador, "to implore you to *destroy* Lampsacus." Alexander, pleased with the readiness of the embassador in giving his language such a sudden turn, and perhaps influenced by his oath, spared the city.

He was now fairly in Asia. The Persian forces were gathering to attack him, but so unexpected and sudden had been his invasion that they were not prepared to meet him at his arrival, and he advanced without opposition till he reached the banks of the little river Granicus.

CHAPTER V.

CAMPAIGN IN ASIA MINOR.

ALTHOUGH Alexander had landed safely on the Asiatic shore, the way was not yet fairly open for him to advance into the interior of the country. He was upon a sort of plain, which was separated from the territory beyond by natural barriers. On the south was the range of lofty land called Mount Ida. From the northeastern slopes of this mountain there descended a stream which flowed north into the sea, thus hemming Alexander's army in. He must either scale the mountain or cross the river before he could penetrate into the interior.

He thought it would be easiest to cross the river. It is very difficult to get a large body of horsemen and of heavy-armed soldiers, with all their attendants and baggage, over high elevations of land. This was the reason why the army turned to the northward after landing upon the Asiatic shore. Alexander thought the Granicus less of an obstacle than Mount

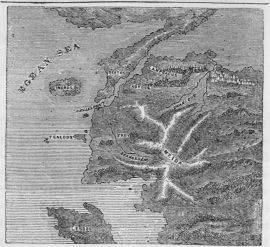

THE GRANICUS

Ida. It was not a large stream, and was easi
ly fordable.

It was the custom in those days, as it is now
when armies are marching, to send forward
small bodies of men in every direction to explore the roads, remove obstacles, and discover
sources of danger. These men are called, in
modern times, *scouts;* in Alexander's day, and
in the Greek language, they were called *pro
dromi*, which means forerunners. It is the
duty of these pioneers to send messengers back

continually to the main body of the army, informing the officers of every thing important which comes under their observation.

In this case, when the army was gradually drawing near to the river, the *prodromi* came in with the news that they had been to the river, and found the whole opposite shore, at the place of crossing, lined with Persian troops, collected there to dispute the passage. The army continued their advance, while Alexander called the leading generals around him, to consider what was to be done.

Parmenio recommended that they should not attempt to pass the river immediately. The Persian army consisted chiefly of cavalry. Now cavalry, though very terrible as an enemy on the field of battle by day, are peculiarly exposed and defenseless in an encampment by night. The horses are scattered, feeding or at rest. The arms of the men are light, and they are not accustomed to fighting on foot; and on a sudden incursion of an enemy at midnight into their camp, their horses and their horsemanship are alike useless, and they fall an easy prey to resolute invaders. Parmenio thought, therefore, that the Persians would not dare to remain and encamp many days in the vicinity

of Alexander's army, and that, accordingly, if
they waited a little, the enemy would retreat,
and Alexander could then cross the river without incurring the danger of a battle.

But Alexander was unwilling to adopt any
such policy. He felt confident that his army
was courageous and strong enough to march on,
directly through the river, ascend the bank upon
the other side, and force their way through all
the opposition which the Persians could make.
He knew, too, that if this were done it would
create a strong sensation throughout the whole
country, impressing every one with a sense of
the energy and power of the army which he
was conducting, and would thus tend to intimi-
date the enemy, and facilitate all future operations. But this was not all ; he had a more
powerful motive still for wishing to march right
on, across the river, and force his way through
the vast bodies of cavalry on the opposite shore,
and this was the pleasure of performing the exploit.

Accordingly, as the army advanced to the
banks, they maneuvered to form in order of battle, and prepared to continue their march as if
there were no obstacle to oppose them. The
general order of battle of the Macedonian army

was this. There was a certain body of troops,
armed and organized in a peculiar manner, called the Phalanx. This body was placed in the
center. The men composing it were very heavily armed. They had shields upon the left arm,
and they carried spears sixteen feet long, and
pointed with iron, which they held firmly in
their two hands, with the points projecting far
before them. The men were arranged in lines,
one behind the other, and all facing the enemy
—sixteen lines, and a thousand in each line, or,
as it is expressed in military phrase, a thousand
in rank and sixteen in file, so that the phalanx
contained sixteen thousand men.

The spears were so long that when the men
stood in close order, the rear ranks being brought
up near to those before them, the points of the
spears of eight or ten of the ranks projected in
front, forming a bristling wall of points of steel,
each one of which was held in its place by the
strong arms of an athletic and well-trained soldier. This wall no force which could in those
days be brought against it could penetrate.
Men, horses, elephants, every thing that attempted to rush upon it, rushed only to their own
destruction. Every spear, feeling the impulse
of the vigorous arms which held it, seemed to

be alive, and darted into its enemy, when an enemy was at hand, as if it felt itself the fierce hostility which directed it. If the enemy remained at a distance, and threw javelins or darts at the phalanx, they fell harmless, stopped by the shields which the soldiers wore upon the left arm, and which were held in such a manner as to form a system of scales, which covered and protected the whole mass, and made the men almost invulnerable. The phalanx was thus, when only defending itself and in a state of rest, an army and a fortification all in one, and it was almost impregnable. But when it took an aggressive form, put itself in motion, and advanced to an attack, it was infinitely more formidable. It became then a terrible monster, covered with scales of brass, from beneath which there projected forward ten thousand living, darting points of iron. It advanced deliberately and calmly, but with a prodigious momentum and force. There was nothing human in its appearance at all. It was a huge animal, ferocious, dogged, stubborn, insensible to pain, knowing no fear, and bearing down with resistless and merciless destruction upon every thing that came in its way. The phalanx was the center and soul of Alexander's army. Powerful and impregnable as it was, however, in ancient days, it would be helpless and defenseless on a modern battle-field. Solid balls of iron, flying through the air with a velocity which makes them invisible, would tear their way through the pikes and the shields, and the bodies of the men who bore them, without even feeling the obstruction.

The phalanx was subdivided into brigades, regiments, and battalions, and regularly officered. In marching, it was separated into these its constituent parts, and sometimes in battle it acted in divisions. It was stationed in the center of the army on the field, and on the two sides of it were bodies of cavalry and foot soldiers, more lightly armed than the soldiers of the phalanx, who could accordingly move with more alertness and speed, and carry their action readily wherever it might be called for. Those troops on the sides were called the wings. Alexander himself was accustomed to command one wing and Parmenio the other, while the phalanx crept along slowly but terribly between

The army, thus arranged and organized, advanced to the river. It was a broad and shallow stream. The Persians had assembled in vast numbers on the opposite shore. Some his-

torians say there were one hundred thousand
men, others say two hundred thousand, and others six hundred thousand. However this may
be, there is no doubt their numbers were vastly
superior to those of Alexander's army, which it
will be recollected was less than forty thousand.
There was a narrow plain on the opposite side
of the river, next to the shore, and a range of
hills beyond. The Persian cavalry covered the
plain, and were ready to dash upon the Macedonian troops the moment they should emerge
from the water and attempt to ascend the bank

The army, led by Alexander, descended into
the stream, and moved on through the water.
They encountered the onset of their enemies on
the opposite shore. A terrible and a protracted
struggle ensued, but the coolness, courage, and
strength of Alexander's army carried the day.
The Persians were driven back, the Greeks effected their landing, reorganized and formed on
the shore, and the Persians, finding that all was
lost, fled in all directions.

Alexander himself took a conspicuous and a
very active part in the contest. He was easily
recognized on the field of battle by his dress, and
by a white plume which he wore in his helmet
He exposed himself to the most imminent dan

ger. At one time, when desperately engaged
with a troop of horse, which had galloped down
upon him, a Persian horseman aimed a blow at
his head with a sword. Alexander saved his
head from the blow, but it took off his plume
and a part of his helmet. Alexander immediately thrust his antagonist through the body.
At the same moment, another horseman, on another side, had his sword raised, and would have
killed Alexander before he could have turned to
defend himself, had no help intervened ; but
just at this instant a third combatant, one of
Alexander's friends, seeing the danger, brought
down so terrible a blow upon the shoulder of
this second assailant as to separate his arm from
his body.

Such are the stories that are told. They
may have been literally and fully true, or they
may have been exaggerations of circumstances
somewhat resembling them which really occurred, or they may have been fictitious altogether. Great generals, like other great men, have
often the credit of many exploits which they
never perform. It is the special business of
poets and historians to magnify and embellish
the actions of the great, and this art was understood as well in ancient days as it is now

26

We must remember, too, in reading the accounts of these transactions, that it is only the Greek side of the story that we hear. The Persian narratives have not come down to us.

At any rate, the Persian army was defeated, and that, too, without the assistance of the phalanx. The horsemen and the light troops were alone engaged. The phalanx could not be formed, nor could it act in such a position. The men, on emerging from the water, had to climb up the banks, and rush on to the attack of an enemy consisting of squadrons of horse ready to dash at once upon them.

The Persian army was defeated and driven away. Alexander did not pursue them. He felt that he had struck a very heavy blow. The news of this defeat of the Persians would go with the speed of the wind all over Asia Minor, and operate most powerfully in his favor. He sent home to Greece an account of the victory, and with the account he forwarded three hundred suits of armor, taken from the Persian horsemen killed on the field. These suits of armor were to be hung up in the Parthenon, a great temple at Athens; the most conspicuous position for them, perhaps, which all Europe could afford.

The name of the Persian general who commanded at the battle of the Granicus was Memnon. He had been opposed to the plan of hazarding a battle. Alexander had come to Asia with no provisions and no money. He had relied on being able to sustain his army by his victories. Memnon, therefore, strongly urged that the Persians should retreat slowly, carrying off all the valuable property, and destroying all that could not be removed, taking especial care to leave no provisions behind them. In this way he thought that the army of Alexander would be reduced by privation and want, and would, in the end, fall an easy prey. His opinion was, however, overruled by the views of the other commanders, and the battle of the Granicus was the consequence.

Alexander encamped to refresh his army and to take care of the wounded. He went to see the wounded men one by one, inquired into the circumstances of each case, and listened to each one who was able to talk, while he gave an account of his adventures in the battle, and the manner in which he received his wound. To be able thus to tell their story to their general, and to see him listening to it with interest and pleasure, filled their hearts with pride and joy:

H

and the whole army was inspired with the highest spirit of enthusiasm, and with eager desires
to have another opportunity occur in which they
could encounter danger and death in the service
of such a leader. It is in such traits as these
that the true greatness of the soul of Alexander
shines. It must be remembered that all this
time he was but little more than twenty-one.
He was but just of age.

From his encampment on the Granicus Alexander turned to the southward, and moved along
on the eastern shores of the Ægean Sea. The
country generally surrendered to him without
opposition. In fact, it was hardly Persian territory at all. The inhabitants were mainly of
Greek extraction, and had been sometimes
under Greek and sometimes under Persian rule.
The conquest of the country resulted simply in
a change of the executive officer of each province. Alexander took special pains to lead the
people to feel that they had nothing to fear from
him. He would not allow the soldiers to do
any injury. He protected all private property
He took possession only of the citadels, and of
such governmental property as he found there,
and he continued the same taxes, the same
laws, and the same tribunals as had existed be

fore his invasion. The cities and the provinces accordingly surrendered to him as he passed along, and in a very short time all the western part of Asia Minor submitted peacefully to his sway.

The narrative of this progress, as given by the ancient historians, is diversified by a great variety of adventures and incidents, which give great interest to the story, and strikingly illustrate the character of Alexander and the spirit of the times. In some places there would be a contest between the Greek and the Persian parties before Alexander's arrival. At Ephesus the animosity had been so great that a sort of civil war had broken out. The Greek party had gained the ascendency, and were threatening a general massacre of the Persian inhabitants. Alexander promptly interposed to protect them, though they were his enemies. The intelligence of this act of forbearance and generosity spread all over the land, and added greatly to the influence of Alexander's name, and to the estimation in which he was held.

It was the custom in those days for the mass of the common soldiers to be greatly influenced by what they called *omens*, that is, signs and tokens which they observed in the flight or the

actions of birds, and other similar appearances.
In one case, the fleet, which had come along the
sea, accompanying the march of the army on
land, was pent up in a harbor by a stronger
Persian fleet outside. One of the vessels of the
Macedonian fleet was aground. An eagle lighted upon the mast, and stood perched there for
a long time, looking toward the sea. Parmenio said that, as the eagle looked toward the
sea, it indicated that victory lay in that quarter, and he recommended that they should arm
their ships and push boldly out to attack the
Persians. But Alexander maintained that, as
the eagle alighted on a ship which was aground,
it indicated that they were to look for their success on the shore. The omens could thus almost always be interpreted any way, and sagacious generals only sought in them the means
of confirming the courage and confidence of
their soldiers, in respect to the plans which they
adopted under the influence of other considerations altogether. Alexander knew very well
that he was not a sailor, and had no desire to
embark in contests from which, however they
might end, he would himself personally obtain
no glory.

When the winter came on, Alexander and

his army were about three or four hundred miles from home; and, as he did not intend to advance much farther until the spring should open, he announced to the army that all those persons, both officers and soldiers who had been married within the year, might go home if they chose, and spend the winter with their brides, and return to the army in the spring. No doubt this was an admirable stroke of policy; for, as the number could not be large, their absence could not materially weaken his force, and they would, of course, fill all Greece with tales of Alexander's energy and courage, and of the nobleness and generosity of his character. It was the most effectual way possible of disseminating through Europe the most brilliant accounts of what he had already done.

Besides, it must have awakened a new bond of sympathy and fellow-feeling between himself and his soldiers, and greatly increased the attachment to him felt both by those who went and those who remained. And though Alexander must have been aware of all these advantages of the act, still no one could have thought of or adopted such a plan unless he was accustomed to consider and regard, in his dealings with others, the feelings and affections of the heart, and

to cherish a warm sympathy for them. The
bridegroom soldiers, full of exultation and pleasure, set forth on their return to Greece, in a detachment under the charge of three generals,
themselves bridegrooms too.

Alexander, however, had no idea of remaining idle during the winter. He marched on
from province to province, and from city to city,
meeting with every variety of adventures. He
went first along the southern coast, until at
length he came to a place where a mountain
chain, called Taurus, comes down to the sea-
coast, where it terminates abruptly in cliffs and
precipices, leaving only a narrow beach between
them and the water below. This beach was
sometimes covered and sometimes bare. It is
true, there is very little tide in the Mediterranean, but the level of the water along the shores
is altered considerably by the long-continued
pressure exerted in one direction or another by
winds and storms. The water was *up* when
Alexander reached this pass; still he determined to march his army through it. There was
another way, back among the mountains, but
Alexander seemed disposed to gratify the love
of adventure which his army felt, by introducing
them to a novel scene of danger. They accord

ingly defiled along under these cliffs, marching, as they say, sometimes up to the waist in water, the swell rolling in upon them all the time from the offing.

Having at length succeeded in passing safely round this frowning buttress of the mountains, Alexander turned northward, and advanced into the very heart of Asia Minor. In doing this he had to pass *over* the range which he had come *round* before; and, as it was winter, his army were, for a time, enveloped in snows and storms among the wild and frightful defiles. They had here, in addition to the dangers and hardships of the way and of the season, to encounter the hostility of their foes, as the tribes who inhabited these mountains assembled to dispute the passage. Alexander was victorious, and reached a valley through which there flows a river which has handed down its name to the English language and literature. This river was the Meander. Its beautiful windings through verdant and fertile valleys were so renowned, that every stream which imitates its example is said to *meander* to the present day.

During all this time Parmenio had remained in the western part of Asia Minor with a considerable body of the army. As the spring ap-

proached, Alexander sent him orders to go to
Gordium, whither he was himself proceeding,
and meet him there. He also directed that the
detachment which had gone home should, on
recrossing the Hellespont on their return, proceed eastward to Gordium, thus making that
city the general rendezvous for the commencement of his next campaign.

One reason why Alexander desired to go to
Gordium was that he wished to untie the famous Gordian knot. The story of the Gordian
knot was this. Gordius was a sort of mountain
farmer. One day he was plowing, and an eagle
came down and alighted upon his yoke, and remained there until he had finished his plowing.
This was an omen, but what was the significa-
tion of it? Gordius did not know, and he accordingly went to a neighboring town in order
to consult the prophets and soothsayers. On
his way he met a damsel, who, like Rebecca in
the days of Abraham, was going forth to draw
water. Gordius fell into conversation with her,
and related to her the occurrence which had interested him so strongly. The maiden advised
him to go back and offer a sacrifice to Jupiter.
Finally, she consented to go back with him and
aid him. The affair ended in her becoming his

wife, and they lived together in peace for many years upon their farm.

They had a son named Midas. The father and mother were accustomed to go out sometimes in their cart or wagon, drawn by the oxen, Midas driving. One day they were going into the town in this way, at a time when it happened that there was an assembly convened, which was in a state of great perplexity on account of the civil dissensions and contests which prevailed in the country. They had just inquired of an oracle what they should do. The oracle said that " a cart would bring them a king, who would terminate their eternal broils." Just then Midas came up, driving the cart in which his father and mother were seated. The assembly thought at once that this must be the cart meant by the oracle, and they made Gordius king by acclamation. They took the cart and the yoke to preserve as sacred relics, consecrating them to Jupiter; and Gordius tied the yoke to the pole of the cart by a thong of leather, making a knot so close and complicated that nobody could untie it again. It was called the Gordian knot. The oracle afterward said that whoever should untie this knot should become monarch of all Asia. Thus far, nobody had succeeded.

Alexander felt a great desire to see this knot and try what he could do. He went, accordingly, into the temple where the sacred cart had been deposited, and, after looking at the knot, and satisfying himself that the task of untying it was hopeless, he cut it to pieces with his sword. How far the circumstances of this whole story are true, and how far fictitious, no one can tell; the story itself, however, as thus related, has come down from generation to generation, in every country of Europe, for two thousand years, and any extrication of one's self from a difficulty by violent means has been called cutting the Gordian knot to the present day.

At length the whole army was assembled, and the king recommenced his progress. He went on successfully for some weeks, moving in a southeasterly direction, and bringing the whole country under his dominion, until, at length, when he reached Tarsus, an event occurred which nearly terminated his career. There were some circumstances which caused him to press forward with the utmost effort in approaching Tarsus, and, as the day was warm, he got very much overcome with heat and fatigue. In

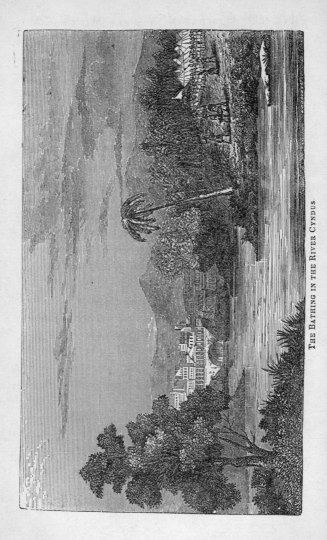

THE BATHING IN THE RIVER CYNDUS.

this state, he went and plunged suddenly into
the River Cydnus to bathe.

Now the Cydnus is a small stream, flowing
by Tarsus, and it comes down from Mount Taurus at a short distance back from the city.
Such streams are always very cold. Alexander
was immediately seized with a very violent chill,
and was taken out of the water shivering ex-
cessively, and, at length, fainted away. They
thought he was dying. They bore him to his
tent, and, as tidings of their leader's danger
spread through the camp, the whole army, officers and soldiers, were thrown into the greatest
consternation and grief.

A violent and protracted fever came on. In
the course of it, an incident occurred which
strikingly illustrates the boldness and originality of Alexander's character. The name of his
physician was Philip. Philip had been preparing a particular medicine for him, which, it
seems, required some days to make ready. Just
before it was presented, Alexander received a
letter from Parmenio, informing him that he
had good reason to believe that Philip had been
bribed by the Persians to murder him, during
his sickness, by administering poison in the
name of medicine. He wrote, he said, to put

him on his guard against any medicine which
Philip might offer him.

Alexander put the letter under his pillow, and
communicated its contents to no one. At length,
when the medicine was ready, Philip brought it
in. Alexander took the cup containing it with
one hand, and with the other he handed Philip
the communication which he had received from
Parmenio, saying, "Read that letter." As soon
as Philip had finished reading it, and was ready
to look up, Alexander drank off the draught in
full, and laid down the cup with an air of perfect confidence that he had nothing to fear.

Some persons think that Alexander watched
the countenance of his physician while he was
reading the letter, and that he was led to take
the medicine by his confidence in his power to
determine the guilt or the innocence of a person
thus accused by his looks. Others suppose that
the act was an expression of his implicit faith
in the integrity and fidelity of his servant, and
that he intended it as testimony, given in a very
pointed and decisive, and, at the same time, delicate manner, that he was not suspicious of his
friends, or easily led to distrust their faithfulness. Philip was, at any rate, extremely gratified at the procedure, and Alexander recovered.

Alexander had now traversed the whole extent of Asia Minor, and had subdued the entire country to his sway. He was now advancing to another district, that of Syria and Palestine, which lies on the eastern shores of the Mediterranean Sea. To enter this new territory, he had to pass over a narrow plain which lay between the mountains and the sea, at a place called Issus. Here he was met by the main body of the Persian army, and the great battle of Issus was fought. This battle will be the subject of the next chapter.

27

128 ALEXANDER THE GREAT. [B.C. 333

Darius's opinion of Alexander.   He prepares to meet him

CHAPTER VI.

DEFEAT OF DARIUS.

THUS far Alexander had had only the lieu-
tenants and generals of the Persian monarch to contend with. Darius had at first looked
upon the invasion of his vast dominions by such
a mere boy, as he called him, and by so small
an army, with contempt. He sent word to his
generals in Asia Minor to seize the young fool,
and send him to Persia bound hand and foot.
By the time, however, that Alexander had possessed himself of all Asia Minor, Darius began
to find that, though young, he was no fool, and
that it was not likely to be very easy to seize
him.

Accordingly, Darius collected an immense
army himself, and advanced to meet the Macedonians in person. Nothing could exceed the
pomp and magnificence of his preparations.
There were immense numbers of troops, and
they were of all nations. There were even a
great many Greeks among his forces, many of
them enlisted from the Greeks of Asia Minor.
There were some from Greece itself—mercena

ries, as they were called; that is, soldiers who fought for pay, and who were willing to enter into any service which would pay them best.

There were even some Greek officers and counselors in the family and court of Darius. One of them, named Charidemus, offended the king very much by the free opinion which he expressed of the uselessness of all his pomp and parade in preparing for an encounter with such an enemy as Alexander. "Perhaps," said Charidemus, "you may not be pleased with my speaking to you plainly, but if I do not do it now, it will be too late hereafter. This great parade and pomp, and this enormous multitude of men, might be formidable to your Asiatic neighbors; but such sort of preparation will be of little avail against Alexander and his Greeks. Your army is resplendent with purple and gold. No one who had not seen it could conceive of its magnificence; but it will not be of any avail against the terrible energy of the Greeks. Their minds are bent on something very different from idle show. They are intent on securing the substantial excellence of their weapons, and on acquiring the discipline and the hardihood essential for the most efficient use of them. They will despise all your parade of purple and gold

I

They will not even value it as plunder. They glory in their ability to dispense with all the luxuries and conveniences of life. They live upon the coarsest food. At night they sleep upon the bare ground. By day they are always on the march. They brave hunger, cold, and every species of exposure with pride and pleasure, having the greatest contempt for any thing like softness and effeminacy of character. All this pomp and pageantry, with inefficient weapons, and inefficient men to wield them, will be of no avail against their invincible courage and energy; and the best disposition that you can make of all your gold, and silver, and other treasures, is to send it away and procure good soldiers with it, if indeed gold and silver will procure them."

The Greeks were habituated to energetic speaking as well as acting, but Charidemus did not sufficiently consider that the Persians were not accustomed to hear such plain language as this. Darius was very much displeased. In his anger he condemned him to death. "Very well," said Charidemus, "I can die. But my avenger is at hand. My advice is good, and Alexander will soon punish you for not regarding it."

Very gorgeous descriptions are given of the pomp and magnificence of the army of Darius, as he commenced his march from the Euphrates to the Mediterranean. The Persians worship the sun and fire. Over the king's tent there was an image of the sun in crystal, and supported in such a manner as to be in the view of the whole army. They had also silver altars, on which they kept constantly burning what they called the sacred fire. These altars were borne by persons appointed for the purpose, who were clothed in magnificent costumes. Then came a long procession of priests and magi, who were dressed also in very splendid robes. They performed the services of public worship. Following them came a chariot consecrated to the sun. It was drawn by white horses, and was followed by a single white horse of large size and noble form, which was a sacred animal, being called the horse of the sun. The equerries, that is, the attendants who had charge of this horse, were also all dressed in white, and each carried a golden rod in his hand.

There were bodies of troops distinguished from the rest, and occupying positions of high honor, but these were selected and advanced above the others, not on account of their cour

age, or strength, or superior martial efficiency,
but from considerations connected with their
birth, and rank, and other aristocratic qualities.
There was one body called the Kinsmen, who
were the relatives of the king, or, at least, so considered, though, as there were fifteen thousand
of them, it would seem that the relationship
could not have been, in all cases, very near.
They were dressed with great magnificence,
and prided themselves on their rank, their
wealth, and the splendor of their armor. There
was also a corps called the Immortals. They
were ten thousand in number. They wore a
dress of gold tissue, which glittered with span
gles and precious stones.

These bodies of men, thus dressed, made an
appearance more like that of a civic procession,
on an occasion of ceremony and rejoicing, than
like the march of an army. The appearance of
the king in his chariot was still more like an
exhibition of pomp and parade. The carriage
was very large, elaborately carved and gilded,
and ornamented with statues and sculptures.
Here the king sat on a very elevated seat, in
sight of all. He was clothed in a vest of purple, striped with silver, and over his vest he
wore a robe glittering with gold and precious

stones. Around his waist was a golden girdle, from which was suspended his cimeter—a species of sword—the scabbard of which was resplendent with gems. He wore a tiara upon his head of very costly and elegant workmanship, and enriched, like the rest of his dress, with brilliant ornaments. The guards who preceded and followed him had pikes of silver, mounted and tipped with gold.

It is very extraordinary that King Darius took his wife and all his family with him, and a large portion of his treasures, on this expedition against Alexander. His mother, whose name was Sysigambis, was in his family, and she and his wife came, each in her own chariot, immediately after the king. Then there were fifteen carriages filled with the children and their attendants, and three or four hundred ladies of the court, all dressed like queens. After the family there came a train of many hundreds of camels and mules, carrying the royal treasures.

It was in this style that Darius set out upon his expedition, and he advanced by a slow progress toward the westward, until at length he approached the shores of the Mediterranean Sea. He left his treasures in the city of Da-

134 ALEXANDER THE GREAT. [B.C. 333

Darius advances to meet Alexander.   Map of the plain of Issus

mascus, where they were deposited under the charge of a sufficient force to protect them, as he supposed. He then advanced to meet Alexander, going himself from Syria toward Asia Minor just at the time that Alexander was coming from Asia Minor into Syria.

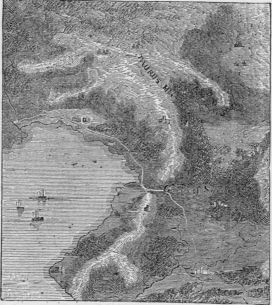

PLAIN OF ISSUS

It will be observed by looking upon the map,

that the chain of mountains called Mount Taurus extends down near to the coast, at the
northeastern corner of the Mediterranean
Among these mountains there are various tracts
of open country, through which an army may
march to and fro, between Syria and Asia Minor. Now it happened that Darius, in going
toward the west, took a more inland route than
Alexander, who, on coming eastward, kept nearer to the sea. Alexander did not know that
Darius was so near; and as for Darius, he was
confident that Alexander was retreating before
him; for, as the Macedonian army was so small,
and his own forces constituted such an innu-
merable host, the idea that Alexander would
remain to brave a battle was, in his opinion, entirely out of the question. He had, therefore,
no doubt that Alexander was retreating. It is,
of course, always difficult for two armies, fifty
miles apart, to obtain correct ideas of each other's movements. All the ordinary intercommu-
nications of the country are of course stopped,
and each general has his scouts out, with orders to intercept all travelers, and to interrupt
the communication of intelligence by every
means in their power.

In consequence of these and other circum-

stances of a similar nature, it happened that
Alexander and Darius actually passed each other, without either of them being aware of it
Alexander advanced into Syria by the plains of
Issus, marked *a* upon the map, and a narrow
pass beyond, called the Gates of Syria, while
Darius went farther to the north, and arrived
at Issus after Alexander had left it. Here each
army learned to their astonishment that their
enemy was in their rear. Alexander could not
credit this report when he first heard it. He
dispatched a galley with thirty oars along the
shore, up the Gulf of Issus, to ascertain the
truth. The galley soon came back and reported that, beyond the Gates of Syria, they saw
the whole country, which was nearly level land,
though gently rising from the sea, covered with
the vast encampments of the Persian army.

The king then called his generals and counselors together, informed them of the facts, and
made known to them his determination to return immediately through the Gates of Syria
and attack the Persian army. The officers received the intelligence with enthusiastic expressions of joy.

It was now near the evening. Alexander
sent forward a strong reconnoitering party, or-

dering them to proceed cautiously, to ascend
eminences and look far before them, to guard
carefully against surprise, and to send back
word immediately if they came upon any traces
of the enemy. At the present day the operations of such a reconnoitering party are very
much aided by the use of spy-glasses, which are
made now with great care expressly for military purposes. The instrument, however, was
not known in Alexander's day.

When the evening came on, Alexander followed the reconnoitering party with the main
body of the army. At midnight they reached
the defile. When they were secure in the possession of it, they halted. Strong watches were
stationed on all the surrounding heights to guard
against any possible surprise. Alexander himself ascended one of the eminences, from whence
he could look down upon the great plain beyond,
which was dimly illuminated in every part by
the smouldering fires of the Persian encampment. An encampment at night is a spectacle
which is always grand, and often sublime. It
must have appeared sublime to Alexander in
the highest degree, on this occasion. To stand
stealthily among these dark and somber mountains, with the defiles and passes below filled

with the columns of his small but undaunted
army, and to look onward, a few miles beyond,
and see the countless fires of the vast hosts
which had got between him and all hope of retreat to his native land; to feel, as he must
have done, that his fate, and that of all who
were with him, depended upon the events of
the day that was soon to dawn—to see and feel
these things must have made this night one of
the most exciting and solemn scenes in the conqueror's life. He had a soul to enjoy its excitement and sublimity. He gloried in it; and,
as if he wished to add to the solemnity of the
scene, he caused an altar to be erected, and offered a sacrifice, by torch-light, to the deities on
whose aid his soldiers imagined themselves most
dependent for success on the morrow. Of course
a place was selected where the lights of the
torches would not attract the attention of the
enemy, and sentinels were stationed at every
advantageous point to watch the Persian camp
for the slightest indications of movement or
alarm.

In the morning, at break of day, Alexander
commenced his march down to the plain. In
the evening, at sunset, all the valleys and defiles
among the mountains around the plain of Issus

were thronged with vast masses of the Persian army, broken, disordered, and in confusion, all pressing forward to escape from the victorious Macedonians. They crowded all the roads, they choked up the mountain passes, they trampled upon one another, they fell, exhausted with fatigue and mental agitation. Darius was among them, though his flight had been so sudden that he had left his mother, and his wife, and all his family behind. He pressed on in his chariot as far as the road allowed his chariot to go, and then, leaving every thing behind, he mounted a horse and rode on for his life.

Alexander and his army soon abandoned the pursuit, and returned to take possession of the Persian camp. The tents of King Darius and his household were inconceivably splendid, and were filled with gold and silver vessels, caskets, vases, boxes of perfumes, and every imaginable article of luxury and show. The mother and wife of Darius bewailed their hard fate with cries and tears, and continued all the evening in an agony of consternation and despair.

Alexander, hearing of this, sent Leonnatus, his former teacher, a man of years and gravity, to quiet their fears and comfort them, so far as it was possible to comfort them. In addition

to their own captivity, they supposed that Darius was killed, and the mother was mourning
bitterly for her son, and the wife for her husband. Leonnatus, attended by some soldiers,
advanced toward the tent where these mourn-
ers were dwelling. The attendants at the door
ran in and informed them that a body of Greeks
were coming. This threw them into the greatest consternation. They anticipated violence
and death, and threw themselves upon the
ground in agony. Leonnatus waited some time
at the door for the attendants to return. At
length he entered the tent. This renewed the
terrors of the women. They began to entreat
him to spare their lives, at least until there
should be time for them to see the remains of
the son and husband whom they mourned, and
to pay the last sad tribute to his memory.

Leonnatus soon relieved their fears. He told
them that he was charged by Alexander to say
to them that Darius was alive, having made his
escape in safety. As to themselves, Alexander
assured them, he said, that they should not be
injured; that not only were their persons and
lives to be protected, but no change was to be
made in their condition or mode of life; they
should continue to be treated like queens. He

added, moreover, that Alexander wished him to
say that he felt no animosity or ill will whatever against Darius He was but technically his
enemy, being only engaged in a generous and
honorable contest with him for the empire of
Asia. Saying these things, Leonnatus raised
the disconsolate ladies from the ground, and they
gradually regained some degree of composure.

Alexander himself went to pay a visit to the
captive princesses the next day. He took with
him Hephæstion. Hephæstion was Alexander's
personal friend. The two young men were of
the same age, and, though Alexander had the
good sense to retain in power all the old and
experienced officers which his father had employed, both in the court and army, he showed
that, after all, ambition had not overwhelmed
and stifled all the kindlier feelings of the heart,
by his strong attachment to this young companion. Hephæstion was his confidant, his asso-
ciate, his personal friend. He did what very
few monarchs have done, either before or since,
in securing for himself the pleasures of friendship, and of intimate social communion with a
heart kindred to his own, without ruining himself by committing to a favorite powers which
he was not qualified to wield. Alexander left

142 ALEXANDER THE GREAT. [B.C. 333

Alexander's interview with the queens.   A mistake

the wise and experienced. Parmenio to manage
the camp, while he took the young and handsome Hephæstion to accompany him on his visit
to the captive queens.

When the two friends entered the tent, the
ladies were, from some cause, deceived, and mis-
took Hephæstion for Alexander, and addressed
him, accordingly, with tokens of high respect and
homage. One of their attendants immediately
rectified the mistake, telling them that the other was Alexander. The ladies were at first overwhelmed with confusion, and attempted to apologize ; but the king reassured them at once by
the easy and good-natured manner with which
he passed over the mistake, saying it was no
mistake at all. "It is true," said he, "that I
am Alexander, but then he is Alexander too."

The wife of Darius was young and very beautiful, and they had a little son who was with
them in the camp. It seems almost unaccountable that Darius should have brought such a
helpless and defenseless charge with him into
camps and fields of battle. But the truth was
that he had no idea of even a battle with Alexander, and as to defeat, he did not contemplate
the remotest possibility of it. He regarded Alexander as a mere boy—energetic and daring,

it is true, and at the head of a desperate band
of adventurers; but he considered his whole
force as altogether too insignificant to make any
stand against such a vast military power as he
was bringing against him. He presumed that
he would retreat as fast as possible before the
Persian army came near him. The idea of
such a boy coming down at break of day, from
narrow defiles of the mountains, upon his vast
encampment covering all the plains, and in
twelve hours putting the whole mighty mass
to flight, was what never entered his imagina
tion at all. The exploit was, indeed, a very extraordinary one. Alexander's forces may have
consisted of forty or fifty thousand men, and,
if we may believe their story, there were over
a hundred thousand Persians left dead upon the
field. Many of these were, however, killed by
the dreadful confusion and violence of the retreat
as vast bodies of horsemen, pressing through the
defiles, rode over and trampled down the foot
soldiers who were toiling in awful confusion
along the way, having fled before the horsemen
left the field.

Alexander had heard that Darius had left the
greater part of his royal treasures in Damas-
cus, and he sent Parmenio there to seize them.

28

This expedition was successful. An enormous amount of gold and silver fell into Alexander's hands. The plate was coined into money, and many of the treasures were sent to Greece.

Darius got together a small remnant of his army and continued his flight. He did not stop until he had crossed the Euphrates. He then sent an embassador to Alexander to make propositions for peace. He remonstrated with him, in the communication which he made, for coming thus to invade his dominions, and urged him to withdraw and be satisfied with his own kingdom. He offered him any sum he might name as a ransom for his mother, wife, and child, and agreed that if he would deliver them up to him on the payment of the ransom, and depart from his dominions, he would thenceforth regard him as an ally and a friend.

Alexander replied by a letter, expressed in brief but very decided language. He said that the Persians had, under the ancestors of Darius, crossed the Hellespont, invaded Greece, laid waste the country, and destroyed cities and towns, and had thus done them incalculable injury; and that Darius himself had been plotting against his (Alexander's) life, and offering rewards to any one who would kill him. " I am acting, then," continued Alexander, "only on the defensive. The gods, who always favor the right, have given me the victory. I am now monarch of a large part of Asia, and your sovereign king. If you will admit this, and come to me as my subject, I will restore to you your mother, your wife, and your child, without any ransom. And, at any rate, whatever you decide in respect to these proposals, if you wish to communicate with me on any subject hereafter, I shall pay no attention to what you send unless you address it to me as your king."

One circumstance occurred at the close of this great victory which illustrates the magnanimity of Alexander's character, and helps to explain the very strong personal attachment which every body within the circle of his influence so obviously felt for him. He found a great number of envoys and embassadors from the various states of Greece at the Persian court, and these persons fell into his hands among the other captives. Now the states and cities of Greece, all except Sparta and Thebes, which last city he had destroyed, were combined ostensibly in the confederation by which Alexander was sustained. It seems, however, that there was a secret enmity against him in Greece, and vari-

K

ous parties had sent messengers and agents to
the Persian court to aid in plots and schemes
to interfere with and defeat Alexander's plans.
The Thebans, scattered and disorganized as they
were, had sent envoys in this way. Now Alexander, in considering what disposition he
should make of these emissaries from his own
land, decided to regard them all as traitors except the Thebans. All except the Thebans
were *traitors*, he maintained, for acting secretly against him, while ostensibly, and by solemn
covenants, they were his friends. "The case
of the Thebans is very different," said he. "I
have destroyed their city, and they have a right
to consider me their enemy, and to do all they
can to oppose my progress, and to regain their
own lost existence and their former power." So
he gave them their liberty and sent them away
with marks of consideration and honor.

As the vast army of the Persian monarch
had now been defeated, of course none of the
smaller kingdoms or provinces thought of resist-
ing. They yielded one after another, and Alexander appointed governors of his own to rule
over them. He advanced in this manner along
the eastern shores of the Mediterranean Sea,
meeting with no obstruction until he reached
the great and powerful city of Tyre.

B.C. 333.] THE SIEGE OF TYRE. 147

The city of Tyre. Its situation and extent

CHAPTER VII.

THE SIEGE OF TYRE.

THE city of Tyre stood on a small island, three or four miles in diameter,* on the eastern shores of the Mediterranean Sea. It was, in those days, the greatest commercial city in the world, and it exercised a great maritime power by means of its fleets and ships, which traversed every part of the Mediterranean.

Tyre had been built originally on the mainland; but in some of the wars which it had to encounter with the kings of Babylon in the East, this old city had been abandoned by the inhabitants, and a new one built upon an island not far from the shore, which could be more easily defended from an enemy. The old city had gone to ruin, and its place was occupied by old walls, fallen towers, stones, columns, arches, and other remains of the ancient magnifi. cence of the place.

The island on which the Tyre of Alexander's

* There are different statements in respect to the size of this island, varying from three to nine miles in circumference

day had been built was about half a mile from
the shore. The water between was about
eighteen feet deep, and formed a harbor for the
vessels. The great business of the Tyrians
was commerce. They bought and sold merchandise in all the ports of the Mediterranean
Sea, and transported it by their merchant vessels to and fro. They had also fleets of war
galleys, which they used to protect their interests on the high seas, and in the various ports
which their merchant vessels visited. They
were thus wealthy and powerful, and yet they
lived shut up upon their little island, and were
almost entirely independent of the main-land.

The city itself, however, though contracted
in extent on account of the small dimensions
of the island, was very compactly built and
strongly fortified, and it contained a vast number of stately and magnificent edifices, which
were filled with stores of wealth that had been
accumulated by the mercantile enterprise and
thrift of many generations. Extravagant stories are told by the historians and geographers
of those days, in respect to the scale on which
the structures of Tyre were built. It was said,
for instance, that the walls were one hundred
and fifty feet high. It is true that the walls

rose directly from the surface of the water, and
of course a considerable part of their elevation
was required to bring them up to the level of
the surface of the land; and then, in addition to
this, they had to be carried up the whole ordinary height of a city wall to afford the usual
protection to the edifices and dwellings within.
There might have been some places where the
walls themselves, or structures connected with
them, were carried up to the elevation above
named, though it is scarcely to be supposed that
such could have been their ordinary dimensions.

At any rate, Tyre was a very wealthy, magnificent, and powerful city, intent on its com
mercial operations, and well furnished with
means of protecting them at sea, but feeling
little interest, and taking little part, in the contentions continually arising among the rival
powers which had possession of the land. Their
policy was to retain their independence, and yet
to keep on good terms with all other powers,
so that their commercial intercourse with the
ports of all nations might go on undisturbed.

It was, of course, a very serious question
with Alexander, as his route lay now through
Phœnicia and in the neighborhood of Tyre, what
he should do in respect to such a port. He did

not like to leave it behind him and proceed to
the eastward; for, in case of any reverses happening to him, the Tyrians would be very likely to act decidedly against him, and their power on the Mediterranean would enable them to
act very efficiently against him on all the coasts
of Greece and Asia Minor. On the other hand,
it seemed a desperate undertaking to attack the
city. He had none but land forces, and the isl-
and was half a mile from the shore. Besides
its enormous walls, rising perpendicularly out of
the water, it was defended by ships well armed
and manned. It was not possible to surround
the city and starve it into submission, as the
inhabitants had wealth to buy, and ships to
bring in, any quantity of provisions and stores
by sea. Alexander, however, determined not
to follow Darius toward the east, and leave such
a stronghold as this behind him.

The Tyrians wished to avoid a quarrel if it
were possible. They sent complimentary messages to Alexander, congratulating him on his
conquests, and disavowing all feelings of hostility to him. They also sent him a golden crown,
as many of the other states of Asia had done,
in token of their yielding a general submission
to his authority. Alexander returned very gra-

cious replies, and expressed to them his intention of coming to Tyre for the purpose of offering sacrifices, as he said, to Hercules, a god
whom the Tyrians worshiped.

The Tyrians knew that wherever Alexander
went he went at the head of his army, and his
coming into Tyre at all implied necessarily his
taking military possession of it. They thought
it might, perhaps, be somewhat difficult to dis-
possess such a visitor after he should once get
installed in their castles and palaces. So they
sent him word that it would not be in their
power to receive him in the city itself, but that
he could offer the sacrifice which he intended on
the main-land, as there was a temple sacred to
Hercules among the ruins there.

Alexander then called a council of his officers, and stated to them his views. He said
that, on reflecting fully upon the subject, he had
come to the conclusion that it was best to postpone pushing his expedition forward into the
heart of Persia until he should have subdued
Tyre completely, and made himself master of
the Mediterranean Sea. He said, also, that he
should take possession of Egypt before turning
his arms toward the forces that Darius was
gathering against him in the East. The gen-

erals of the army concurred in this opinion, and
Alexander advanced toward Tyre. The Tyrians prepared for their defense.

After examining carefully all the circumstances of the case, Alexander conceived the very
bold plan of building a broad causeway from the
main-land to the island on which the city was
founded, out of the ruins of old Tyre, and then
marching his army over upon it to the walls of
the city, where he could then plant his engines
and make a breach. This would seem to be a
very desperate undertaking. It is true the
stones remaining on the site of the old city afforded sufficient materials for the construction
of the pier, but then the work must go on against
a tremendous opposition, both from the walls of
the city itself and from the Tyrian ships in the
harbor. It would seem to be almost impossible
to protect the men from these attacks so as to
allow the operations to proceed at all, and the
difficulty and danger must increase very rapidly
as the work should approach the walls of the
city. But, notwithstanding these objections,
Alexander determined to proceed. Tyre must
be taken, and this was obviously the only possible mode of taking it.

The soldiers advanced to undertake the work

with great readiness. Their strong personal attachment to Alexander; their confidence that whatever he should plan and attempt would succeed; the novelty and boldness of this design of reaching an island by building an isthmus to it from the main-land—these and other similar considerations excited the ardor and enthusiasm of the troops to the highest degree.

In constructing works of this kind in the water, the material used is sometimes stone and sometimes earth. So far as earth is employed, it is necessary to resort to some means to prevent its spreading under the water, or being washed away by the dash of the waves at its sides. This is usually effected by driving what are called *piles*, which are long beams of wood, pointed at the end, and driven into the earth by means of powerful engines. Alexander sent parties of men into the mountains of Lebanon, where were vast forests of cedars, which were very celebrated in ancient times, and which are often alluded to in the sacred scriptures. They cut down these trees, and brought the stems of them to the shore, where they sharpened them at one end and drove them into the sand, in order to protect the sides of their embankment. Others brought stones from the ruins and tum

bled them into the sea in the direction where
the pier was to be built.   It was some time before the work made such progress as to attract
much attention from Tyre.   At length, however, when the people of the city saw it gradually
increasing in size and advancing toward them,
they concluded that they must engage in earnest in the work of arresting its progress.

They accordingly constructed engines on the
walls to throw heavy darts and stones over the
water to the men upon the pier.   They sent
secretly to the tribes that inhabited the valleys
and ravines among the mountains, to attack
the parties at work there, and they landed forces from the city at some distance from the
pier, and then marched along the shore, and attempted to drive away the men that were engaged in carrying stones from the ruins.   They
also fitted up and manned some galleys of large
size, and brought them up near to the pier itself, and attacked the men who were at work
upon it with stones, darts, arrows, and missiles
of every description.

But all was of no avail.   The work, though
impeded, still went on.   Alexander built large
screens of wood upon the pier, covering them
with hides, which protected his soldiers from the

weapons of the enemy, so that they could carry on their operations safely behind them. By these means the work advanced for some distance further. As it advanced, various structures were erected upon it, especially along the sides and at the end toward the city. These structures consisted of great engines for driving piles, and machines for throwing stones and darts, and towers carried up to a great height, to enable the men to throw stones and heavy weapons down upon the galleys which might attempt to approach them.

At length the Tyrians determined on attempting to destroy all these wooden works by means of what is called in modern times a *fire ship*. They took a large galley, and filled it with combustibles of every kind. They loaded it first with light dry wood, and they poured pitch, and tar, and oil over all this wood to make it burn with fiercer flames. They saturated the sails and the cordage in the same manner, and laid trains of combustible materials through all parts of the vessel, so that when fire should be set in one part it would immediately spread every where, and set the whole mass in flames at once. They towed this ship, on a windy day, near to the enemy's works, and on the side from

which the wind was blowing. They then put
it in motion toward the pier at a point where
there was the greatest collection of engines and
machines, and when they had got as near as
they dared to go themselves, the men who were
on board set the trains on fire, and made their
escape in boats. The flames ran all over the
vessel with inconceivable rapidity. The vessel
itself drifted down upon Alexander's works, notwithstanding the most strenuous exertions of
his soldiers to keep it away. The frames and
engines, and the enormous and complicated machines which had been erected, took fire, and
the whole mass was soon enveloped in a general conflagration.

The men made desperate attempts to defend
their works, but all in vain. Some were killed
by arrows and darts, some were burned to
death, and others, in the confusion, fell into
the sea. Finally, the army was obliged to draw
back, and to abandon all that was combustible
in the vast construction they had reared, to the
devouring flames.

Not long after this the sea itself came to the
aid of the Tyrians. There was a storm; and,
as a consequence of it, a heavy swell rolled in
from the offing, which soon undermined and

THE SIEGE OF TYRE

washed away a large part of the pier. The effects of a heavy sea on the most massive and substantial structures, when they are fairly exposed to its impulse, are far greater than would be conceived possible by those who had not witnessed them. The most ponderous stones are removed, the strongest fastenings are torn asunder, and embankments the most compact and solid are undermined and washed away. The storm, in this case, destroyed in a few hours the work of many months, while the army of Alexander looked on from the shore witnessing its ravages in dismay.

When the storm was over, and the first shock of chagrin and disappointment had passed from the minds of the men, Alexander prepared to resume the work with fresh vigor and energy The men commenced repairing the pier and widening it, so as to increase its strength and capacity. They dragged whole trees to the edges of it, and sunk them, branches and all, to the bottom, to form a sort of platform there, to prevent the stones from sinking into the slime. They built new towers and engines, covering them with green hides to make them fire-proof; and thus they were soon advancing again, and gradually drawing nearer to the city, and in a

29

more threatening and formidable manner than ever.

Alexander, finding that his efforts were impeded very much by the ships of the Tyrians, determined on collecting and equipping a fleet of his own. This he did at Sidon, which was a town a short distance north of Tyre. He embarked on board this fleet himself, and came down with it into the Tyrian seas. With this fleet he had various success. He chained many of the ships together, two and two, at a little distance apart, covering the inclosed space with a platform, on which the soldiers could stand to fight. The men also erected engines on these platforms to attack the city. These engines were of various kinds. There was what they called the battering ram, which was a long and very heavy beam of wood, headed with iron or brass. This beam was suspended by a chain in the middle, so that it could be swung back and forth by the soldiers, its head striking against the wall each time, by which means the wall would sometimes be soon battered down. They had also machines for throwing great stones, or beams of wood, by means of the elastic force of strong bars of wood, or of steel, or that of twisted ropes. The part of the machine

upon which the stone was placed would be
drawn back by the united strength of many of
the soldiers, and then, as it recovered itself when
released, the stone would be thrown off into the
air with prodigious velocity and force.

Alexander's double galleys answered very
well as long as the water was smooth; but
sometimes, when they were caught out in a
swell, the rolling of the waves would rack and
twist them so as to tear the platforms asunder, and sink the men in the sea. Thus difficulties unexpected and formidable were continually arising. Alexander, however, persevered
through them all. The Tyrians, finding themselves pressed more and more, and seeing that
the dangers impending became more and more
formidable every day, at length concluded to
send a great number of the women and children
away to Carthage, which was a great commercial city in Africa. They were determined not
to submit to Alexander, but to carry their resistance to the very last extremity. And as
the closing scenes of a siege, especially if the
place is at last taken by storm, are awful beyond description, they wished to save their wives,
and daughters, and helpless babes from having
to witness them.

In the mean time, as the siege advanced, the
parties became more and more incensed against
each other. They treated the captives which
they took on either side with greater and great
er cruelty, each thinking that they were only
retaliating worse injuries from the other. The
Macedonians approached nearer and nearer.
The resources of the unhappy city were gradually cut off and its strength worn away. The
engines approached nearer and nearer to the
walls, until the battering rams bore directly
upon them, and breaches began to be made.
At length one great breach on the southern side
was found to be " practicable," as they call it.
Alexander began to prepare for the final assault,
and the Tyrians saw before them the horrible
prospect of being taken by storm.

Still they would not submit. Submission
would now have done but little good, though it
might have saved some of the final horrors of
the scene. Alexander had become greatly exasperated by the long resistance which the Tyrians had made. They probably could not now
have averted destruction, but they might, perhaps, have prevented its coming upon them in
so terrible a shape as the irruption of thirty
thousand frantic and infuriated soldiers through

{the breaches in their walls to take their city by storm.

The breach by which Alexander proposed to force his entrance was on the southern side. He prepared a number of ships, with platforms raised upon them in such a manner that, on getting near the walls, they could be let down, and form a sort of bridge, over which the men could pass to the broken fragments of the wall, and thence ascend through the breach above.

The plan succeeded. The ships advanced to the proposed place of landing. The bridges were let down. The men crowded over them to the foot of the wall. They clambered up through the breach to the battlements above, although the Tyrians thronged the passage and made the most desperate resistance. Hundreds were killed by darts, and arrows, and falling stones, and their bodies tumbled into the sea. The others, paying no attention to their falling comrades, and drowning the horrid screams of the crushed and the dying with their own frantic shouts of rage and fury, pressed on up the broken wall till they reached the battlements above. The vast throng then rolled along upon the top of the wall till they came to stairways and slopes by which they could descend into the

city, and, pouring down through all these avenues, they spread over the streets, and satiated
the hatred and rage, which had been gathering
strength for seven long months, in bursting into
houses, and killing and destroying all that came
in their way. Thus the city was stormed.

After the soldiers were weary with the work
of slaughtering the wretched inhabitants of the
city, they found that many still remained alive,
and Alexander tarnished the character for generosity and forbearance for which he had thus
far been distinguished by the cruelty with which
he treated them. Some were executed, some
thrown into the sea; and it is even said that
two thousand were *crucified* along the sea-shore.
This may mean that their bodies were placed
upon crosses after life had been destroyed by
some more humane method than crucifixion.
At any rate, we find frequent indications from
this time that prosperity and power were beginning to exert their usual unfavorable influence upon Alexander's character He became
haughty, imperious, and cruel. He lost the
modesty and gentleness which seemed to char
acterize him in the earlier part of his life, and
began to assume the moral character, as well
as perform the exploits, of a military hero.

A good illustration of this is afforded by the answer that he sent to Darius, about the time of the storming of Tyre, in reply to a second communication which he had received from him proposing terms of peace. Darius offered him a very large sum of money for the ransom of his mother, wife, and child, and agreed to give up to him all the country he had conquered, including the whole territory west of the Euphrates. He also offered him his daughter Statira in marriage. He recommended to him to accept these terms, and be content with the possessions he had already acquired; that he could not expect to succeed, if he should try, in crossing the mighty rivers of the East, which were in the way of his march toward the Persian dominions.

Alexander replied, that if he wished to marry his daughter he could do it without his consent; as to the ransom, he was not in want of money; in respect to Darius's offering to give him up all west of the Euphrates, it was absurd for a man to speak of giving what was no longer his own; that he had crossed too many seas in his military expeditions, since he left Macedon, to feel any concern about the *rivers* that he might find in his way; and that he should continue to pursue Darius wherever he might retreat in search of safety and protection, and he had no fear but that he should find and conquer him at last.

It was a harsh and cruel message to send to the unhappy monarch whom he had already so greatly injured. Parmenio advised him to accept Darius's offers. "I would," said he, "if I were Alexander." "Yes," said Alexander, "and so would I if I were Parmenio." What a reply from a youth of twenty-two to a venerable general of sixty, who had been so tried and faithful a friend, and so efficient a coadjutor both to his father and to himself, for so many years.

The siege and storming of Tyre has always been considered one of the greatest of Alexander's exploits. The boldness, the perseverance, the indomitable energy which he himself and all his army manifested, during the seven months of their Herculean toil, attracted the admiration of the world. And yet we find our feelings of sympathy for his character, and interest in his fate, somewhat alienated by the indications of pride, imperiousness, and cruelty which begin to appear. While he rises in our estimation as a military hero, he begins to sink somewhat as a man.

And yet the change was not sudden. He
bore during the siege his part in the privations
and difficulties which the soldiers had to endure ; and the dangers to which they had to be
exposed, he was always willing to share. One
night he was out with a party upon the mountains. Among his few immediate attendants
was Lysimachus, one of his former teachers,
who always loved to accompany him at such
times. Lysimachus was advanced in life, and
somewhat infirm, and consequently could not
keep up with the rest in the march. Alexander remained with Lysimachus, and ordered the
rest to go on. The road at length became so
rugged that they had to dismount from their
horses and walk. Finally they lost their way,
and found themselves obliged to stop for the
night. They had no fire. They saw, however, at a distance, some camp fires blazing which
belonged to the barbarian tribes against whom
the expedition was directed. Alexander went
to the nearest one. There were two men lying
by it, who had been stationed to take care of it
He advanced stealthily to them and killed them
both, probably while they were asleep. He then
took a brand from their fire, carried it back to
his own encampment, where he made a blazing

fire for himself and Lysimachus, and they passed
the night in comfort and safety. This is the
story. How far we are to give credit to it, each
reader must judge for himself. One thing is
certain, however, that there are many military
heroes of whom such stories would not be even
fabricated

B.C. 332.] ALEXANDER IN EGYPT. 169

Alexander in Judea.   Josephus, and the character of his writings

CHAPTER VIII.
ALEXANDER IN EGYPT.

AFTER completing the subjugation of Tyre, Alexander commenced his march for Egypt. His route led him through Judea. The time was about three hundred years before the birth of Christ, and, of course, this passage of the great conqueror through the land of Israel took place between the historical periods of the Old Testament and of the New, so that no account of it is given in the sacred volume.

There was a Jewish writer named Josephus, who lived and wrote a few years after Christ, and, of course, more than three hundred years after Alexander. He wrote a history of the Jews, which is a very entertaining book to read; but he liked so much to magnify the importance of the events in the history of his country, and to embellish them with marvelous and supernatural incidents, that his narratives have not always been received with implicit faith. Josephus says that, as Alexander passed through Palestine, he went to pay a visit to Jerusalem.

The circumstances of this visit, according to his account, were these.

The city of Tyre, before Alexander besieged it, as it lived entirely by commerce, and was surrounded by the sea, had to depend on the neighboring countries for a supply of food. The people were accordingly accustomed to purchase grain in Phœnicia, in Judea, and in Egypt, and transport it by their ships to the island. Alexander, in the same manner, when besieging the city, found that he must depend upon the neighboring countries for supplies of food; and he accordingly sent requisitions for such supplies to several places, and, among others, to Judea. The Jews, as Josephus says, refused to send any such supplies, saying that it would be inconsistent with fidelity to Darius, under whose government they were.

Alexander took no notice of this reply at the time, being occupied with the siege of Tyre; but, as soon as that city was taken, and he was ready to pass through Judea, he directed his march toward Jerusalem with the intention of destroying the city

Now the chief magistrate at Jerusalem at this time, the one who had the command of the city, ruling it, of course, under a general responsibility to the Persian government, was the high priest. His name was Jaddus. In the time of Christ, about three hundred years after this, the name of the high-priest, as the reader will recollect, was Caiaphas. Jaddus and all the inhabitants of Jerusalem were very much alarmed. They knew not what to do. The siege and capture of Tyre had impressed them all with a strong sense of Alexander's terrible energy and martial power, and they began to anticipate certain destruction.

Jaddus caused great sacrifices to be offered to Almighty God, and public and solemn prayers were made, to implore his guidance and protection. The next day after these services, he told the people that they had nothing to fear. God had appeared to him in a dream, and directed him what to do. "We are not to resist the conqueror," said he, "but to go forth to meet him and welcome him. We are to strew the city with flowers, and adorn it as for a festive celebration. The priests are to be dressed in their pontifical robes and go forth, and the inhabitants are to follow them in a civic procession. In this way we are to go out to meet Alexander as he advances—and all will be well."

These directions were followed. Alexander

was coming on with a full determination to destroy the city. When, however, he saw this
procession, and came near enough to distinguish
the appearance and dress of the high priest, he
stopped, seemed surprised and pleased, and advanced toward him with an air of the profound-
est deference and respect. He seemed to pay
him almost religious homage and adoration.
Every one was astonished. Parmenio asked
him for an explanation. Alexander made the
following extraordinary statement:

"When I was in Macedon, before setting out
on this expedition, while I was revolving the
subject in my mind, musing day after day on
the means of conquering Asia, one night I had
a remarkable dream. In my dream this very
priest appeared before me, dressed just as he is
now. He exhorted me to banish every fear, to
cross the Hellespont boldly, and to push forward
into the heart of Asia. He said that God would
march at the head of my army, and give me the
victory over all the Persians. I recognize this
priest as the same person that appeared to me
then. He has the same countenance, the same
dress, the same stature, the same air. It is
through his encouragement and aid that I am
here, and I am ready to worship and adore the
God whose service he administers."

Alexander joined the high priest in the procession, and they returned to Jerusalem together. There Alexander united with them and with the Jews of the city in the celebration of religious rites, by offering sacrifices and oblations in the Jewish manner. The writings which are now printed together in our Bibles, as the Old Testament, were, in those days, written separately on parchment rolls, and kept in the temple. The priests produced from the rolls the one containing the prophecies of Daniel, and they read and interpreted some of these prophecies to Alexander, which they considered to have reference to him, though written many hundred years before. Alexander was, as Josephus relates, very much pleased at the sight of these ancient predictions, and the interpretation put upon them by the priests. He assured the Jews that they should be protected in the exercise of all their rights, and especially in their religious worship, and he also promised them that he would take their brethren who resided in Media and Babylon under his special charge when he should come into possession of those places. These Jews of Media and Babylon were the descendants of captives which had been carried away from their native land in former wars

Such is the story which Josephus relates.
The Greek historians, on the other hand, make
no mention of this visit to Jerusalem; and some
persons think that it was never made, but that
the story arose and was propagated from generation to generation among the Jews, through
the influence of their desire to magnify the importance and influence of their worship, and
that Josephus incorporated the account into his
history without sufficiently verifying the facts.

However it may be in regard to Jerusalem,
Alexander was delayed at Gaza, which, as may
be seen upon the map, is on the shore of the
Mediterranean Sea. It was a place of considerable commerce and wealth, and was, at this
time, under the command of a governor whom
Darius had stationed there. His name was
Betis. Betis refused to surrender the place.
Alexander stopped to besiege it, and the siege
delayed him two months. He was very much
exasperated at this, both against Betis and
against the city.

His unreasonable anger was very much increased by a wound which he received. He
was near a mound which his soldiers had been
constructing near the city, to place engines upon
for an attack upon the walls, when an arrow

B.C. 332.] ALEXANDER IN EGYPT. 175

Alexander receives a wound.   Gaza taken by storm.

shot from one of the engines upon the walls,
struck him in the breast. It penetrated his armor, and wounded him deeply in the shoulder.
The wound was very painful for some time, and
the suffering which he endured from it only added fuel to the flame of his anger against the city.

At last breaches were made in the walls, and
the place was taken by storm. Alexander treated the wretched captives with extreme cruelty.
He cut the garrison to pieces, and sold the inhabitants to slavery. As for Betis, he dealt
with him in a manner almost too horrible to be
described. The reader will recollect that Achilles, at the siege of Troy, after killing Hector,
dragged his dead body around the walls of the
city. Alexander, growing more cruel as he became more accustomed to war and bloodshed,
had been intending to imitate this example so
soon as he could find an enemy worthy of such
a fate. He now determined to carry his plan
into execution with Betis. He ordered him into
his presence. A few years before, he would have
rewarded him for his fidelity in his master's service; but now, grown selfish, hard hearted, and
revengeful, he looked upon him with a countenance full of vindictive exultation, and said,

"You are not going to die the simple death
30

that you desire. You have got the worst torments that revenge can invent to suffer."

Betis did not reply, but looked upon Alexander with a calm, and composed, and unsubdued
air, which incensed the conqueror more and
more.

"Observe his dumb arrogance," said Alexander; "but I will conquer him. I will show
him that I can draw groans from him, if nothing else."

He then ordered holes to be made through the
heels of his unhappy captive, and, passing a rope
through them, had the body fastened to a chariot, and dragged about the city till no life remained.

Alexander found many rich treasures in Gaza.
He sent a large part of them to his mother Olympias, whom he had left in Macedon. Alexander's affection for his mother seems to have been
more permanent than almost any other good
trait in his character. He found, in addition to
other stores of valuable merchandise, a large
quantity of frankincense and myrrh. These are
gums which were brought from Arabia, and
were very costly. They were used chiefly in
making offerings and in burning incense to the
gods.

When Alexander was a young man in Macedon, before his father's death, he was one day present at the offering of sacrifices, and one of his teachers and guardians, named Leonnatus, who was standing by, thought he was rather profuse in his consumption of frankincense and myrrh. He was taking it up by handfuls and throwing it upon the fire. Leonnatus reproved him for this extravagance, and told him that when he became master of the countries where these costly gums were procured, he might be as prodigal of them as he pleased, but that in the mean time it would be proper for him to be more prudent and economical. Alexander remembered this reproof, and, finding vast stores of these expensive gums in Gaza, he sent the whole quantity to Leonnatus, telling him that he sent him this abundant supply that he might not have occasion to be so reserved and sparing for the future in his sacrifices to the gods.

After this conquest and destruction of Gaza Alexander continued his march southward to the frontiers of Egypt. He reached these frontiers at the city of Pelusium. The Egyptians had been under the Persian dominion, but they abhorred it, and were very ready to submit to Alexander's sway. They sent embassadors to

M

meet him upon the frontiers. The governors of the cities, as he advanced into the country, finding that it would be useless to resist, and warned by the terrible example of Thebes, Tyre, and Gaza, surrendered to him as fast as he summoned them.

He went to Memphis. Memphis was a great and powerful city, situated in what was called Lower Egypt, on the Nile, just above where the branches which form the mouths of the Nile separate from the main stream. All that part of Egypt is flat country, having been formed by the deposits brought down by the Nile. Such land is called *alluvial;* it is always level, and, as it consists of successive deposits from the turbid waters of the river, made in the successive inundations, it forms always a very rich soil, deep and inexhaustible, and is, of course, extremely fertile. Egypt has been celebrated for its unexampled fertility from the earliest times. It waves with fields of corn and grain, and is adorned with groves of the most luxuriant growth and richest verdure.

It is only, however, so far as the land is formed by the deposits of the Nile, that this scene of verdure and beauty extends. On the east it is bounded by ranges of barren and rocky hills

and on the west by vast deserts, consisting of
moving sands, from which no animal or vegeta-
ble life can derive the means of existence. The
reason of this sterility seems to be the absence
of water. The geological formation of the land
is such that it furnishes few springs of water,
and no streams, and in that climate it seldom
or never rains. If there is water, the most barren sands will clothe themselves with some species of vegetation, which, in its decay, will form
a soil that will nourish more and more fully each
succeeding generation of plants. But in the absence of water, any surface of earth will soon
become a barren sand. The wind will drive
away every thing imponderable, leaving only
the heavy sands, to drift in storms, like fields of
snow.

Among these African deserts, however, there
are some fertile spots. They are occasioned by
springs which arise in little dells, and which
saturate the ground with moisture for some distance around them. The water from these
springs flows for some distance, in many cases,
in a little stream, before it is finally lost and
absorbed in the sands. The whole tract under
the influence of this irrigation clothes itself
with verdure. Trees grow up to shade it. It

180 ALEXANDER THE GREAT. [B.C. 332

The Great Oasis.   Oasis of Siwah.   Jupiter Ammon

forms a spot whose beauty, absolutely great, is heightened by the contrast which it presents to the gloomy and desolate desert by which it is surrounded. Such a green spot in the desert is called an Oasis. They are the resort and the refuge of the traveler and the pilgrim, who seek shelter and repose upon them in their weary journeys over the trackless wilds.

Nor must it be supposed that these islands of fertility and verdure are always *small*. Some of them are very extensive, and contain a considerable population. There is one called the Great Oasis, which consists of a chain of fertile tracts of about a hundred miles in length Another, called the Oasis of Siwah, has, in modern times, a population of eight thousand souls This last is situated not far from the shores of the Mediterranean Sea—at least not very far; perhaps two or three hundred miles—and it was a very celebrated spot in Alexander's day.

The cause of its celebrity was that it was the seat and center of the worship of a famous deity called Jupiter Ammon. This god was said to be the son of Jupiter, though there were all sorts of stories about his origin and early history. He had the form of a ram, and was worshiped by the people of Egypt, and also by the

Carthaginians, and by the people of Northern
Africa generally.   His temple was in this Oasis,
and it was surrounded by a considerable population, which was supported, in a great degree,
by the expenditures of the worshipers who came
as pilgrims, or otherwise, to sacrifice at his
shrine.

It is said that Alexander, finding that the various objects of human ambition which he had
been so rapidly attaining by his victories and
conquests for the past few years were insufficient to satisfy him, began now to aspire for
some supernatural honors, and he accordingly
conceived the design of having himself declared
to be the son of a god.   The heroes of Homer
were sons of the gods.   Alexander envied them
the fame and honor which this distinction gave
them in the opinion of mankind.   He determined to visit the temple of Jupiter Ammon in
the Oasis of Siwah, and to have the declaration
of his divine origin made by the priests there.

He proceeded, accordingly, to the mouth of
the Nile, where he found a very eligible place,
as he believed, for the foundation of a commercial city, and he determined to build it on his
return.   Thence he marched along the shores
of the Mediterranean, toward the west, until

he reached a place called Parætonium, which will be found upon the map. He then left the sea-shore and marched south, striking at once into the desert when he left the sea. He was accompanied by a small detachment of his army as an escort, and they journeyed eleven days before they reached the Oasis.

They had a variety of perilous adventures in crossing the desert. For the first two days the soldiers were excited and pleased with the novelty and romantic grandeur of the scene. The desert has, in some degree, the sublimity of the ocean. There is the same boundless expanse, the same vast, unbroken curve of the horizon, the same tracklessness, the same solitude. There is, in addition, a certain profound and awful stillness and repose, which imparts to it a new element of impressiveness and grandeur. Its dread and solemn silence is far more imposing and sublime than the loudest thunders of the seas.

The third day the soldiers began to be weary of such a march. They seemed afraid to penetrate any further into such boundless and terrible solitudes. They had been obliged to bring water with them in goat-skins, which were carried by camels. The camel is the only beast of burden which can be employed upon the deserts. There is a peculiarity in the anatomical structure of this animal by which he can take in, at one time, a supply of water for many days. He is formed, in fact, for the desert. In his native state he lives in the oases and in the valleys. He eats the herbage which grows among the rocks and hills that alternate with the great sandy plains in all these countries. In passing from one of his scanty pasturages to another, he has long journeys to make across the sands, where, though he can find food here and there, there is no water. Providence has formed him with a structure adapted to this exigency, and by means of it he becomes extremely useful to man.

The soldiers of Alexander did not take a sufficient supply of water, and were reduced, at one time, to great distress. They were relieved, the story says, by a rain, though rain is extremely unusual in the deserts. Alexander attributed this supply to the miraculous interposition of Heaven. They catch the rain, in such cases, with cloths, and afterward wring out the water; though in this instance, as the historians of that day say, the soldiers did not wait for this tardy method of supply, but the whole detachment held back their heads and opened

their mouths, to catch the drops of rain as they
fell.

There was another danger to which they
were exposed in their march, more terrible even
than the scarcity of water. It was that of being overwhelmed in the clouds of sand and dust
which sometimes swept over the desert in gales
of wind. These were called sand-storms. The
fine sand flew, in such cases, in driving clouds,
which filled the eyes and stopped the breath of
the traveler, and finally buried his body under
its drifts when he laid down to die. A large
army of fifty thousand men, under a former Persian king, had been overwhelmed and destroyed
in this way, some years before, in some of the
Egyptian deserts. Alexander's soldiers had
heard of this calamity, and they were threatened sometimes with the same fate. They,
however, at length escaped all the dangers of
the desert, and began to approach the green and
fertile land of the Oasis.

The change from the barren and dismal lone-
liness of the sandy plains to the groves and the
villages, the beauty and the verdure of the Oasis, was delightful both to Alexander himself
and to all his men. The priests at the great
temple of Jupiter Ammon received them all

with marks of great distinction and honor. The
most solemn and magnificent ceremonies were
performed, with offerings, oblations, and sacrifices. The priests, after conferring in secret
with the god in the temple, came out with the
annunciation that Alexander was indeed his
son, and they paid him, accordingly, almost divine honors. He is supposed to have bribed
them to do this by presents and pay. Alexander returned at length to Memphis, and in all
his subsequent orders and decrees he styled himself Alexander king, son of Jupiter Ammon.

But, though Alexander was thus willing to
impress his ignorant soldiers with a mysterious
veneration for his fictitious divinity, he was not
deceived himself on the subject; he sometimes
even made his pretensions to the divine character a subject of joke. For instance, they one
day brought him in too little fire in the *focus*.
The focus, or fire-place used in Alexander's day

A Focus.

was a small metallic stand, on which the fire was
built. It was placed wherever convenient in
the tent, and the smoke escaped above. They
had put upon the focus too little fuel one day
when they brought it in. Alexander asked the
officer to let him have either some wood or some
frankincense; they might consider him, he said,
as a god or as a man, whichever they pleased,
but he wished to be treated either like one or
the other.

On his return from the Oasis Alexander carried forward his plan of building a city at the
mouth of the Nile. He drew the plan, it is
said, with his own hands. He superintended
the constructions, and invited artisans and me-
chanics from all nations to come and reside in it.
They accepted the invitation in great numbers,
and the city soon became large, and wealthy,
and powerful. It was intended as a commercial post, and the wisdom and sagacity which
Alexander manifested in the selection of the site,
is shown by the fact that the city rose immediately to the rank of the great seat of trade and
commerce for all those shores, and has continued to hold that rank now for twenty centuries

There was an island near the coast, opposite
the city, called the island of Pharos. They

built a most magnificent light-house upon one
extremity of this island, which was considered,
in those days, one of the wonders of the world
It was said to be five hundred feet high. This
may have been an exaggeration. At any rate,
it was celebrated throughout the world in its
day, and its existence and its greatness made an
impression on the human mind which has not
yet been effaced. Pharos is the name for light-
house, in many languages, to the present day.

In building the city of Alexandria, Alexander
laid aside, for a time, his natural and proper
character, and assumed a mode of action in
strong contrast with the ordinary course of his
life. He was, throughout most of his career, a
destroyer. He roamed over the world to interrupt commerce, to break in upon and disturb
the peaceful pursuits of industry, to batter down
city walls, and burn dwellings, and kill men.
This is the true vocation of a hero and a conqueror; but at the mouth of the Nile Alexander
laid aside this character. He turned his ener
gies to the work of planning means to do good
He constructed a port; he built warehouses,
he provided accommodations and protection for
merchants and artisans. The nations exchanged their commodities far more easily and exten-

sively in consequence of these facilities, and the means of comfort and enjoyment were multiplied and increased in thousands and thousands of huts in the great cities of Egypt, and in the rural districts along the banks of the Nile. The good, too, which he thus commenced, has perpetuated itself. Alexandria has continued to fulfill its beneficent function for two thousand years. It is the only monument of his greatness which remains. Every thing else which he accomplished perished when he died. How much better would it have been for the happiness of mankind, as well as for his own true fame and glory, if doing good had been the rule of his life instead of the exception.

CHAPTER IX.

THE GREAT VICTORY.

ALL the western part of Asia was now in Alexander's power. He was undisputed master of Asia Minor, Phœnicia, Judea, and Egypt. He returned from Egypt to Tyre, leaving governors to rule in his name in all the conquered provinces. The injuries which had been done to Tyre, during the siege and at the assault, were repaired, and it was again a wealthy, powerful, and prosperous city. Alexander rested and refreshed his army there, and spent some weeks in most splendid festivities and rejoicings. The princes and potentates of all the neighboring countries assembled to partake of his hospitality, to be entertained by the games, the plays, the spectacles, and the feastings, and to unite in swelling his court and doing him honor. In a word, he was the general center of attraction for all eyes, and the object of universal homage.

All this time, however, he was very far from being satisfied, or feeling that his work was done. Darius, whom he considered his great

enemy, was still in the field unsubdued. He
had retreated across the Euphrates, and was
employed in assembling a vast collection of forces from all the Eastern nations which were under his sway, to meet Alexander in the final
contest. Alexander therefore made arrangements at Tyre for the proper government of the
various kingdoms and provinces which he had
already conquered, and then began to prepare
for marching eastward with the main body of
his army.

During all this time the ladies of Darius's
family, who had been taken captive at Issus,
had been retained in captivity, and made to accompany Alexander's army in its marches. Alexander refused to accede to any of the plans
and propositions which Darius made and offered
for the redemption of his wife and mother, but
insisted on retaining them as his prisoners. He,
however, treated them with respect and high
consideration. He provided them with royal
tents of great magnificence, and had them conveyed from place to place, when his army moved, with all the royal state to which they had
been accustomed when in the court of Darius.

It has been generally thought a proof of nobleness of spirit and generosity in Alexander

B.C. 331.] The Great Victory. 191

Alexander's treatment of the queens.   Death of Statira

that he treated his captives in this manner. It would seem, however, that true generosity would have prompted the restoration of these unhappy and harmless prisoners to the husband and father who mourned their separation from him, and their cruel sufferings, with bitter grief. It is more probable, therefore, that policy, and a regard for his own aggrandizement, rather than compassion for the suffering, led him to honor his captive queens. It was a great glory to him, in a martial point of view, to have such trophies of his victory in his train; and, of course, the more highly he honored the personages, the more glorious the trophy appeared. Accordingly, Alexander did every thing in his power to magnify the importance of his royal captives, by the splendor of their retinue, and the pomp and pageantry with which he invested their movements.

A short time after leaving Tyre, on the march eastward, Statira, the wife of Darius, was taken suddenly ill and died.* The tidings were immediately brought to Alexander, and he repaired without delay to Sysigambis's tent.

* It was the birth of an infant that caused her death, exhausted and worn down as she doubtless was, by her captivity and her sorrows

31

Sysigambis was the mother of Darius. She was in the greatest agony of grief. She was lying upon the floor of her tent, surrounded by the ladies of her court, and entirely overwhelm ed with sorrow. Alexander did all in his power to calm and comfort her.

One of the officers of Queen Statira's household* made his escape from the camp immediately after his mistress's death, and fled across the country to Darius, to carry him the heavy tidings. Darius was overwhelmed with affliction. The officer, however, in farther interviews, gave him such an account of the kind and respectful treatment which the ladies had received from Alexander, during all the time of their captivity, as greatly to relieve his mind, and to afford him a high degree of comfort and consolation. He expressed a very strong sense of gratitude to Alexander for his generosity and kindness, and said that if his kingdom of Persia *must* be conquered, he sincerely wished that it might fall into the hands of such a conqueror as Alexander.

By looking at the map at the commencement of the volume, it will be seen that the Tigris

---

* A eunuch, a sort of officer employed in Eastern nations in attendance upon ladies of high rank.

B.C. 331.] THE GREAT VICTORY. 193

Alexander crosses the Euphrates.   Darius crosses the Tigris

and the Euphrates are parallel streams, flowing through the heart of the western part of Asia toward the southeast, and emptying into the Persian Gulf. The country between these two rivers, which was extremely populous and fertile, was called Mesopotamia. Darius had collected an immense army here. The various detachments filled all the plains of Mesopotamia. Alexander turned his course a little northward, intending to pass the River Euphrates at a famous ancient crossing at Thapsacus, which may be seen upon the map. When he arrived at this place he found a small Persian army there. They, however, retired as he approached. Alexander built two bridges across the river, and passed his army safely over.

In the mean time, Darius, with his enormous host, passed across the Tigris, and moved toward the northward, along the eastern side of the river. He had to cross the various branches of the Tigris as he advanced. At one of them, called the Lycus, which may also be seen upon the map, there was a bridge. It took the vast host which Darius had collected *five days* to pass this bridge.

While Darius had been thus advancing to the northward into the latitude where he knew

N

194 ALEXANDER THE GREAT. [B.C. 331

Alexander reaches the Tigris.   He crosses the river

that Alexander must cross the rivers, Alexan
der himself, and his small but compact and fearless body of Grecian troops, were moving eastward, toward the same region to which Darius's
line of march was tending. Alexander at length
reached the Tigris. He was obliged to ford this
stream. The banks were steep and the current
was rapid, and the men were in great danger of
being swept away. To prevent this danger,
the ranks, as they advanced, linked their arms
together, so that each man might be sustained
by his comrades. They held their shields above
their heads to keep them from the water. Alexander waded like the rest, though he kept in
front, and reached the bank before the others
Standing there, he indicated to the advancing
column, by gesticulation, where to land, the
noise of the water being too great to allow his
voice to be heard. To see him standing there,
safely landed, and with an expression of confidence and triumph in his attitude and air,
awakened fresh energy in the heart of every
soldier in the columns which were crossing the
stream.

Notwithstanding this encouragement, however, the passage of the troops and the landing
on the bank produced a scene of greet confusion

Many of the soldiers had tied up a portion of
their clothes in bundles, which they held above
their heads, together with their arms, as they
waded along through the swift current of the
stream. They, however, found it impossible to
carry these bundles, but had to abandon them
at last in order to save themselves, as they
staggered along through deep and rapid water,
and over a concealed bottom of slippery stones.
Thousands of these bundles, mingled with spears,
darts, and every other sort of weapon that would
float, were swept down by the current, to impede and embarrass the men who were passing
below.

At length, however, the men themselves succeeded in getting over in safety, though a large
quantity of arms and of clothing was lost.
There was no enemy upon the bank to oppose
them. Darius could not, in fact, well meet
and oppose Alexander in his attempt to cross
the river, because he could not determine at
what point he would probably make the attempt, in season to concentrate so large an army
to oppose him. Alexander's troops, being a
comparatively small and compact body, and being accustomed to move with great promptness
and celerity, could easily evade any attempt of

such an unwieldy mass of forces to oppose his
crossing at any particular point upon the stream
At any rate, Darius did not make any such attempt, and Alexander had no difficulties to encounter in crossing the Tigris other than the
physical obstacles presented by the current of
the stream.

Darius's plan was, therefore, not to intercept
Alexander on his march, but to choose some
great and convenient battle-field, where he
could collect his forces, and marshal them ad-
vantageously and so await an attack there.
He knew very well that his enemy would seek
him out, wherever he was, and, consequently,
that he might choose his position. He found
such a field in an extensive plain at Guagame-
la, not far from the city of Arbela. The spot
has received historical immortality under the
name of the plain of Arbela.

Darius was several days in concentrating his
vast armies upon this plain. He constructed
encampments; he leveled the inequalities which
would interfere with the movements of his great
bodies of cavalry; he guarded the approaches,
too, as much as possible. There is a little instrument used in war called a *caltrop.** It

* It receives its name from a kind of thistle called the caltrop

consists of a small ball of iron, with several sharp points projecting from it one or two inches each way. If these instruments are

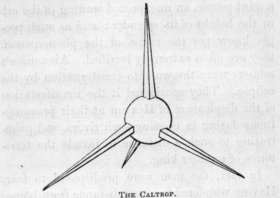

THE CALTROP.

thrown upon the ground at random, one of the points must necessarily be upward, and the horses that tread upon them are lamed and disabled at once. Darius caused caltrops to be scattered in the grass and along the roads, wherever the army of Alexander would be likely to approach his troops on the field of battle.

Alexander, having crossed the river, encamped for a day or two on the banks, to rest and refresh, and to rearrange his army. While here, the soldiers were one night thrown into consternation by an eclipse of the moon. Whenever an eclipse of the moon takes place, it is, of course, when the moon is full, so that the eclipse is always a sudden, and, among an ignorant people, an unexpected waning of the orb in the height of its splendor ; and as such people know not the cause of the phenomenon, they are often extremely terrified. Alexander's soldiers were thrown into consternation by the eclipse. They considered it the manifestation of the displeasure of Heaven at their presumptuous daring in crossing such rivers, and penetrating to such a distance to invade the territories of another king.

In fact, the men were predisposed to fear. Having wandered to a vast distance from home, having passed over such mountains and deserts, and now, at last, having crossed a deep and dangerous river, and thrown themselves into the immediate vicinity of a foe ten times as numerous as themselves, it was natural that they should feel some misgivings. And when, at night, impressed with the sense of solemnity which night always imparts to strange and novel scenes, they looked up to the bright round moon, pleased with the expression of cheerfulness and companionship which beams always in her light, to find her suddenly waning, changing her form, withdrawing her bright beams, and looking down upon them with a lurid and murky light, it was not surprising that they felt an emotion of terror. In fact, there is always an element of terror in the emotion excited by looking upon an eclipse, which an instinctive feeling of the heart inspires. It invests the spectacle with a solemn grandeur. It holds the spectator, however cultivated and refined, in silence while he gazes at it. It mingles with a scientific appreciation of the vastness of the movements and magnitudes by which the effect is produced, and while the one occupies the intellect, the other impresses the soul. The mind that has lost, through its philosophy, the power of feeling this emotion of awe in such scenes, has sunk, not risen. Its possessor has made himself inferior, not superior, to the rest of his species, by having paralyzed one of his susceptibilities of pleasure. To him an eclipse is only curious and wonderful; to others it is sublime.

The soldiers of Alexander were extremely terrified. A great panic spread throughout the encampment. Alexander himself, instead of attempting to allay their fears by reasoning, or treating them as of no importance, immediately gave the subject his most serious attention. He

called together the soothsayers, and directed them
to consult together, and let him know what this
great phenomenon portended. This mere com·
mitting of the subject to the attention of the
soothsayers had a great effect among all the
soldiers of the army. It calmed them. It
changed their agitation and terror into a feeling of suspense, in awaiting the answer of the
soothsayers, which was far less painful and dangerous; and at length, when the answer came,
it allayed their anxiety and fear altogether
The soothsayers said that the sun was on Alexander's side, and the moon on that of the Persians, and that this sudden waning of her light
foreshadowed the defeat and destruction which
the Persians were about to undergo. The army
were satisfied with this decision, and were inspired with new confidence and ardor. It is
often idle to attempt to oppose ignorance and
absurdity by such feeble instruments as truth
and reason, and the wisest managers of mankind have generally been most successful when
their plan has been to counteract one folly by
means of the influence of another.

Alexander's army consisted of about fifty
thousand men, with the phalanx in the center
This army moved along down the eastern bank

of the Tigris, the scouts pressing forward as far
as possible in every direction in front of the main
army, in order to get intelligence of the foe. It
is in this way that two great armies *feel* after
each other, as it were, like insects creeping over
the ground, exploring the way before them with
their *antennæ.* At length, after three days' advance, the scouts came in with intelligence of
the enemy. Alexander pressed forward with a
detachment of his army to meet them. They
proved to be, however, not the main body of Darius's army, but only a single corps of a thousand
men, in advance of the rest. They retreated
as Alexander approached. He, however, succeeded in capturing some horsemen, who gave
the information that Darius had assembled his
vast forces on the plain of Arbela, and was waiting there in readiness to give his advancing enemy battle.

Alexander halted his troops. He formed an
encampment, and made arrangements for de-
positing his baggage there. He refreshed the
men, examined and repaired their arms, and
made the arrangements for battle. These operations consumed several days. At the end of
that time, early one morning, long before day,
the camp was in motion, and the columns, armed

and equipped for immediate contest, moved forward.

They expected to have reached the camp of Darius at daybreak, but the distance was greater than they had supposed. At length, however, the Macedonians, in their march, came upon the brow of a range of hills, from which they looked down upon numberless and endless lines of infantry and cavalry, and ranges after ranges of tents, which filled the plain. Here the army paused while Alexander examined the field, studying for a long time, and with great attention, the numbers and disposition of the enemy. They were four miles distant still, but the murmuring sounds of their voices and movements came to the ears of the Macedonians through the calm autumnal air.

Alexander called the leading officers together, and held a consultation on the question whether to march down and attack the Persians on the plain that night, or to wait till the next day. Parmenio was in favor of a night attack, in order to surprise the enemy by coming upon them at an unexpected time. But Alexander said no. He was sure of victory. He had got his enemies all before him; they were fully in his power He would, therefore, take no advant-

age, but would attack them fairly and in open
day. Alexander had fifty thousand men; the
Persians were variously estimated between five
hundred thousand and a million. There is something sublime in the idea of such a pause, made
by the Macedonian phalanx and its wings, on
the slopes of the hills, suspending its attack upon
ten times its number, to give the mighty mass
of their enemies the chances of a fair and equal
contest.

Alexander made congratulatory addresses to
his soldiers on the occasion of their having now
at last before them, what they had so long toiled
and labored to attain, the whole concentrated
force of the Persian empire. They were now
going to contend, not for single provinces and
kingdoms, as heretofore, but for general empire;
and the victory which they were about to achieve
would place them on the summit of human glory. In all that he said on the subject, the unquestionable certainty of victory was assumed.

Alexander completed his arrangements, and
then retired to rest. He went to sleep—at least
he appeared to do so. Early in the morning
Parmenio arose, summoned the men to their
posts, and arranged every thing for the march.
He then went to Alexander's tent. Alexander

was still asleep. He awoke him, and told him
that all was ready. Parmenio expressed surprise at his sleeping so quietly at a time when
such vast issues were at stake. " You seem as
calm," said he, " as if you had had the battle
and gained the victory." "I have done so,"
said Alexander. "I consider the whole work
done when we have gained access to Darius and
his forces, and find him ready to give us battle."

Alexander soon appeared at the head of his
troops. Of course this day was one of the most
important ones of his life, and one of the historians of the time has preserved an account of
his dress as he went into battle. He wore a
short tunic, girt close around him, and over it
a linen breast-plate, strongly quilted. The belt
by which the tunic was held was embossed with
figures of beautiful workmanship. This belt
was a present to him from some of the people
of the conquered countries through which he had
passed, and it was very much admired. He
had a helmet upon his head, of polished steel,
with a neck piece, also of steel, ornamented with
precious stones. His helmet was surmounted
with a white plume. His sword, which was a
present to him from the King of Cyprus, was
very light and slender, and of the most perfect

temper. He carried, also, a shield and a lance, made in the best possible manner for use, not for display. Thus his dress corresponded with the character of his action. It was simple, compact, and whatever of value it possessed consisted in those substantial excellences which would give the bearer the greatest efficiency on the field of battle.

The Persians were accustomed to make use of elephants in their wars. They also had chariots, with scythes placed at the axles, which they were accustomed to drive among their enemies and mow them down. Alexander resorted to none of these contrivances. There was the phalanx—the terrible phalanx—advancing irresistibly either in one body or in detachments, with columns of infantry and flying troops of horsemen on the wings. Alexander relied simply on the strength, the courage, the energy, and the calm and steady, but resistless ardor of his men, arranging them in simple combinations, and leading them forward directly to their work.

The Macedonians cut their way through the mighty mass of their enemies with irresistible force. The elephants turned and fled. The foot soldiers seized the horses of some of the

scythe-armed chariots and cut the traces. In
respect to others, they opened to the right and
left and let them pass through, when they were
easily captured by the men in the rear. In the
mean time the phalanx pressed on, enjoying a
great advantage in the level nature of the
ground. The Persian troops were broken in
upon and driven away wherever they were attacked. In a word, before night the whole
mighty mass was scattering every where in confusion, except some hundreds of thousands left
trampled upon and dead, or else writhing upon
the ground, and groaning in their dying ago-
nies. Darius himself fled. Alexander pursued
him with a troop of horse as far as Arbela,
which had been Darius's head-quarters, and
where he had deposited immense treasures
Darius had gone through and escaped when
Alexander arrived at Arbela, but the city and
the treasures fell into Alexander's hands.

Although Alexander had been so completely
victorious over his enemies on the day of battle,
and had maintained his ground against them
with such invincible power, he was, neverthe-
less, a few days afterward, driven entirely off
the field, and completely away from the region
where the battle had been fought. What the

B.C. 331.] THE GREAT VICTORY. 207

Alexander driven from the field.   March to Babylon

living men, standing erect in arms, and full of
martial vigor, could not do, was easily and effectually accomplished by their dead bodies cor-
rupting on the plain. The corpses of three
hundred thousand men, and an equal bulk of
the bodies of elephants and horses, was too
enormous a mass to be buried. It had to be
abandoned; and the horrible effluvia and pestilence which it emitted drove all the inhabitants
of the country away. Alexander marched his
troops rapidly off the ground, leaving, as the direct result of the battle, a wide extent of coun
try depopulated and desolate, with this vast
mass of putrefaction and pestilence reigning in
awful silence and solitude in the midst of it.

Alexander went to Babylon. The governor
of the city prepared to receive him as a conqueror. The people came out in throngs to
meet him, and all the avenues of approach were
crowded with spectators. All the city walls,
too, were covered with men and women, assembled to witness the scene. As for Alexander
himself, he was filled with pride and pleasure at
thus arriving at the full accomplishment of his
earliest and long-cherished dreams of glory.

The great store-house of the royal treasures
of Persia was at Susa, a strong city east of Bab-

32

ylon. Susa was the winter residence of the Persian kings, as Ecbatana, further north, among
the mountains, was their summer residence
There was a magnificent palace and a very
strong citadel at Susa, and the treasures were
kept in the citadel. It is said that in times of
peace the Persian monarchs had been accustomed to collect coin, melt it down, and cast the
gold in earthen jars. The jars were afterward
broken off from the gold, leaving the bullion in
the form of the interior of the jars. An enormous amount of gold and silver, and of other
treasures, had been thus collected. Alexander
was aware of this depository before he advanced
to meet Darius, and, on the day of the battle
of Arbela, as soon as the victory was decided,
he sent an officer from the very field to summon
Susa to surrender. They obeyed the summons,
and Alexander, soon after his great public entrance into Babylon, marched to Susa, and took
possession of the vast stores of wealth accumulated there. The amount was enormous, both
in quantity and value, and the seizing of it was
a very magnificent act of plunder. In fact, it
is probable that Alexander's slaughter of the
Persian army at Arbela, and subsequent spoli-
ation of Susa, constitute, taken together, the

most gigantic case of murder and robbery which
was ever committed by man; so that, in performing these deeds, the great hero attained at
last to the glory of having perpetrated the grandest and most imposing of all human crimes.
That these deeds were really crimes there can
be no doubt, when we consider that Alexander
did not pretend to have any other motive in this
invasion than love of conquest, which is, in other words, love of violence and plunder. They
are only technically shielded from being called
crimes by the fact that the earth has no laws
and no tribunals high enough to condemn such
enormous burglaries as that of one quarter of
the globe breaking violently and murderously in
upon and robbing the other.

Besides the treasures, Alexander found also
at Susa a number of trophies which had been
brought by Xerxes from Greece; for Xerxes
had invaded Greece some hundred years before
Alexander's day, and had brought to Susa the
spoils and the trophies of his victories. Alexander sent them all back to Greece again.

From Susa the conqueror moved on to Persepolis, the great Persian capital. On his march
he had to pass through a defile of the mountains. The mountaineers had been accustomed

O

to exact tribute here of all who passed, having a sort of right, derived from ancient usage, to the payment of a toll. They sent to Alexander when they heard that he was approaching, and informed him that he could not pass with his army without paying the customary toll. Alexander sent back word that he would meet them at the pass, and give them *their due*.

They understood this, and prepared to defend the pass. Some Persian troops joined them They built walls and barricades across the narrow passages. They collected great stones on the brinks of precipices, and on the declivities of the mountains, to roll down upon the heads of their enemies. By these and every other means they attempted to stop Alexander's passage. But he had contrived to send detachments around by circuitous and precipitous paths, which even the mountaineers had deemed impracticable, and thus attack his enemies suddenly and unexpectedly from above their own positions. As usual, his plan succeeded. The mountaineers were driven away, and the conqueror advanced toward the great Persian capital.

ALEXANDER AT THE PASS OF SUSA

CHAPTER X.

THE DEATH OF DARIUS.

ALEXANDER'S march from Susa to Persepolis was less a march than a triumphal progress. He felt the pride and elation so naturally resulting from success very strongly. The moderation and forbearance which had characterized him in his earlier years, gradually disappeared as he became great and powerful. He was intoxicated with his success. He became haughty, vain, capricious, and cruel. As he approached Persepolis, he conceived the idea that, as this city was the capital and center of the Persian monarchy, and, as such, the point from which had emanated all the Persian hostility to Greece, he owed it some signal retribution. Accordingly, although the inhabitants made no opposition to his entrance, he marched in with the phalanx formed, and gave the soldiers liberty to kill and plunder as they pleased.

There was another very striking instance of the capricious recklessness now beginning to appear in Alexander's character, which occurred

soon after he had taken possession of Persepolis.
He was giving a great banquet to his friends,
the officers of the army, and to Persians of dis
tinction among those who had submitted to him
There was, among other women at this banquet,
a very beautiful and accomplished female named
Thais. Alexander made her his favorite and
companion, though she was not his wife. Thais
did all in her power to captivate and please Alexander during the feast by her vivacity, her
wit, her adroit attentions to him, and the display of her charms, and at length, when he himself, as well as the other guests, were excited
with wine, she asked him to allow her to have
the pleasure of going herself and setting fire,
with her own hands, to the great palace of the
Persian kings in the city. Thais was a native
of Attica in Greece, a kingdom of which Athens was the capital. Xerxes, who had built the
great palace of Persepolis, had formerly invaded
Greece and had burned Athens, and now Thais
desired to burn his palace in Persepolis, to gratify her revenge, by making, of its conflagration
an evening spectacle to entertain the Macedonian party after their supper. Alexander agreed
to the proposal, and the whole company moved
forward. Taking the torches from the banquet

ing halls, they sallied forth, alarming the city
with their shouts, and with the flashing of the
lights they bore. The plan of Thais was carried fully into effect, every half-intoxicated guest
assisting, by putting fire to the immense pile
wherever they could get access to it. They performed the barbarous deed with shouts of vengeance and exultation.

There is, however, something very solemn
and awful in a great conflagration at night, and
very few incendiaries can gaze upon the fury of
the lurid and frightful flames which they have
caused to ascend without some misgivings and
some remorse. Alexander was sobered by the
grand and sublime, but terrible spectacle. He
was awed by it. He repented. He ordered the
fire to be extinguished ; but it was too late.
The palace was destroyed, and one new blot,
which has never since been effaced, was cast
upon Alexander's character and fame.

And yet, notwithstanding these increasing
proofs of pride and cruelty, which were beginning to be developed, Alexander still preserved
some of the early traits of character which had
made him so great a favorite in the commencement of his career. He loved his mother, and
sent her presents continually from the treasures

which were falling all the time into his possession. She was a woman of a proud, imperious,
and ungovernable character, and she made Ar-
tipater, whom Alexander had left in command
in Macedon, infinite trouble. She wanted to
exercise the powers of government herself, and
was continually urging this. Alexander would
not comply with these wishes, but he paid her
personally every attention in his power, and
bore all her invectives and reproaches with great
patience and good humor. At one time he received a long letter from Antipater, full of complaints against her; but Alexander, after reading it, said that they were heavy charges it was
true, but that a single one of his mother's tears
would outweigh ten thousand such accusations.

Olympias used to write very frequently to
Alexander, and in these letters she would criti-
cise and discuss his proceedings, and make com-
ments upon the characters and actions of his
generals. Alexander kept these letters very secret, never showing them to any one. One day
however, when he was reading one of these letters, Hephæstion, the personal friend and companion who has been already several times mentioned, came up, half playfully, and began to
look over his shoulder. Alexander went on, al

lowing him to read, and then, when the letter
was finished he took the signet ring from his
finger and pressed it upon Hephæstion's lips, a
signal for silence and secrecy.

Alexander was very kind to Sysigambis, the
mother of Darius, and also to Darius's children.
He would not give these unhappy captives their
liberty, but in every other respect he treated
them with the greatest possible kindness and
consideration. He called Sysigambis mother,
loaded her with presents—presents, it is true,
which he had plundered from her son, but to
which it was considered, in those days, that he
had acquired a just and perfect title. When he
reached Susa, he established Sysigambis and
the children there in great state. This had been
their usual residence in most seasons of the year,
when not at Persepolis, so that here they were,
as it were, at home. Ecbatana* was, as has
been already mentioned, further north, among
the mountains. After the battle of Arbela,
while Alexander marched to Babylon and to
Susa, Darius had fled to Ecbatana, and was now
there, his family being thus at one of the royal
palaces under the command of the conqueror,
and he himself independent, but insecure, in the

* The modern Ispahan.

other. He had with him about forty thousand men, who still remained faithful to his fallen fortunes. Among these were several thousand Greeks, whom he had collected in Asia Minor and other Grecian countries, and whom he had attached to his service by means of pay.

He called the officers of his army together, and explained to them the determination that he had come to in respect to his future movements. " A large part of those," said he, " who formerly served as officers of my government, have abandoned me in my adversity, and gone over to Alexander's side. They have surrendered to him the towns, and citadels, and provinces which I intrusted to their fidelity. You alone remain faithful and true. As for myself, I might yield to the conqueror, and have him assign to me some province or kingdom to govern as his subordinate ; but I will never submit to such a degradation. I can die in the struggle, but never will yield. I will wear no crown which another puts upon my brow, nor give up my right to reign over the empire of my ancestors till I give up my life. If you agree with me in this determination, let us act energetically upon it. We have it in our power to terminate the injuries we are suffering, or else to avenge them "

The army responded most cordially to this appeal. They were ready, they said, to follow him wherever he should lead. All this apparent enthusiasm, however, was very delusive and unsubstantial. A general named Bessus, combining with some other officers in the army, conceived the plan of seizing Darius and making him a prisoner, and then taking command of the army himself. If Alexander should pursue him, and be likely to overtake and conquer him, he then thought that, by giving up Darius as a prisoner, he could stipulate for liberty and safety, and perhaps great rewards, both for himself and for those who acted with him. If, on the other hand, they should succeed in increasing their own forces so as to make head against Alexander, and finally to drive him away, then Bessus was to usurp the throne, and dispose of Darius by assassinating him, or imprisoning him for life in some remote and solitary castle.

Bessus communicated his plans, very cautiously at first, to the leading officers of the army. The Greek soldiers were not included in the plot. They, however, heard and saw enough to lead them to suspect what was in preparation. They warned Darius, and urged him to rely upon them more than he had done:

to make them his body-guard, and to pitch his
tent in their part of the encampment. But Darius declined these proposals. He would not,
he said, distrust and abandon his countrymen,
who were his natural protectors, and put himself in the hands of strangers. He would not
betray and desert his friends in anticipation of
their deserting and betraying him.

In the mean time, as Alexander advanced toward Ecbatana, Darius and his forces retreated
from it toward the eastward, through the great
tract of country lying south of the Caspian Sea.
There is a mountainous region here, with a defile traversing it, through which it would be
necessary for Darius to pass. This defile was
called the Caspian Gates,* the name referring
to rocks on each side. The marching of an
army through a narrow and dangerous defile
like this always causes detention and delay, and
Alexander hastened forward in hopes to overtake Darius before he should reach it. He advanced with such speed that only the strongest
and most robust of his army could keep up
Thousands, worn out with exertion and toil,
were left behind, and many of the horses sank
down by the road side, exhausted with heat and

* *Pylæ Caspiæ* on the map, which means the Caspian Gates

fatigue, to die. Alexander pressed desperately
on with all who were able to follow.

It was all in vain, however; it was too late
when he arrived at the pass. Darius had gone
through with all his army. Alexander stopped
to rest his men, and to allow time for those behind to come up. He then went on for a couple
of days, when he encamped, in order to send out
foraging parties—that is to say, small detachments, dispatched to explore the surrounding
country in search of grain and other food for the
horses. Food for the horses of an army being
too bulky to be transported far, has to be collected day by day from the neighborhood of the
line of march.

While halting for these foraging parties to
return, a Persian nobleman came into the camp,
and informed Alexander that Darius and the
forces accompanying him were encamped about
two days' march in advance, but that Bessus
was in command—the conspiracy having been
successful, and Darius having been deposed and
made a prisoner. The Greeks, who had ad
hered to their fidelity, finding that all the army
were combined against them, and that they
were not strong enough to resist, had abandoned the Persian camp, and had retired to the

mountains, where they were awaiting the result.

Alexander determined to set forward immediately in pursuit of Bessus and his prisoner He did not wait for the return of the foraging parties. He selected the ablest and most active, both of foot soldiers and horsemen, ordered them to take two days' provisions, and then set forth with them that very evening. The party pressed on all that night, and the next day till noon. They halted till evening, and then set forth again. Very early the next morning they arrived at the encampment which the Persian nobleman had described. They found the remains of the camp-fires, and all the marks usually left upon a spot which has been used as the bivouac of an army. The army itself, however, was gone.

The pursuers were now too much fatigued to go any further without rest. Alexander remained here, accordingly, through the day, to give his men and his horses refreshment and repose. That night they set forward again, and the next day at noon they arrived at another encampment of the Persians, which they had left scarcely twenty-four hours before. The officers of Alexander's army were excited and animated in

the highest degree, as they found themselves
thus drawing so near to the great object of their
pursuit. They were ready for any exertions,
any privation and fatigue, any measures, however extraordinary, to accomplish their end.

Alexander inquired of the inhabitants of the
place whether there were not some shorter road
than the one along which the enemy were moving. There was one cross-road, but it led
through a desolate and desert tract of land, destitute of water. In the march of an army, as
the men are always heavily loaded with arms
and provisions, and water can not be carried, it
is always considered essential to choose routes
which will furnish supplies of water by the way.
Alexander, however, disregarded this consideration here, and prepared at once to push into the
cross-road with a small detachment. He had
been now two years advancing from Macedon
into the heart of Asia, always in quest of Darius as his great opponent and enemy. He had
conquered his armies, taken his cities, plundered his palaces, and made himself master of his
whole realm. Still, so long as Darius himself
remained at liberty and in the field, no victories
could be considered as complete. To capture
Darius himself would be the last and crowning

act of his conquest.   He had now been pursuing him for eighteen hundred miles, advancing
slowly from province to province, and from kingdom to kingdom.   During all this time the
strength of his flying foe had been wasting
away.   His armies had been broken up, his
courage and hope had gradually failed, while
the animation and hope of the pursuer had been
gathering fresh and increasing strength from his
successes, and were excited to wild enthusiasm
now, as the hour for the final consummation of
all his desires seemed to be drawing nigh.

Guides were ordered to be furnished by the
inhabitants, to show the detachment the way
across the solitary and desert country.   The
detachment was to consist of horsemen entirely,
that they might advance with the utmost celerity.   To get as efficient a corps as possible, Alexander dismounted five hundred of the cavalry,
and gave their horses to five hundred men—officers and others—selected for their strength and
courage from among the foot soldiers.   All were
ambitious of being designated for this service
Besides the honor of being so selected, there
was an intense excitement, as usual toward the
close of a chase, to arrive at the end.

This body of horsemen were ready to set out

in the evening. Alexander took the command, and, following the guides, they trotted off in the direction which the guides indicated. They traveled all night. When the day dawned, they saw, from an elevation to which they had attained, the body of the Persian troops moving at a short distance before them, foot soldiers, chariots, and horsemen pressing on together in great confusion and disorder.

As soon as Bessus and his company found that their pursuers were close upon them, they attempted at first to hurry forward, in the vain hope of still effecting their escape. Darius was in a chariot. They urged this chariot on, but it moved heavily. Then they concluded to abandon it, and they called upon Darius to mount a horse and ride off with them, leaving the rest of the army and the baggage to its fate. But Darius refused. He said he would rather trust himself in the hands of Alexander than in thos of such traitors as they. Rendered desperate by their situation, and exasperated by this reply, Bessus and his confederates thrust their spears into Darius's body, as he sat in his chariot, and then galloped away. They divided into different parties, each taking a different road. Their object in doing this was to increase their

P

chances of escape by confusing Alexander in his plans for pursuing them. Alexander pressed on toward the ground which the enemy were abandoning, and sent off separate detachments after the various divisions of the flying army.

In the mean time Darius remained in his chariot wounded and bleeding. He was worn out and exhausted, both in body and mind, by his complicated sufferings and sorrows. His kingdom lost; his family in captivity; his beloved wife in the grave, where the sorrows and sufferings of separation from her husband had borne her; his cities sacked; his palaces and treasures plundered; and now he himself, in the last hour of his extremity, abandoned and betrayed by all in whom he had placed his confidence and trust, his heart sunk within him in despair. At such a time the soul turns from traitorous friends to an open foe with something like a feeling of confidence and attachment. Darius's exasperation against Bessus was so intense, that his hostility to Alexander became a species of friendship in comparison. He felt that Alexander was a sovereign like himself, and would have some sympathy and fellow-feeling for a sovereign's misfortunes. He thought, too, of his mother, his wife, and his children, and the kindness with which Alexander had treated them went to his heart. He lay there, accordingly, faint and bleeding in his chariot, and looking for the coming of Alexander as for that of a protector and friend, the only one to whom he could now look for any relief in the extremity of his distress.

The Macedonians searched about in various places, thinking it possible that in the sudden dispersion of the enemy Darius might have been left behind. At last the chariot in which he was lying was found. Darius was in it, pierced with spears. The floor of the chariot was covered with blood. They raised him a little, and he spoke. He called for water.

Men wounded and dying on the field of battle are tormented always with an insatiable and intolerable thirst, the manifestations of which constitute one of the greatest horrors of the scene. They cry piteously to all who pass to bring them water, or else to kill them. They crawl along the ground to get at the canteens of their dead companions, in hopes to find, remaining in them, some drops to drink ; and if there is a little brook meandering through the battle-field, its bed gets filled and choked up with the bodies of those who crawled there, in

their agony, to quench their horrible thirst, and
die. Darius was suffering this thirst. It bore
down and silenced, for the time, every other suffering, so that his first cry, when his enemies
came around him with shouts of exultation, was
not for his life, not for mercy, not for relief from
the pain and anguish of his wounds—he begged
them to give him some water.

He spoke through an interpreter. The interpreter was a Persian prisoner whom the Macedonian army had taken some time before, and
who had learned the Greek language in the
Macedonian camp. Anticipating some occasion
for his services, they had brought him with
them now, and it was through him that Darius
called for water. A Macedonian soldier went
immediately to get some. Others hurried away
in search of Alexander, to bring him to the spot
where the great object of his hostility, and of
his long and protracted pursuit, was dying.

Darius received the drink. He then said that
he was extremely glad that they had an interpreter with them, who could understand him,
and bear his message to Alexander. He had
been afraid that he should have had to die without being able to communicate what he had to
say. "Tell Alexander," said he, then, "that

I feel under the strongest obligations to him, which I can now never repay, for his kindness to my wife, my mother, and my children. He not only spared their lives, but treated them with the greatest consideration and care, and did all in his power to make them happy. The last feeling in my heart is gratitude to him for these favors. I hope now that he will go on prosperously, and finish his conquests as triumphantly as he has begun them." He would have made one last request, he added, if he had thought it necessary, and that was, that Alexander would pursue the traitor Bessus, and avenge the murder he had committed; but he was sure that Alexander would do this of his own accord, as the punishment of such treachery was an object of common interest for every king.

Darius then took Polystratus, the Macedonian who had brought him the water, by the hand, saying, " Give Alexander thy hand as I now give thee mine; it is the pledge of my gratitude and affection."

Darius was too weak to say much more. They gathered around him, endeavoring to sustain his strength until Alexander should arrive: but it was all in vain. He sank gradually, and soon ceased to breathe. Alexander came up a few minutes after all was over. He was at first shocked at the spectacle before him, and then overwhelmed with grief. He wept bitterly. Some compunctions of conscience may have visited his heart at seeing thus before him the ruin he had made. Darius had never injured him or done him any wrong, and yet here he lay, hunted to death by a persevering and relentless hostility, for which his conqueror had no excuse but his innate love of dominion over his fellow-men. Alexander spread his own military cloak over the dead body. He immediately made arrangements for having the body embalmed, and then sent it to Susa, for Sysigambis, in a very costly coffin, and with a procession of royal magnificence. He sent it to her that she might have the satisfaction of seeing it deposited in the tombs of the Persian kings. What a present! The killer of a son sending the dead body, in a splendid coffin, to the mother, as a token of respectful regard!

Alexander pressed on to the northward and eastward in pursuit of Bessus, who had soon collected the scattered remains of his army, and was doing his utmost to get into a posture of defense. He did not, however, overtake him til.

he had crossed the Oxus, a large river which will be found upon the map, flowing to the northward and westward into the Caspian Sea. He had great difficulty in crossing this river, as it was too deep to be forded, and the banks and bottom were so sandy and yielding that he could not make the foundations of bridges stand. He accordingly made floats and rafts, which were supported by skins made buoyant by inflation, or by being stuffed with straw and hay. After getting his army, which had been in the mean time greatly re-enforced and strengthened, across this river, he moved on. The generals under Bessus, finding all hope of escape failing them, resolved on betraying him as he had betrayed his commander. They sent word to Alexander that if he would send forward a small force where they should indicate, they would give up Bessus to his hands. Alexander did so, intrusting the command to an officer named Ptolemy. Ptolemy found Bessus in a small walled town whither he had fled for refuge, and easily took him prisoner. He sent back word to Alexander that Bessus was at his disposal, and asked for orders. The answer was, "Put a rope around his neck and send him to me."

When the wretched prisoner was brought

into Alexander's presence, Alexander demanded of him how he could have been so base as to
have seized, bound, and at last murdered his
kinsman and benefactor. It is a curious instance in proof of the permanence and stability
of the great characteristics of human nature,
through all the changes of civilization and lapses
of time, that Bessus gave the same answer that
wrong-doers almost always give when brought
to account for their wrongs. He laid the fault
upon his accomplices and friends. It was not
his act, it was theirs.

Alexander ordered him to be publicly scourg-
ed; then he caused his face to be mutilated in
a manner customary in those days, when a tyrant wished to stamp upon his victim a perpetual mark of infamy. In this condition, and
with a mind in an agony of suspense and fear
at the thought of worse tortures which he knew
were to come, Alexander sent him as a second
present to Sysigambis, to be dealt with, at Susa,
as her revenge might direct. She inflicted upon
him the most extreme tortures, and finally,
when satiated with the pleasure of seeing him
suffer, the story is that they chose four very
elastic trees, growing at a little distance from
each other, and bent down the tops of them to

ward the central point between them. They
fastened the exhausted and dying Bessus to
these trees, one limb of his body to each, and
then releasing the stems from their confinement,
they flew upward, tearing the body asunder,
each holding its own dissevered portion, as if in
triumph, far over the heads of the multitude
assembled to witness the spectacle.

234 ALEXANDER THE GREAT. [B.C. 329

Alexander at the summit of his ambition.   Sad changes

CHAPTER XI.

DETERIORATION OF CHARACTER.

ALEXANDER was now twenty-six years
of age. He had accomplished fully the
great objects which had been the aim of his ambition. Darius was dead, and he was himself
the undisputed master of all western Asia. His
wealth was almost boundless. His power was
supreme over what was, in his view, the whole
known world. But, during the process of rising to this ascendency, his character was sadly
changed. He lost the simplicity, the temper-
ance, the moderation, and the sense of justice
which characterized his early years. He adopted the dress and the luxurious manners of the
Persians. He lived in the palaces of the Persian kings, imitating all their state and splendor. He became very fond of convivial entertainments and of wine, and often drank to excess. He provided himself a seraglio of three
hundred and sixty young females, in whose company he spent his time, giving himself up to every form of effeminacy and dissipation. In a

word, he was no longer the same man. The de
cision, the energy of character, the steady pur
suit of great ends by prudence, forethought,
patient effort, and self-denial, all disappeared;
nothing now seemed to interest him but banquets, carousals, parties of pleasure, and whole
days and nights spent in dissipation and vice.

This state of things was a great cause of mor-
tification and chagrin to the officers of his army.
Many of them were older than himself, and better able to resist these temptations to luxury,
effeminacy, and vice. They therefore remained firm in their original simplicity and integrity,
and after some respectful but ineffectual remon-
strances, they stood aloof, alienated from their
commander in heart, and condemning very
strongly, among themselves, his wickedness and
folly.

On the other hand, many of the *younger* officers followed Alexander's example, and became
as vain, as irregular, and as fond of vicious indulgence as he. But then, though they joined
him in his pleasures, there was no strong bond
of union between him and them. The tie which
binds mere companions in pleasure together is
always very slight and frail. Thus Alexander
gradually lost the confidence and affection of his

old friends, and gained no new ones. His officers either disapproved his conduct, and were
distant and cold, or else joined him in his dissipation and vice, without feeling any real respect
for his character, or being bound to him by any
principle of fidelity.

Parmenio and his son Philotas were, respectively, striking examples of these two kinds of
character. Parmenio was an old general, now
considerably advanced in life. He had served,
as has already been stated, under Philip, Alexander's father, and had acquired great experience and great fame before Alexander succeeded to the throne. During the whole of Alexander's career Parmenio had been his principal
lieutenant general, and he had always placed
his greatest reliance upon him in all trying emergencies. He was cool, calm, intrepid, sagacious.
He held Alexander back from many rash enterprises, and was the efficient means of his accomplishing most of his plans. It is the custom
among all nations to give kings the glory of all
that is effected by their generals and officers;
and the writers of those days would, of course,
in narrating the exploits of the Macedonian
army, exaggerate the share which Alexander
had in their performances, and underrate those

of Parmenio. But in modern times, many impartial readers, in reviewing calmly these events,
think that there is reason to doubt whether Alexander, if he had set out on his great expedition without Parmenio, would have succeeded
at all.

Philotas was the son of Parmenio, but he
was of a very different character. The difference was one which is very often, in all ages of
the world, to be observed between those who
inherit greatness and those who acquire it for
themselves. We see the same analogy reigning at the present day, when the sons of the
wealthy, who are *born* to fortune, substitute
pride, and arrogance, and vicious self-indulgence
and waste for the modesty, and prudence, and
virtue of their sires, by means of which the fortune was acquired. Philotas was proud, boastful, extravagant, and addicted, like Alexander
his master, to every species of indulgence and
dissipation. He was universally hated. His
father, out of patience with his haughty airs,
his boastings, and his pomp and parade, advised
him, one day, to "make himself less." But
Parmenio's prudent advice to his son was thrown
away. Philotas spoke of himself as Alexander's
great reliance. "What would Philip have been

or have done," said he, " without my father Par
menio? and what would Alexander have been,
or have done, without me?" These things were
reported to Alexander, and thus the mind of
each was filled with suspicion, fear, and hatred
toward the other.

Courts and camps are always the scenes of
conspiracy and treason, and Alexander was continually hearing of conspiracies and plots formed against him. The strong sentiment of love
and devotion with which he inspired all around
him at the commencement of his career, was
now gone, and his generals and officers were
continually planning schemes to depose him
from the power which he seemed no longer to
have the energy to wield; or, at least, Alexander was continually suspecting that such plans
were formed, and he was kept in a continual
state of uneasiness and anxiety in discovering
and punishing them.

At last a conspiracy occurred in which Philotas was implicated. Alexander was informed
one day that a plot had been formed to depose
and destroy him; that Philotas had been made
acquainted with it by a friend of Alexander's,
in order that he might make it known to the
king; that he had neglected to do so, thus mak

ing it probable that he was himself in league
with the conspirators. Alexander was informed
that the leader and originator of this conspiracy
was one of his generals named Dymnus.

He immediately sent an officer to Dymnus to
summon him into his presence. Dymnus appeared to be struck with consternation at this
summons. Instead of obeying it, he drew his
sword, thrust it into his own heart, and fell
dead upon the ground.

Alexander then sent for Philotas, and asked
him if it was indeed true that he had been informed of this conspiracy, and had neglected to
make it known.

Philotas replied that he had been told that
such a plot was formed, but that he did not believe it; that such stories were continually invented by the malice of evil-disposed men, and
that he had not considered the report which
came to his ears as worthy of any attention.
He was, however, now convinced, by the terror
which Dymnus had manifested, and by his sui-
cide, that all was true, and he asked Alexander's pardon for not having taken immediate
measures for communicating promptly the information he had received.

Alexander gave him his hand, said that he was
34

convinced that he was innocent, and had acted
as he did from disbelief in the existence of the
conspiracy, and not from any guilty participa-
tion in it. So Philotas went away to his tent.

Alexander, however, did not drop the subject
here. He called a council of his ablest and best
friends and advisers, consisting of the principal
officers of his army, and laid the facts before
them. They came to a different conclusion from
his in respect to the guilt of Philotas. They
believed him implicated in the crime, and demanded his trial. Trial in such a case, in those
days, meant putting the accused to the torture,
with a view of forcing him to confess his guilt

Alexander yielded to this proposal. Perhaps
he had secretly instigated it. The advisers of
kings and conquerors, in such circumstances as
this, generally have the sagacity to discover
what advice will be agreeable. At all events,
Alexander followed the advice of his counselors,
and made arrangements for arresting Philotas
on that very evening.

These circumstances occurred at a time when
the army was preparing for a march, the various generals lodging in tents pitched for the purpose. Alexander placed extra guards in various parts of the encampment, as if to impress

the whole army with a sense of the importance
and solemnity of the occasion. He then sent
officers to the tent of Philotas, late at night, to
arrest him. The officers found their unhappy
victim asleep. They awoke him, and made
known their errand. Philotas arose, and obeyed
the summons, dejected and distressed, aware,
apparently, that his destruction was impending.

The next morning Alexander called together
a large assembly, consisting of the principal and
most important portions of the army, to the number of several thousands. They came together
with an air of impressive solemnity, expecting,
from the preliminary preparations, that business
of very solemn moment was to come before them,
though they knew not what it was.

These impressions of awe and solemnity were
very much increased by the spectacle which first
met the eyes of the assembly after they were
convened. This spectacle was that of the dead
body of Dymnus, bloody and ghastly, which Alexander ordered to be brought in and exposed
to view. The death of Dymnus had been kept
a secret, so that the appearance of his body was
an unexpected as well as a shocking sight.
When the first feeling of surprise and wonder
had a little subsided, Alexander explained to the

Q

assembly the nature of the conspiracy, and the
circumstances connected with the self-execution
of one of the guilty participators in it. The
spectacle of the body, and the statement of the
king, produced a scene of great and universal
excitement in the assembly, and this excitement
was raised to the highest pitch by the announcement which Alexander now made, that he had
reason to believe that Philotas and his father
Parmenio, officers who had enjoyed his highest
favor, and in whom he had placed the most unbounded confidence, were the authors and orig-
inators of the whole design.

He then ordered Philotas to be brought in
He came guarded as a criminal, with his hands
tied behind him, and his head covered with a
coarse cloth. He was in a state of great dejection and despondency. It is true that he was
brought forward for trial, but he knew very well
that trial meant torture, and that there was no
hope for him as to the result. Alexander said
that he would leave the accused to be dealt with
by the assembly, and withdrew.

The authorities of the army, who now had
the proud and domineering spirit which had so
long excited their hatred and envy completely
in their power, listened for a time to what Phi-

lotas had to say in his own justification. He
showed that there was no evidence whatever
against him, and appealed to their sense of justice not to condemn him on mere vague surmi-
ses. In reply, they decided to put him to the
torture. There was no evidence, it was true,
and they wished, accordingly, to supply its place
by his own confession, extorted by pain. Of
course, his most inveterate and implacable enemies were appointed to conduct the operation.
They put Philotas upon the rack. The rack is
an instrument of wheels and pulleys, into which
the victim is placed, and his limbs and tendons
are stretched by it in a manner which produces
most excruciating pain.

Philotas bore the beginning of his torture with
great resolution and fortitude. He made no
complaint, he uttered no cry: this was the signal to his executioners to increase the tension
and the agony. Of course, in such a trial as
this, there was no question of guilt or innocence
at issue. The only question was, which could
stand out the longest, his enemies in witnessing horrible sufferings, or he himself in enduring them. In this contest the unhappy Philotas was vanquished at last. He begged them
to release him from the rack, saying he would

confess whatever they required, on condition of being allowed to die in peace.

They accordingly released him, and, in an swer to their questions, he confessed that he him self and his father were involved in the plot.   He said yes to various other inquiries relating to the circumstances of the conspiracy, and to the guilt of various individuals whom those that managed the torture had suspected, or who, at any rate, they wished to have condemned.   The answers of Philotas to all these questions were written down, and he was himself sentenced to be stoned. The sentence was put in execution without any delay.

During all this time Parmenio was in Media, in command of a very important part of Alexander's army.   It was decreed that he must die; but some careful management was necessary to secure his execution while he was at so great a distance, and at the head of so great a force.   The affair had to be conducted with great secrecy as well as dispatch.   The plan adopted was as follows:

There was a certain man, named Polydamas, who was regarded as Parmenio's particular friend.   Polydamas was commissioned to go to Media and see the execution performed.   He

was selected, because it was supposed that if
any enemy, or a stranger, had been sent, Parmenio would have received him with suspicion,
or at least with caution, and kept himself on
his guard. They gave Polydamas several letters to Parmenio, as if from his friends, and to
one of them they attached the seal of his son
Philotas, the more completely to deceive the
unhappy father. Polydamas was eleven days
on his journey into Media. He had letters to
Cleander, the governor of the province of Media,
which contained the king's warrant for Parmenio's execution. He arrived at the house of
Cleander in the night. He delivered his letters,
and they together concerted the plans for carrying the execution into effect.

After having taken all the precautions necessary, Polydamas went, with many attendants
accompanying him, to the quarters of Parmenio. The old general, for he was at this time
eighty years of age, was walking in his grounds.
Polydamas being admitted, ran up to accost
him, with great appearance of cordiality and
friendship. He delivered to him his letters, and
Parmenio read them. He seemed much pleased with their contents, especially with the one
which had been written in the name of his son

He had no means of detecting the imposture, for it was very customary in those days for letters to be written by secretaries, and to be authenticated solely by the seal.

Parmenio was much pleased to get good tidings from Alexander, and from his son, and began conversing upon the contents of the letters, when Polydamas, watching his opportunity, drew forth a dagger which he had concealed upon his person, and plunged it into Parmenio's side. He drew it forth immediately and struck it at his throat. The attendants rushed on at this signal, and thrust their swords again and again into the fallen body until it ceased to breathe.

The death of Parmenio and of his son in this violent manner, when, too, there was so little evidence of their guilt, made a very general and a very unfavorable impression in respect to Alexander; and not long afterward another case occurred, in some respects still more painful, as it evinced still more strikingly that the mind of Alexander, which had been in his earlier days filled with such noble and lofty sentiments of justice and generosity, was gradually getting to be under the supreme dominion of selfish and ungovernable passions: it was the case of Clitus

Clitus was a very celebrated general of Alexander's army, and a great favorite with the king. He had, in fact, on one occasion saved Alexander's life. It was at the battle of the Granicus. Alexander had exposed himself in the thickest of the combat, and was surrounded by enemies. The sword of one of them was actually raised over his head, and would have fallen and killed him on the spot, if Clitus had not rushed forward and cut the man down just at the instant when he was about striking the blow. Such acts of fidelity and courage as this had given Alexander great confidence in Clitus. It happened, shortly after the death of Parmenio, that the governor of one of the most important provinces of the empire resigned his post. Alexander appointed Clitus to fill the vacancy.

The evening before his departure to take charge of his government, Alexander invited him to a banquet, made, partly at least, in honor of his elevation. Clitus and the other guests assembled. They drank wine, as usual, with great freedom. Alexander became excited, and began to speak, as he was now often accustomed to do, boastingly of his own exploits, and to disparage those of his father Philip in comparison.

Men half intoxicated are very prone to quar-

rel, and not the less so for being excellent friends
when sober. Clitus had served under Philip.
He was now an old man, and, like other old men,
was very tenacious of the glory that belonged to
the exploits of his youth. He was very restless
and uneasy at hearing Alexander claim for himself the merit of his father Philip's victory at
Chæronea, and began to murmur something to
those who sat next to him about kings claiming
and getting a great deal of glory which did not
belong to them.

Alexander asked what it was that Clitus said.
No one replied. Clitus, however, went on talking, speaking more and more audibly as he became gradually more and more excited. He
praised the character of Philip, and applauded
his military exploits, saying that they were far
superior to any of the enterprises of *their* day
The different parties at the table took up the
subject, and began to dispute, the old men taking the part of Philip and former days, and the
younger defending Alexander. Clitus became
more and more excited. He praised Parmenio,
who had been Philip's greatest general, and began to impugn the justice of his late condemnation and death.

Alexander retorted, and Clitus, rising from

his seat, and losing now all self-command, reproached him with severe and bitter words
"Here is the hand," said he, extending his arm,
"that saved your life at the battle of the Granicus, and the fate of Parmenio shows what sort
of gratitude and what rewards faithful servants
are to expect at your hands." Alexander, burning with rage, commanded Clitus to leave the
table. Clitus obeyed, saying, as he moved away,
"He is right not to bear freeborn men at his table who can only tell him the truth. He is right.
It is fitting for him to pass his life among barbarians and slaves, who will be proud to pay
their adoration to his Persian girdle and his
splendid robe."

Alexander seized a javelin to hurl at Clitus's
head. The guests rose in confusion, and with
many outcries pressed around him. Some seized
Alexander's arm, some began to hurry Clitus
out of the room, and some were engaged in
loudly criminating and threatening each other.
They got Clitus out of the apartment, but as
soon as he was in the hall he broke away from
them, returned by another door, and began to renew his insults to Alexander. The king hurled
his javelin and struck Clitus down, saying, at
the same time, "Go, then, and join Philip and

Parmenio." The company rushed to the rescue of the unhappy man, but it was too late. He died almost immediately.

Alexander, as soon as he came to himself, was overwhelmed with remorse and despair. He mourned bitterly, for many days, the death of his long-tried and faithful friend, and execrated the intoxication and passion, on his part, which had caused it. He could not, however, restore Clitus to life, nor remove from his own character the indelible stains which such deeds necessarily fixed upon it.

B.C. 326.] ALEXANDER'S END. 251

Alexander's invasion of India.   Insubordination of the army

CHAPTER XII.

ALEXANDER'S END.

AFTER the events narrated in the last chapter, Alexander continued, for two or three years, his expeditions and conquests in Asia, and in the course of them he met with a great variety of adventures which can not be here particularly described. He penetrated into India as far as the banks of the Indus, and, not content with this, was preparing to cross the Indus and go on to the Ganges. His soldiers, however, resisted this design. They were alarmed at the stories which they heard of the Indian armies, with elephants bearing castles upon their backs, and soldiers armed with strange and unheard-of weapons. These rumors, and the natural desire of the soldiers not to go away any further from their native land, produced almost a mutiny in the army. At length, Alexander, learning how strong and how extensive the spirit of insubordination was becoming, summoned his officers to his own tent, and then ordering the whole army to gather around, he went out to meet them.

He made an address to them, in which he re-
counted all their past exploits, praised the courage and perseverance which they had shown
thus far, and endeavored to animate them with
a desire to proceed. They listened in silence,
and no one attempted to reply. This solemn
pause was followed by marks of great agitation
throughout the assembly. The army loved
their commander, notwithstanding his faults
and failings. They were extremely unwilling
to make any resistance to his authority; but
they had lost that extreme and unbounded confidence in his energy and virtue which made
them ready, in the former part of his career, to
press forward into any difficulties and dangers
whatever, where he led the way.

At last one of the army approached the king
and addressed him somewhat as follows :

"We are not changed, sir, in our affection
for you. We still have, and shall always retain, the same zeal and the same fidelity. We
are ready to follow you at the hazard of our
lives, and to march wherever you may lead us.
Still we must ask you, most respectfully, to
consider the circumstances in which we are
placed. We have done all for you that it was
possible for man to do. We have crossed seas

and land. We have marched to the end of the world, and you are now meditating the conquest of another, by going in search of new Indias, unknown to the Indians themselves. Such a thought may be worthy of your courage and resolution, but it surpasses ours, and our strength still more. Look at these ghastly faces, and these bodies covered with wounds and scars. Remember how numerous we were when first we set out with you, and see how few of us remain. The few who have escaped so many toils and dangers have neither courage nor strength to follow you any further. They all long to revisit their country and their homes, and to enjoy, for the remainder of their lives, the fruits of all their toils. Forgive them these desires, so natural to man."

The expression of these sentiments confirmed and strengthened them in the minds of all the soldiers. Alexander was greatly troubled and distressed. A disaffection in a small part of an army may be put down by decisive measures; but when the determination to resist is universal, it is useless for any commander, however imperious and absolute in temper, to attempt to withstand it. Alexander, however, was extremely unwilling to yield. He remained two

days shut up in his tent, the prey to disappoint‑
ment and chagrin.

The result, however, was, that he abandoned
plans of further conquest, and turned his steps
again toward the west. He met with various
adventures as he went on, and incurred many
dangers, often in a rash and foolish manner, and
for no good end. At one time, while attacking
a small town, he seized a scaling ladder and
mounted with the troops. In doing this, how‑
ever, he put himself forward so rashly and in‑
considerately that his ladder was broken, and
while the rest retreated he was left alone upon
the wall, whence he descended into the town,
and was immediately surrounded by enemies.
His friends raised their ladders again, and press‑
ed on desperately to find and rescue him. Some
gathered around him and defended him, while
others contrived to open a small gate, by which
the rest of the army gained admission. By this
means Alexander was saved; though, when they
brought him out of the city, there was an arrow
three feet long, which could not be extracted,
sticking into his side through his coat of mail.

The surgeons first very carefully cut off the
wooden shaft of the arrow, and then, enlarging
the wound by incisions, they drew out the barbed

point. The soldiers were indignant that Alexander should expose his person in such a foolhardy way, only to endanger himself, and to compel them to rush into danger to rescue him. The wound very nearly proved fatal. The loss of blood was attended with extreme exhaustion; still, in the course of a few weeks he recovered.

Alexander's habits of intoxication and vicious excess of all kinds were, in the mean time, continually increasing. He not only indulged in such excesses himself, but he encouraged them in others. He would offer prizes at his banquets to those who would drink the most. On one of these occasions, the man who conquered drank, it is said, eighteen or twenty pints of wine, after which he lingered in misery for three days, and then died; and more than forty others, present at the same entertainment, died in consequence of their excesses.

Alexander returned toward Babylon. His friend Hephæstion was with him, sharing with him every where in all the vicious indulgences to which he had become so prone. Alexander gradually separated himself more and more from his old Macedonian friends, and linked himself more and more closely with Persian associates. He married Statira, the oldest daughter of Da-

35

rius, and gave the youngest daughter to Hephæstion. He encouraged similar marriages between Macedonian officers and Persian maidens,
as far as he could. In a word, he seemed intent in merging, in every way, his original character and habits of action in the effeminacy, luxury, and vice of the Eastern world, which he had
at first so looked down upon and despised.

Alexander's entrance into Babylon, on his return from his Indian campaigns, was a scene of
great magnificence and splendor. Embassadors
and princes had assembled there from almost all
the nations of the earth to receive and welcome
him, and the most ample preparations were
made for processions, shows, parades, and spectacles to do him honor. The whole country
was in a state of extreme excitement, and the
most expensive preparations were made to give
him a reception worthy of one who was the conqueror and monarch of the world, and the son
of a god.

When Alexander approached the city, however, he was met by a deputation of Chaldean
astrologers. The astrologers were a class of
philosophers who pretended, in those days, to
foretell human events by means of the motions
of the stars. The motions of the stars were

studied very closely in early times, and in those
Eastern countries, by the shepherds, who had
often to remain in the open air, through the
summer nights, to watch their flocks.   These
shepherds observed that nearly all the stars were
fixed in relation to each other, that is, although
they rose successively in the east, and, passing
over, set in the west, they did not change in relation to each other.   There were, however, a
few that wandered about among the rest in
an irregular and unaccountable manner.   They
called these stars the wanderers — that is, in
their language, *the planets* — and they watched
their mysterious movements with great interest
and awe.   They naturally imagined that these
changes had some connection with human affairs, and they endeavored to prognosticate from
them the events, whether prosperous or adverse,
which were to befall mankind.   Whenever a
comet or an eclipse appeared, they thought it
portended some terrible calamity.   The study
of the motions and appearances of the stars, with
a view to foretell the course of human affairs,
was the science of astrology.

The astrologers came, in a very solemn and
imposing procession, to meet Alexander on his
march.   They informed him that they had

R

found indubitable evidence in the stars that, if
he came into Babylon, he would hazard his life
They accordingly begged him not to approach
any nearer, but to choose some other city for
his capital. Alexander was very much perplex
ed by this announcement. His mind, weakened by effeminacy and dissipation, was very susceptible to superstitious fears. It was not merely by the debilitating influence of vicious indulgence on the nervous constitution that this effect
was produced. It was, in part, the moral influence of conscious guilt. Guilt makes men
afraid. It not only increases the power of real
dangers, but predisposes the mind to all sorts
of imaginary fears.

Alexander was very much troubled at this
announcement of the astrologers. He suspended his march, and began anxiously to consider
what to do. At length the Greek philosophers
came to him and reasoned with him on the subject, persuading him that the science of astrology was not worthy of any belief. The Greeks
had no faith in astrology. They foretold future
events by the flight of birds, or by the appearances presented in the dissection of beasts offered in sacrifice!

At length, however, Alexander's fears were

so far allayed that he concluded to enter the
city. He advanced, accordingly, with his whole
army, and made his entry under circumstances
of the greatest possible parade and splendor
As soon, however, as the excitement of the first
few days had passed away, his mind relapsed
again, and he became anxious, troubled, and
unhappy.

Hephæstion, his great personal friend and
companion, had died while he was on the march
toward Babylon. He was brought to the grave
by diseases produced by dissipation and vice.
Alexander was very much moved by his death.
It threw him at once into a fit of despondency
and gloom. It was some time before he could
at all overcome the melancholy reflections and
forebodings which this event produced. He determined that, as soon as he arrived in Babylon,
he would do all possible honor to Hephæstion's
memory by a magnificent funeral.

He accordingly now sent orders to all the cities and kingdoms around, and collected a vast
sum for this purpose. He had a part of the
city wall pulled down to furnish a site for a mon-
umental edifice. This edifice was constructed
of an enormous size and most elaborate archi-
tecture. It was ornamented with long rows of

prows of ships, taken by Alexander in his victories, and by statues, and columns, and sculptures, and gilded ornaments of every kind.
There were images of sirens on the entabla-
tures near the roof, which, by means of a mech-
anism concealed within, were made to sing dirg-
es and mournful songs. The expense of this
edifice, and of the games, shows, and spectacles
connected with its consecration, is said by the
historians of the day to have been a sum which,
on calculation, is found equal to about ten millions of dollars.

There were, however, some limits still to Alexander's extravagance and folly. There was
a mountain in Greece, Mount Athos, which a
certain projector said could be carved and fash-
ioned into the form of a man—probably in a re-
cumbent posture. There was a city on one of
the declivities of the mountain, and a small river, issuing from springs in the ground, came
down on the other side. The artist who conceived of this prodigious piece of sculpture said
that he would so shape the figure that the city
should be in one of its hands, and the river
should flow out from the other.

Alexander listened to this proposal. The
name Mount Athos recalled to his mind the

PROPOSED IMPROVEMENT OF MOUNT ATHOS

attempt of Xerxes, a former Persian king, who had attempted to cut a road through the rocks upon a part of Mount Athos, in the invasion of Greece. He did not succeed, but left the unfinished work a lasting memorial both of the attempt and the failure. Alexander concluded at length that he would not attempt such a sculpture. "Mount Athos," said he, "is already the monument of one king's folly; I will not make it that of another."

As soon as the excitement connected with the funeral obsequies of Hephæstion were over, Alexander's mind relapsed again into a state of gloomy melancholy. This depression, caused, as it was, by previous dissipation and vice, seemed to admit of no remedy or relief but in new excesses. The traces, however, of his former energy so far remained that he began to form magnificent plans for the improvement of Babylon He commenced the execution of some of these plans. His time was spent, in short, in strange alternations: resolution and energy in forming vast plans one day, and utter abandonment to all the excesses of dissipation and vice the next. It was a mournful spectacle to see his former greatness of soul still struggling on. though more and more faintly, as it became gradually

overborne by the resistless inroads of intemper-
ance and sin. The scene was at length sud-
lenly terminated in the following manner:

On one occasion, after he had spent a whole
night in drinking and carousing, the guests,
when the usual time arrived for separating, proposed that, instead of this, they should begin
anew, and commence a second banquet at the
end of the first. Alexander, half intoxicated already, entered warmly into this proposal. They
assembled, accordingly, in a very short time.
There were twenty present at this new feast.
Alexander, to show how far he was from having
exhausted his powers of drinking, began to
pledge each one of the company individually.
Then he drank to them all together. There
was a very large cup, called the bowl of Hercules, which he now called for, and, after having filled it to the brim, he drank it off to the
health of one of the company present, a Macedonian named Proteas. This feat being received by the company with great applause, he ordered the great bowl to be filled again, and
drank it off as before.

The work was now done. His faculties and
his strength soon failed him, and he sank down
to the floor. They bore him away to his pal-

ace. A violent fever intervened, which the phy-
sicians did all in their power to allay. As soon
as his reason returned a little, Alexander aroused himself from his lethargy, and tried to persuade himself that he should recover. He began
to issue orders in regard to the army, and to his
ships, as if such a turning of his mind to the
thoughts of power and empire would help bring
him back from the brink of the grave toward
which he had been so obviously tending. He
was determined, in fact, that he would not die.

He soon found, however, notwithstanding his
efforts to be vigorous and resolute, that his
strength was fast ebbing away. The vital powers had received a fatal wound, and he soon felt
that they could sustain themselves but little
longer. He came to the conclusion that he
must die. He drew his signet ring off from his
finger; it was a token that he felt that all was
over. He handed the ring to one of his friends
who stood by his bed-side. "When I am gone,"
said he, "take my body to the Temple of Jupiter Ammon, and inter it there."

The generals who were around him advanced
to his bed-side, and one after another kissed his
hand. Their old affection for him revived as
they saw him about to take leave of them for-

ever. They asked him to whom he wished to leave his empire. "To the most worthy," said he. He meant, doubtless, by this evasion, that he was too weak and exhausted to think of such affairs. He knew, probably, that it was useless for him to attempt to control the government of his empire after his death. He said, in fact, that he foresaw that the decision of such questions would give rise to some strange funeral games after his decease. Soon after this he died.

The palaces of Babylon were immediately filled with cries of mourning at the death of the prince, followed by bitter and interminable disputes about the succession. It had not been the aim of Alexander's life to establish firm and well-settled governments in the countries that he conquered, to encourage order, and peace, and industry among men, and to introduce system and regularity in human affairs, so as to leave the world in a better condition than he found it. In this respect his course of conduct presents a strong contrast with that of Washington. It was Washington's aim to mature and perfect organizations which would move on prosperously of themselves, without him; and he was continually withdrawing his hand from

action and control in public affairs, taking a
higher pleasure in the independent working of
the institutions which he had formed and protected, than in exercising, himself, a high personal power. Alexander, on the other hand, was all
his life intent solely on enlarging and strengthening his own personal power. *He* was all in
all. He wished to make himself so. He never
thought of the welfare of the countries which he
had subjected to his sway, or did any thing to
guard against the anarchy and civil wars which
he knew full well would break out at once over
all his vast dominions, as soon as his power came
to an end.

The result was as might have been foreseen.
The whole vast field of his conquests became,
for many long and weary years after Alexander's death, the prey to the most ferocious and
protracted civil wars. Each general and governor seized the power which Alexander's death
left in his hands, and endeavored to defend himself in the possession of it against the others.
Thus the devastation and misery which the
making of these conquests brought upon Europe and Asia were continued for many years,
during the slow and terrible process of their return to their original condition.

In the exigency of the moment, however, at
Alexander's death, the generals who were in
his court at the time assembled forthwith, and
made an attempt to appoint some one to take
the immediate command. They spent a week
in stormy debates on this subject. Alexander
had left no legitimate heir, and he had declined,
when on his death-bed, as we have already seen,
to appoint a successor. Among his wives—if,
indeed, they may be called wives—there was
one named Roxana, who had a son not long
after his death. This son was ultimately named his successor; but, in the mean time, a cer
tain relative named Aridæus was chosen by the
generals to assume the command. The selection of Aridæus was a sort of compromise. He
had no talents or capacity whatever, and was
chosen by the rest on that very account, each
one thinking that if such an imbecile as Aridæus was nominally the king, he could himself
manage to get possession of the real power.
Aridæus accepted the appointment, but he was
never able to make himself king in any thing
but the name.

In the mean time, as the tidings of Alexander's death spread over the empire, it produced
very various effects, according to the personal

feelings in respect to Alexander entertained by
the various personages and powers to which th :
intelligence came. Some, who had admired his
greatness, and the splendor of his exploits, with
out having themselves experienced the bitter
fruits of them, mourned and lamented his death.
Others, whose fortunes had been ruined, and
whose friends and relatives had been destroyed,
in the course, or in the sequel of his victories,
rejoiced that he who had been such a scourge
and curse to others, had himself sunk, at last,
under the just judgment of Heaven.

We should have expected that Sysigambis,
the bereaved and widowed mother of Darius,
would have been among those who would have
exulted most highly at the conqueror's death :
but history tells us that, instead of this, she
mourned over it with a protracted and inconsolable grief. Alexander had been, in fact,
though the implacable enemy of her son, a faithful and generous friend to her. He had treated
her, at all times, with the utmost respect and
consideration, had supplied all her wants, and
ministered, in every way, to her comfort and
happiness. She had gradually learned to think
of him and to love him as a son; he, in fact,
always called her mother; and when she learn-

ed that he was gone, she felt as if her last
earthly protector was gone. Her life had been
one continued scene of affliction and sorrow, and
this last blow brought her to her end. She
pined away, perpetually restless and distressed.
She lost all desire for food, and refused, like
others who are suffering great mental anguish,
to take the sustenance which her friends and
attendants offered and urged upon her. At
length she died. They said she starved herself
to death; but it was, probably, grief and de
spair at being thus left, in her declining years,
so hopelessly friendless and alone, and not hunger, that destroyed her.

In striking contrast to this mournful scene of
sorrow in the palace of Sysigambis, there was
an exhibition of the most wild and tumultuous
joy in the streets, and in all the public places
of resort in the city of Athens, when the tidings
of the death of the great Macedonian king arrived there. The Athenian commonwealth, as
well as all the other states of Southern Greece,
had submitted very reluctantly to the Macedonian supremacy. They had resisted Philip, and
they had resisted Alexander. Their opposition
had been at last suppressed and silenced by Alexander's terrible vengeance upon Thebes, but

it never was really subdued. Demosthenes, the orator, who had exerted so powerful an influence against the Macedonian kings, had been sent into banishment, and all outward expressions of discontent were restrained. The discontent and hostility existed still, however, as inveterate as ever, and was ready to break out anew, with redoubled violence, the moment that the terrible energy of Alexander himself was no longer to be feared.

When, therefore, the rumor arrived at Athens—for at first it was a mere rumor—that Alexander was dead in Babylon, the whole city was thrown into a state of the most tumultuous joy. The citizens assembled in the public places, and congratulated and harangued each other with expressions of the greatest exultation They were for proclaiming their independence and declaring war against Macedon on the spot. Some of the older and more sagacious of their counselors were, however, more composed and calm They recommended a little delay, in order to see whether the news was really true Phocion, in particular, who was one of the prominent statesmen of the city, endeavored to quiet the excitement of the people. "Do not let us be so precipitate," said he. "There is time

enough. If Alexander is really dead to-day, he
will be dead to-morrow, and the next day, so
that there will be time enough for us to act with
deliberation and discretion."

Just and true as this view of the subject was,
there was too much of rebuke and satire in it
to have much influence with those to whom it
was addressed. The people were resolved on
war. They sent commissioners into all the
states of the Peloponnesus to organize a league,
offensive and defensive, against Macedon. They
recalled Demosthenes from his banishment, and
adopted all the necessary military measures for
establishing and maintaining their freedom.
The consequences of all this would doubtless
have been very serious, if the rumor of Alexan
der's death had proved false; but, fortunately
for Demosthenes and the Athenians, it was soon
abundantly confirmed.

The return of Demosthenes to the city was
like the triumphal entry of a conqueror. At
the time of his recall he was at the island of
Ægina, which is about forty miles southwest
of Athens, in one of the gulfs of the Ægean Sea.
They sent a public galley to receive him, and
to bring him to the land. It was a galley of
three banks of oars, and was fitted up in a style

to do honor to a public guest.   Athens is situ·
ated some distance back from the sea, and has
a small port, called the Piræus, at the shore—a
long, straight avenue leading from the port to
the city. The galley by which Demosthenes
was conveyed landed at the Piræus. All the
civil and religious authorities of the city went
down to the port, in a grand procession, to receive and welcome the exile on his arrival, and
a large portion of the population followed in the
train, to witness the spectacle, and to swell by
their acclamations the general expression of joy.

In the mean time, the preparations for Alexander's funeral had been going on, upon a great
scale of magnificence and splendor. It was two
years before they were complete. The body
had been given, first, to be embalmed, according to the Egyptian and Chaldean art, and then
had been placed in a sort of sarcophagus, in
which it was to be conveyed to its long home.
Alexander, it will be remembered, had given
directions that it should be taken to the temple
of Jupiter Ammon, in the Egyptian oasis, where
he had been pronounced the son of a god. It
would seem incredible that such a mind as his
could really admit such an absurd superstition
as the story of his divine origin, and we must

S

therefore suppose that he gave this direction in
order that the place of his interment might confirm the idea of his superhuman nature in the
general opinion of mankind. At all events, such
were his orders, and the authorities who were
left in power at Babylon after his death, prepared to execute them.

It was a long journey. To convey a body,
by a regular funeral procession, formed as soon
after the death as the arrangements could be
made, from Babylon to the eastern frontiers of
Egypt, a distance of a thousand miles, was
perhaps as grand a plan of interment as was
ever formed. It has something like a parallel
in the removal of Napoleon's body from St. Helena to Paris, though this was not really an interment, but a transfer. Alexander's was a
simple burial procession, going from the palace
where he died to the proper cemetery—a march
of a thousand miles, it is true, but all within
his own dominions. The greatness of it resulted simply from the magnitude of the scale on
which every thing pertaining to the mighty here
was performed, for it was nothing but a simple
passage from the dwelling to the burial-ground
on his own estates, after all.

A very large and elaborately constructed car

riage was built to convey the body. The accounts of the richness and splendor of this vehicle are almost incredible. The spokes and
naves of the wheels were overlaid with gold,
and the extremities of the axles, where they
appeared outside at the centers of the wheels,
were adorned with massive golden ornaments.
The wheels and axle-trees were so large, and
so far apart, that there was supported upon
them a platform or floor for the carriage twelve
feet wide and eighteen feet long. Upon this
platform there was erected a magnificent pavilion, supported by Ionic columns, and profusely
ornamented, both within and without, with purple and gold. The interior constituted an apartment, more or less open at the sides, and resplendent within with gems and precious stones.
The space of twelve feet by eighteen forms a
chamber of no inconsiderable size, and there
was thus ample room for what was required
within. There was a throne, raised some steps,
and placed back upon the platform, profusely
carved and gilded. It was empty; but crowns,
representing the various nations over whom Alexander had reigned, were hung upon it. At
the foot of the throne was the coffin, made, it
is said, of solid gold, and containing, besides

the body, a large quantity of the most costly
spices and aromatic perfumes, which filled the
air with their odor. The arms which Alexan
der wore were laid out in view, also, between
the coffin and the throne.

On the four sides of the carriage were *basso
relievos*, that is, sculptured figures raised from
a surface, representing Alexander himself, with
various military concomitants. There were
Macedonian columns, and Persian squadrons,
and elephants of India, and troops of horse, and
various other emblems of the departed hero's
greatness and power. Around the pavilion, too,
there was a fringe or net-work of golden lace,
to the pendents of which were attached bells,
which tolled continually, with a mournful sound,
as the carriage moved along. A long column
of mules, sixty-four in number, arranged in
sets of four, drew this ponderous car. These
mules were all selected for their great size
and strength, and were splendidly caparisoned
They had collars and harnesses mounted with
gold, and enriched with precious stones.

Before the procession set out from Babylon
an army of pioneers and workmen went for
ward to repair the roads, strengthen the bridg
es, and remove the obstacles along the whole

line of route over which the train was to pass
At length, when all was ready, the solemn procession began to move, and passed out through
the gates of Babylon. No pen can describe the
enormous throngs of spectators that assembled
to witness its departure, and that gathered
along the route, as it passed slowly on from
city to city, in its long and weary way.

Notwithstanding all this pomp and parade,
however, the body never reached its intended
destination. Ptolemy, the officer to whom Egypt
fell in the division of Alexander's empire, came
forth with a grand escort of troops to meet the
funeral procession as it came into Egypt. He
preferred, for some reason or other, that the
body should be interred in the city of Alexandria. It was accordingly deposited there, and
a great monument was erected over the spot.
This monument is said to have remained standing for fifteen hundred years, but all vestiges of
it have now disappeared. The city of Alexandria itself, however, is the conqueror's real monument ; the greatest and best, perhaps, that any
conqueror ever left behind him. It is a monument, too, that time will not destroy ; its position
and character, as Alexander foresaw, by bringing
it a continued renovation, secure its perpetuity

Alexander earned well the name and reputation of THE GREAT. He was truly great in all those powers and capacities which can elevate one man above his fellows. We can not help applauding the extraordinary energy of his genius, though we condemn the selfish and cruel ends to which his life was devoted. He was simply a robber. but yet a robber on so vast a scale, that mankind, in contemplating his career, have generally lost sight of the wickedness of his crimes in their admiration of the enormous magnitude of the scale on which they were perpetrated.

THE END.

P. 16: *Herodotus and Xenophon.*—In this history Mr. Abbott generally follows the account given by Herodotus. The
chief points of difference in the narrative of Xenophon are
the following: He represents Cyrus as brought up at his
grandfather's court, as serving in the Median army under
his uncle Cyaxares, the son and successor of Astyages, of
whom Herodotus and Ctesias know nothing; as making
war upon Babylon simply as the general of Cyaxares, who
remained at home during the latter part of the Assyrian
war, and permitted Cyrus to assume without opposition the
power of state and an independent sovereign at Babylon;
as marrying the daughter of Cyaxares; and at length dying
quietly in his bed after a series of Socratic discourses to his
children and friends. Diodorus, a Roman historian of the
time of Cæsar and Augustus, agrees, for the most part, with
Herodotus. As a means of preparing for his "Universal
History," he travelled over the greater part of Europe and
Asia, and his work embraced a period from the earliest ages
down to the time of Julius Cæsar; but as he made no attempt to exercise any criticism upon the materials which
he gathered, his work gives very little additional authority
to the account of Herodotus. Neither Herodotus nor Xenophon are regarded by the latest and best authorities as affording a really trustworthy narrative of the facts. Xenophon's "Cyropedia" is not unjustly characterized by
Brooke, Foss, and Westcott as "romance." It was written
for the purpose, not of giving an accurate narrative of facts,
but of portraying Xenophon's ideal of a true ruler. Herodotus seems to be more worthy of credit. "Where he
speaks," says Dr. William Smith, "from his own observation, his accounts may be implicitly relied upon;" many of
them which were formerly doubted as impossible have been
confirmed by the researches of modern travellers. Never-
theless, he is not inaptly called by Macaulay "one of the
romantic historians;" and although it is perhaps too much
to say, with Macaulay, that "he is from the first to the last

[i]

chapter an inventor," it is very certain that he does not hesitate to use his invention in narrating those facts respecting which accuracy of knowledge was impossible.

P. 25 : *Herodotus's History.*—The story that Herodotus read his work to the assembled Greeks at Olympia rests upon the authority of Lucian, who states that Thucydides was present, and moved to tears by the recital; but it would appear that, if this story were true, Herodotus could not have been more than thirty-two years of age at the time of this recital, and the work contains numerous historical allusions which belong to a later day than that of the recital, and the hypothesis that he recited parts of it, or a sketch of it, is not sustained by Lucian's description of the event. The best scholars are now of the opinion that Lucian's story is untrustworthy; that the work was finished by Herodotus in his old age, and from allusions in the history, was written in Southern Italy. The division into books is now supposed to have been made by an editor at a later date.

P. 67 : *Birth of Cyrus.*—The facts respecting the birth and ancestry of Cyrus are involved in great uncertainty. The best authorities are generally of the opinion that Astyages had no son; Herodotus distinctly declares that he had not, and there is nothing to give sanction to the statement of Xenophon that he had a son and heir, Cyaxares II. Both Xenophon and Herodotus declare that Mandane, the mother of Cyrus, was the daughter of Astyages; but this statement is doubted by Rawlinson; he thinks that this story was intended to gratify the vanity of the Persians by tracing the descent of their kings to the great Median conqueror Cyaxares I., while at the same time it flattered the Medes, by showing them that the issue of their old monarchs was still sitting on the throne. He adds, "When an Oriental Crown passes from one dynasty to another, however foreign and unconnected, the natives are wont to invent a relationship between the two houses, which both parties are commonly quite ready to accept; as it suits the rising house to be provided with a royal ancestry, and it pleases the fallen one and its partisans to see in the occupants of the throne a branch of the ancient stock—a continuation of the legitimate family. Tales, therefore, of the above-mentioned kind are, historically speaking, valueless, and it must remain uncertain whether the second Median monarch (Astyages) had any child at all, either male or female."

[ii]

Notes to Cyrus the Great.

P. 72: *Median Dress.*—The favorite dress of the Medes is well known to us from the sculptures. The outer garment was a long flowing robe; these robes were of many colors—purple, scarlet, crimson, occasionally a dark gray; they were made of rich materials, often of silk; they wore head-dresses, frequently of an elaborate character, both in-doors and out; they took special delight in the adornment of their persons; they employed cosmetics for the sake of improving the complexion; made use of an abundance of false hair; applied dyes to enhance the brilliancy of the eyes and give them a greater apparent size and softness, and were fond of wearing golden ornaments—chains or collars of gold about their necks, golden bracelets upon their arms, and golden ear-rings. For illustration and further description, see Rawlinson's Ancient Monarchies, vol. ii. pp. 313–317.

P. 142: *Death of Astyages.*—There are various accounts of the death of Astyages. According to some authorities, he died a natural death in captivity; according to others, he was left to perish in a desert region, as described in the text; while according to still others he was succeeded by his son, Cyaxares II., and on his death Cyrus succeeded to the throne. This last is Xenophon's account, and does not agree with such other historical records as we have of these remote events.

P. 143: *Cyrus's Plans.*—Rawlinson supposes that the first object of Cyrus, in his attack upon Astyages, was simply to establish the independence of his own country; but that his successes led him on to transfer the failing and weakened empire of the Medes to himself.

P. 206: *The Capture of Babylon.* —Herodotus and Xenophon differ materially in their account of the campaign of Cyrus against Babylon, and the capture of that city. The account in the text follows mainly Herodotus. According to Xenophon, Cyrus, in his campaign against Babylon, acted simply as the general of Cyaxares, the son and successor of Astyages, and it has been supposed by some critics that this version better accords with the Biblical narrative which attributes the capture of Babylon to Darius the Mede (Dan. vi. 31), who, according to these critics, is supposed to be identical with Cyaxares II.

The better opinion, however, is that the story of Herodotus is the more trustworthy one; that the city was captured under Cyrus, and that Darius, the Mede referred to in

[iii]

Daniel, was a noble Median who held the sovereignty, as the viceroy of Cyrus, until the latter concluded to establish his own court in that city. A difficulty has also been experienced in reconciling the account of the capture of Babylon given by the Bible with that found in Herodotus. According to the Scripture account in Dan. v., Belshazzar, the last king of Babylon, was captured with that city by Cyrus, and was by him put to death. But, according to secular history, the last king of Babylon was one Nabonnedus, or Labynetus, who was defeated in the open plain, and retired to the neighboring city of Borsippa, and was blockaded there; and at length surrendering to Cyrus, his life was spared, and a principality in Carmania was bestowed on him, where he died. But this seeming discrepancy is removed, and the Scripture account is confirmed, by a remarkable discovery made by Colonel Rawlinson in 1854, at Mugheir, the ancient Ur. Documents were brought to light which prove that Nabonnedus, during the last years of his reign, associated his son Bil-shar-uzur with himself in the government, and allowed him the royal title. He then, probably, conducted the defense of Babylon within the walls, while the father commanded without. Bil-shar-uzur was very young at the time; but princes as young as he have held high command in the East. Thus Herod the Great was governor of Galilee at fifteen. In Dan. v. 11, 13, 18, 22, etc., where Nebuchadnezzar is referred to as the *father* of Belshazzar, the word may properly be translated *ancestor,* and is rendered "grandfather" in the margin.

P. 222: *The Character of Cyrus.*—A great deal of interest has been felt in the attempt to form some clear and accurate conception of the character of Cyrus the Great, and particularly of the motives which led him to encourage and provide for the restoration of the Jews, and the rebuilding of their Temple. The materials for a correct estimate of his character are very slight, and not very trustworthy. Skepticism has thrown considerable doubt upon the edict given in the first chapter of the Book of Ezra for the restoration of the Jews, which has been supposed by such writers as Ewald to have been greatly colored by the Jewish historian; and Cyrus has been regarded as a sort of Genghis Khan, and pictured as a furious iconoclast; and in support of this view such passages as Isa. xlvi. 1, 2; Jer. l. 2; li. 44, 52, have been cited. These passages have been supposed to indicate that he broke in pieces the idols which he found in Babylon, and carried away the fragments of them in wagons, which groaned under the weight. See Stanley's *Lectures on the Jewish Church*, Third Series, p. 67. But some recent discoveries tend to throw light upon the act of Cyrus the Great in restoring the Jews to their native land, and at the same time to explain the reason which led him so to do. Last summer (1879) some Arabs obtained from one of the Babylonian ruins a broken clay cylinder, barrel-shaped, about nine inches long, and three and one-fourth inches in diameter at the ends, containing an inscription embodying a proclamation of Cyrus. In this he declares, somewhat self-complacently, the great services that he has rendered to the provinces which have come under his authority. He says, "The gods who dwelt among them, to their places I restored, and I assigned them a permanent habitation; all their people I assembled, and I increased their property; and the gods of Sumer Akkad, whom Nabonidus had introduced at their festivals, and the Lord of the Gods at Kal-Anna, by the command of Merodach the Great Lord, I assigned them an honorable seat in their sanctuaries, as was enjoyed by all the other gods in their own cities; and daily I prayed to Bel and Nebo that they would lengthen my days and increase my good fortunes," etc. In a suggestive article in the *Contemporary Review* for January, 1880, Canon Rawlinson discusses the character of Cyrus the Great, and his motive in the restoration of the Jews, as indicated by this recently discovered proclamation, and concludes that he was a politic prince, cool and cautious, and so broad in his views as to be willing to identify his own supreme deity, the Ormuzd of the Persians, with the chief god of any religious system with which he came into contact. He supposes that Cyrus, finding the Jews to be, like his own nation, professors of a religion based upon a sacred volume, and finding in that volume a prophecy respecting himself, "He is my shepherd, and shall perform all my pleasure: even saying to Jerusalem, Thou shalt be built; and to the temple, Thy foundation shall be laid" (Isa. xliv. 28), gladly accepted this as a charge, and strengthened himself among his Jewish subjects by fulfilling the prophecy, and restoring them to their land and their religion. If this view be correct, then Cyrus was truly *Great*, in that he was the first one to inaugurate that system of religious toleration which Alexander the Great afterward carried out in his kingdom; which Rome subsequently adopted in the administration of her empire; which the English have maintained in their Indian government; and which has preserved unity and peace among the adherents of all the various religious sects in the United States. It should be added that the edict of Cyrus for the return of the Jews is mentioned only in Scripture; but that their restoration actually took place under his reign is not a matter of question by any one.

P. 225: *The Restoration of the Jews.*—It is not easy to trace accurately the connection between the narrative of the Persian domination, as given in secular history, and the narrative of the same epoch as given in the Bible; for the proper names used to designate the same person are different in the secular and in the sacred histories, and the best scholars are not agreed in identifying the two. The following table exhibits the succession of the Persian kings by their ordinary Greek names, with the names which most probably correspond to them in Scripture. I take it from Dr. Smith's Old Testament History; and although some of these are hypothetical, they seem to me, after careful examination, to be more probable than those suggested by any other scheme:

Beginning of each Reign.

1. Cyaxares, King of Media............................. B.C. 634
   Ahasuerus, Dan. ix. 1.
2. Astyages, his son, last King of Media............... " 594
   Darius the Mede.
3. Cyrus, son of his daughter and Cambyses, a Persian noble, founder of the Persian Empire.............. " 559
   Cyrus begins to reign at Babylon................ Jan. 5, 538
4. Cambyses, his son.................................. " 3, 529
   Ahasuerus, Ezra iv. 6–16.
5. Gomates, a Magian usurper (about Jan. 1), who personated Smerdis, the younger son of Cyrus (reigns seven months)...................................... B.C. 522
   Artaxerxes, Ezra iv. 7.
6. Darius, the son of Hystaspes, a Persian noble, raised to the throne on the overthrow of Gomates ...... Jan. 1, 521
   Darius, Ezra iv. 5, 24; v. 6.
7. Xerxes, his son................................... Dec. 23, 486
   Ahasuerus, Esther.
8. Artaxerxes Longimanus, his son.................... Dec. 7, 465
   Artaxerxes, Ezra, vii., Nehemiah, end of reign.... Dec. 17, 423

The restoration begun under Cyrus was not completed until Darius, owing, probably, to the wars of Cyrus in Asia and of his son Cambyses in Egypt, and to the disorders which followed upon the usurpation of Gomates.

P. 13 : *Alexander's Birth.*—Alexander was born 356 B.C., at Pella, the capital of Macedonia; according to Plutarch, on the same day that the Temple of Diana at Ephesus was burned. One of his eulogists declared that it was no wonder that the temple was burned, since Diana was absent, engaged in bringing Alexander into the world. Plutarch describes his complexion as fair, with a tinge of red in his face and on his breast. His proper title was Alexander III., though generally known as Alexander the Great.

P. 17 : *The Macedonians.*—The Macedonians were not pure Greeks, and were never so regarded by the Greeks proper. Their history prior to 490 B.C. is involved in great obscurity. At that time Macedonia was conquered in the Persian invasion by Xerxes, and their king, Alexander I., was compelled to take part with Xerxes in the invasion of Greece. It was first developed into a powerful kingdom under Philip, the father of Alexander; and on Alexander's death, with the rest of his dominions, was ravaged by civil wars, and finally became subject to Rome in 197 B.C., and was made a Roman province in 146 B.C. This was its condition at the time of Paul's visit to it (Acts xvi. 9, 10). It is now a part of Turkey in Europe, but no longer as an independent province.

P. 21 : *Aristotle.*—Aristotle's father, Nicomachus, was a special friend of Amyntas, Philip's father, and it is said that when Alexander was born Philip sent a letter to Aristotle, saying, "I am thankful to the gods, not so much for his birth as that he was born in your time," and inviting the philosopher to take charge of the prince's education. This is somewhat mythical, but it illustrates the probable relations between the royal and the philosophical families. Aristotle may be regarded as the founder of the modern scientific school ; and Plato, his great rival, of the modern metaphysical school. Aristotle studied things, Plato thought; Aristotle gathered knowledge from all quarters, Plato meditated problems the most profound. "History, the human mind, and all departments of nature," says President Seelye, in his admirable though too brief article in "Johnson's Cyclopedia," "furnish Aristotle contributions. He has no rival in the variety and extent of the facts which he has collected, and the patient industry of his investigations." He seems to have had actual charge of Alexander's education from the time when he was thirteen years of age till, in his father's absence, he was appointed regent, at the age of seventeen. For a comprehensive account of Aristotle's life and works, and a brief exposition of his philosophy, see Smith's "Dictionary of Biography and Mythology," art. *Aristotle.*

P. 23 : *Hanging Gardens.* — For fuller description of the Hanging Gardens, see "Cyrus the Great," p. 194.

P. 24 : *Bucephalus.*—The story of Bucephalus is told a little differently by Plutarch. According to him, the horse was offered for sale to Philip for thirteen talents, about twelve thousand dollars. He says that Alexander promised to pay the price of the horse if he should fail to manage him.

P. 32 : *Philip's Wife*—The lady here referred to was Cleopatra, probably the niece of Attalus, though, apparently by mistake, called his daughter by some writers. After the death of Philip, his first wife, Olympias, killed Cleopatra ; some accounts say by hanging, others by boiling her in a brazen kettle.

P. 43 : *Demosthenes.* — Demosthenes was born about 385 B.C., and died 322 B.C., of poison which he took in exile, to avoid being delivered into the hands of his enemies. His father died when he was only seven years of age, and the major part of his fortune was wasted by his guardians. He achieved his success as orator, in spite of a feeble constitution and defects in his organs of speech, by the most laborious and painstaking study. At the age of thirty he was already a successful lawyer. The object of his Philippics was to arouse his countrymen against the ambitious schemes of conquest of Philip of Macedon ; he failed through no fault of his, but because of the apathy of the Athenians, and the rivalries and jealousies between the Grecian States, which prevented their making a common cause against their conquerors. Like Cicero, he lived in the days of his country's decay ; like Cicero, he endeavored in vain to resist the corruption of his age, and restore his country to its old time power and glory; like Cicero, he was exiled, recalled from exile, and finally died to escape his personal and political enemies. For an excellent account of him and his orations, see the volume devoted to "Demosthenes," in the "Ancient Classics for English Readers" (J. B. Lippincott & Co.).

P. 72: *Siege and Destruction of Thebes.*—According to the best authorities, Alexander left the fate of Thebes to be determined by his Greek allies, who were inveterate enemies of the Thebans, and, in determining its entire destruction, meted out to it what they would have received if the Thebans had been victorious. Alexander moderated their wrath by the measures of mercy which are described in the text. The house of Pindar was left standing in the general demolition of the city, which remained without inhabitants for twenty years.

P. 81: *Pelion and Ossa.*—The attempt of the sons of Aloeus to pile Pelion upon Ossa is thus described by Homer, book xi., lines 384-397 (Bryant's Translation):

> "When the twain
> Had seen but nine years of their life, they stood
> In breadth of frame nine cubits, and in height
> Nine fathoms. They against the living gods
> Threatened to wage upon Olympian height
> Fierce and tumultuous battle, and to fling
> Ossa upon Olympus, and to pile
> Pelion, with all its growth of leafy woods,
> On Ossa, that the heavens might thus be scaled.
> And they, if they had reached their prime of youth,
> Had made their menace good. The son of Jove
> And amber-haired Latona took their lives
> Ere yet beneath their temples sprang the down
> And covered with its sprouting tufts the chin."

P. 84: *Greek Worship.*—The principal ceremony of ancient worship, whether public or domestic, was a repast; the former was partaken of in common by all the citizens in honor of the protecting divinities. For a graphic account of such a scene of worship see Homer's "Odyssey," book iii., Bryant's edition, line 538, etc. Festive processions were frequent accompaniments of these religious meals. See De Coulange's "Ancient City," chap. vii.; Guhl and Koner's "Life of the Greeks and Romans," pp. 281-287.

P. 85: *The Muses.*—In the most ancient works we find only three Muses, each with her musical instrument; later, nine Muses, possessing both different attributes and different symbols. They are as follows: (1) Calliope, the Muse of Epic Poetry, with a tablet and stylus, or pen; (2) Clio, the Muse of History, with an open roll of paper or an open chest of books; (3) Euterpe, the Muse of Lyric Poetry, with a flute; (4) Melpomene, the Muse of Tragedy, with a tragic mask; (5) Terpsichore, the Muse of Dance and Song, with a lyre; (6) Erato, the Muse of the Poetry of Love, also sometimes with a lyre; (7) Polyhymnia, the Muse of Sublime Poetry, usually in a pensive attitude; (8) Urania, the Muse of Astronomy, with a staff pointing to a globe; (9) Thalia, the Muse of Comedy, with a comic mask, a shepherd's staff, or a wreath of ivy.

P. 89: *Troy.*—At the time this book was written, the question whether any such poet as Homer ever lived, whether his poems were not legends gathered from various sources, whether there was any historical basis for them, and, if so, what, were grave ones among classical scholars.

The researches of Dr. Schliemann and the literary researches of English Homeric students, prominent among whom is Mr. Gladstone, have now established, almost beyond a doubt, that the poems of Homer have a historical basis, and are, in the highest and best sense, historical as a record of manners and customs, feelings and tastes, principles and institutions, that there was a solid nucleus of fact in his account of the Trojan war, and that the site of ancient Troy is the spot covered with ruins and now known as Hissarlik. Dr. Schliemann's investigations among these ruins have thrown great light on the Homeric poems, and gone far to afford a demonstration of their historical character. The material for the study of this subject will be found in Dr. Schliemann's "Troy and its Ruins," Mr. Gladstone's "Juventus Mundi," "Studies on Homer and the Homeric Age," and "Times and Place of Homer." See also Smith's "Dictionary of Greek and Roman Biography," art. *Ilium.*

P. 107: *Phalanx.*—Philip has been sometimes credited with inventing the phalanx: it seems, however, to have existed prior to his time, though to have been improved and brought to its perfection under him.

P. 119: *Climax.*—Some of the ancient historians attributed the successful march through the sea at Climax to the miraculous interposition of Heaven, which caused the sea to retire; but Alexander himself treated the matter lightly, simply saying that he marched from Phaselis by the way called Climax; and both Strabo and Plutarch repudiate the idea of there having been any miracle.

P. 147: *Tyre.*—Plutarch tells the singular story respecting the manner in which the siege of Tyre was brought to its termination. Aristander, Alexander's principal soothsayer, declared on the very last day of the month that the city would certainly be taken that month. Alexander, perceiving that he was disconcerted by the ridicule which this prophecy brought upon him, and that the faith in his prophecies was liable to be greatly weakened in the army, decreed that the day should be called the twenty-eighth instead of the thirtieth, then ordered an assault which was conducted with so much vigor as to be successful.

The destruction of Tyre is one of the most striking of all the fulfillments of Old Testament prophecies. It was one of the most ancient of the great cities of the East; its glory and its power are graphically described in Ezek. xxvii. While yet a great and prosperous city, and apparently impregnable, its downfall was foretold by the Hebrew prophets (Jer. xxv. 22; xxvii. 3; Joel iii. 4–8; Amos i. 9, 10). These prophecies have become literally fulfilled. The fishermen dry their nets on the rocks of Tyre, as Ezekiel declared they should (Ezek. xxvi. 14); its harbor has been filled up with its ruins; and even if an honest government and a revived commerce should give back prosperity to Palestine, the woe denounced against Tyre, "Thou shalt be built no more," would remain.

P. 174: *The Visit to Jerusalem.*—The story of Alexander's visit to Jerusalem is not mentioned in the "Encyclopædia Britannica," and is discredited in Smith's "Dictionary of Biography." It is probably a legend of Jewish invention. Josephus places this visit subsequent to the siege of Gaza.

P. 181: *Jupiter Ammon.*—Ammon, variously spelled Amon, Amun, and Amen, was the name of an Ethiopian deity whose worship extended over Egypt, and finally into Greece and Rome: in the latter country he took the double name of Jupiter Ammon. His chief temple and oracle in Egypt were in Thebes; and the homage which Alexander paid to him in the oasis was probably in accordance with his policy of ingratiating himself with the priesthood of the various countries which he conquered.

The oasis of Ammonium is about six miles in length, and

three in breadth : the ground is abundantly watered by springs, and the high cultivation of the oasis, which still sustains a population of about 8000, is attested by the abundance of its fruits. Ruins of the Temple of Ammon still remain.

P. 187: *Alexandria.* — This famous city was built upon a strip of land between the sea and a lake ; two main streets, two hundred and forty feet wide, crossing each other at right angles in the centre of the city, left a free passage for the sea-breezes. The most important of all the public buildings of this city, and the ones which have given it a deserved fame in antiquity, were those belonging to the Museum, in which was the great library which became the largest and most famous in the world, and which contained in Cleopatra's time at least four hundred thousand volumes, and rendered Alexandria so illustrious that men in every department of learning resorted thither for instruction.

Among the most notable fruits of Alexandrian learning was the Greek translation of the Old Testament, generally known as the Septuagint, from the legendary account of its translation by seventy-two persons selected for the purpose under the orders of Ptolemy Philadelphus, about fifty years after Alexander's death.

P. 214: *The Burning of Persepolis.* — That Thais had anything to do with the burning of Persepolis is very doubtful. It rests on the sole authority of one of the least trustworthy of the historians of Alexander, and is declared by Smith's "Dictionary" to be, in all probability, a mere fable. The destruction by fire in a drunken bout is unquestionable. Perhaps the story of Thais was invented to relieve Alexander's name somewhat from odium.

P. 251: *Alexander's last Campaigns.* — The statement in the text that Alexander's soldiers refused to cross the Indus and go on to the Ganges, is not exactly accurate. They crossed the western tributary of the Indus and the central tributary of the Indus, and reached the river Ghara, its eastern tributary and the eastern boundary of the Punjaub, but refused to go farther east. At the confluence of the Chenab and the Ghara Alexander founded a city, giving it his name. He then descended to the mouth of the Indus and sailed into the Indian Ocean, from which point he returned to Babylon, where his death occurred as narrated in the text.

BOOKS BY THE ABBOTTS.

THE FRANCONIA STORIES.

By JACOB ABBOTT. In Ten Volumes. Illustrated. 16mo, Cloth, 75 cents per Vol.; the set in a box, $7 50.

1. MALLEVILLE.
2. MARY BELL.
3. ELLEN LINN.
4. WALLACE.
5. BEECHNUT.
6. STUYVESANT.
7. AGNES.
8. MARY ERSKINE.
9. RODOLPHUS.
10. CAROLINE.

MARCO PAUL SERIES.

Marco Paul's Voyages and Travels in the Pursuit of Knowledge. By JACOB ABBOTT. Beautifully Illustrated. Complete in six Volumes, 16mo, Cloth, 75 cents per Volume. Price of the set, in a box, $4 50.

1. IN NEW YORK.
2. ON THE ERIE CANAL.
3. IN THE FORESTS OF MAINE.
4. IN VERMONT.
5. IN BOSTON.
6. THE SPRINGFIELD ARMORY.

RAINBOW AND LUCKY SERIES.

By JACOB ABBOTT. Beautifully Illustrated. 16mo, Cloth, 75 cents each. The set complete, in a box, $3 75.

1. HANDIE.
2. RAINBOW'S JOURNEY.
3. SELLING LUCKY.
4. UP THE RIVER.
5. THE THREE PINES.

YOUNG CHRISTIAN SERIES.

By JACOB ABBOTT. In Four Volumes. Illustrated. 12mo, Cloth, $1 75 per Vol. The set complete, Cloth, $7 00.

1. THE YOUNG CHRISTIAN.
2. THE CORNER STONE.
3. THE WAY TO DO GOOD.
4. HOARYHEAD AND M'DONNER.

THE YOUNG CHRISTIAN.

By JACOB ABBOTT. A Memorial Volume. With a Sketch of the Author by one of his Sons. Illustrated by a Steel-Plate Portrait of the Author, and Woodcuts. 12mo, Cloth, $2 00.

HARPER'S STORY BOOKS.

A Series of Narratives, Biographies, and Tales, for the Instruction and Entertainment of the Young. By JACOB ABBOTT. Embellished with more than One Thousand beautiful Engravings. Square 4to, complete in 12 large Volumes, or 36 small ones.

"HARPER'S STORY BOOKS" can be obtained complete in Twelve Volumes, bound in blue and gold, each one containing Three Stories, for $15 00, or in Thirty-six thin Volumes, bound in crimson and gold, each containing one story, for $27 00. The Volumes may be had separately—the large ones at $1 25 each, the others at 75 cents each.

VOL. I.

BRUNO; or, Lessons of Fidelity, Patience, and Self-Denial Taught by a Dog.

WILLIE AND THE MORTGAGE: showing How Much may be Accomplished by a Boy.

THE STRAIT GATE; or, The Rule of Exclusion from Heaven.

VOL. II.

THE LITTLE LOUVRE; or, The Boys' and Girls' Picture-Gallery.

PRANK; or, The Philosophy of Tricks and Mischief.

EMMA; or, The Three Misfortunes of a Belle.

VOL. III.

VIRGINIA; or, A Little Light on a Very Dark Saying.

TIMBOO AND JOLIBA; or, The Art of Being Useful.

TIMBOO AND FANNY; or, The Art of Self-Instruction.

VOL. IV.

THE HARPER ESTABLISHMENT; or, How the Story Books are Made.

FRANKLIN, the Apprentice-Boy.

THE STUDIO; or, Illustrations of the Theory and Practice of Drawing, for Young Artists at Home.

VOL. V.

THE STORY OF ANCIENT HISTORY, from the Earliest Periods to the Fall of the Roman Empire.

THE STORY OF ENGLISH HISTORY, from the Earliest Periods to the American Revolution.

THE STORY OF AMERICAN HISTORY, from the Earliest Settlement of the Country to the Establishment of the Federal Constitution.

VOL. VI.

JOHN TRUE; or, The Christian Experience of an Honest Boy.
ELFRED; or, The Blind Boy and his Pictures.
THE MUSEUM; or, Curiosities Explained.

VOL. VII.

THE ENGINEER; or, How to Travel in the Woods.
RAMBLES AMONG THE ALPS.
THE THREE GOLD DOLLARS; or, An Account of the Adventures of Robin Green.

VOL. VIII.

THE GIBRALTAR GALLERY: being an Account of Various Things both Curious and Useful.
THE ALCOVE: containing some Farther Account of Timboo, Mark, and Fanny.
DIALOGUES for the Amusement and Instruction of Young Persons.

VOL. IX.

THE GREAT ELM; or, Robin Green and Josiah Lane at School.
AUNT MARGARET; or, How John True kept his Resolutions.
VERNON; or, Conversations about Old Times in England.

VOL. X.

CARL AND JOCKO; or, The Adventures of the Little Italian Boy and his Monkey.
LAPSTONE; or, the Sailor turned Shoemaker.
ORKNEY, THE PEACEMAKER; or, The Various Ways of Settling Disputes.

VOL. XI.

JUDGE JUSTIN; or, The Little Court of Morningdale.
MINIGO; or, The Fairy of Cairnstone Abbey.
JASPER; or, The Spoiled Child Recovered.

VOL. XII.

CONGO; or, Jasper's Experience in Command.
VIOLA and her Little Brother Arno.
LITTLE PAUL; or, How to be Patient in Sickness and Pain.

Some of the Story Books are written particularly for girls, and some for Boys, and the different Volumes are adapted to various ages, so that the work forms a *Complete Library of Story Books* for all the Children of the Family and the Sunday-School.

ABBOTTS' ILLUSTRATED HISTORIES.

Biographical Histories. By Jacob Abbott and John S. C. Abbott. The Volumes of this Series are printed and bound uniformly, and are embellished with numerous Engravings. 16mo, Cloth, $1 00 per Volume. Price of the set (32 Vols.), $32 00.

A series of volumes containing severally full accounts of the lives, characters, and exploits of the most distinguished sovereigns, potentates, and rulers that have been chiefly renowned among mankind, in the various ages of the world, from the earliest periods to the present day.

The successive volumes of the series, though they each contain the life of a single individual, and constitute thus a distinct and independent work, follow each other in the main, in regular historical order, and each one continues the general narrative of history down to the period at which the next volume takes up the story; so that the whole series presents to the reader a connected narrative of the line of general history from the present age back to the remotest times.

CYRUS THE GREAT.

DARIUS THE GREAT.

XERXES.

ALEXANDER THE GREAT.

ROMULUS.

HANNIBAL.

PYRRHUS.

JULIUS CÆSAR.

CLEOPATRA.

NERO.

ALFRED THE GREAT.

WILLIAM THE CONQUEROR.

RICHARD I.

RICHARD II.

RICHARD III.

MARGARET OF ANJOU.

MARY QUEEN OF SCOTS.

QUEEN ELIZABETH.

CHARLES I.

CHARLES II.

HERNANDO CORTEZ.

HENRY IV.

LOUIS XIV.

MARIA ANTOINETTE.

MADAME ROLAND.

JOSEPHINE.

JOSEPH BONAPARTE.

HORTENSE.

LOUIS PHILIPPE.

GENGHIS KHAN.

KING PHILIP.

PETER THE GREAT.

ABRAHAM LINCOLN'S OPINION OF ABBOTTS' HISTORIES. — *In a conversation with the President just before his death, Mr. Lincoln said: "I want to thank you and your brother for Abbotts' Series of Histories. I have not education enough to appreciate the profound works of voluminous historians; and if I had, I have no time to read them. But your Series of Histories gives me, in brief compass, just that knowledge of past men and events which I need. I have read them with the greatest interest. To them I am indebted for about all the historical knowledge I have."*

For the convenience of buyers, these popular Histories have been divided into Six Series, as follows:

I.

Founders of Empires.

CYRUS.
DARIUS.
XERXES.
ALEXANDER.
GENGHIS KHAN.
PETER THE GREAT.

II.

Heroes of Roman History.

ROMULUS.
HANNIBAL.
PYRRHUS.
JULIUS CÆSAR.
NERO.

III.

Earlier British Kings and Queens.

ALFRED.
WILLIAM THE CONQUEROR.
RICHARD I.
RICHARD II.
MARGARET OF ANJOU.

IV.

Later British Kings and Queens.

RICHARD III.
MARY QUEEN OF SCOTS.
ELIZABETH.
CHARLES I.
CHARLES II.

V.

Queens and Heroines.

CLEOPATRA.
MARIA ANTOINETTE.
JOSEPHINE.
HORTENSE.
MADAME ROLAND.

VI.

Rulers of Later Times.

KING PHILIP.
HERNANDO CORTEZ.
HENRY IV.
LOUIS XIV.
JOSEPH BONAPARTE
LOUIS PHILIPPE.

Each Series inclosed in a neat box.

THE LITTLE LEARNER SERIES.

A Series for Very Young Children. Designed to Assist in
the Earliest Development of the Mind of a Child, while under
its Mother's Special Care, during the First Five or Six Years
of its Life. By JACOB ABBOTT. Beautifully Illustrated.
Complete in five small 4to Volumes, Cloth, 75 cents per Vol.
Price of the set, in case, $3 75.

LEARNING TO TALK; or, Entertaining and Instructive
   Lessons in the Use of Language. 170 Engravings.

LEARNING TO THINK: consisting of Easy and Entertaining Lessons, designed to Assist in the First Unfolding
   of the Reflective and Reasoning Powers of Children. 120
   Engravings.

LEARNING TO READ: consisting of Easy and Entertaining Lessons, designed to Assist Young Children in Studying the Forms of the Letters, and in beginning to Read.
   160 Engravings.

LEARNING ABOUT COMMON THINGS; or, Familiar Instruction for Children in Respect to the Objects around
   them that attract their Attention and awaken their Curiosity in the Earliest Years of Life. 120 Engravings.

LEARNING ABOUT RIGHT AND WRONG; or, Entertaining and Instructive Lessons for Young Children in
   Respect to their Duty. 90 Engravings.

KINGS AND QUEENS; or, Life in the Palace: consisting of Historical Sketches of Josephine and Maria Louisa, Louis Philippe, Ferdinand of Austria, Nicholas, Isabella II., Leopold, Victoria, and Louis Napoleon. By JOHN S. C. ABBOTT. Illustrated. 12mo, Cloth, $1 75.

A SUMMER IN SCOTLAND: a Narrative of Observations and Adventures made by the Author during a Summer spent among the Glens and Highlands in Scotland. By JACOB ABBOTT. Illustrated. 12mo, Cloth, $1 75.

THE ROMANCE OF SPANISH HISTORY. By JOHN S. C. ABBOTT. Illustrated. 12mo, Cloth, $2 00.

THE TEACHER. Moral Influences Employed in the Instruction and Government of the Young. By JACOB ABBOTT. Illustrated. 12mo, Cloth, $1 75.

GENTLE MEASURES IN TRAINING THE YOUNG. Gentle Measures in the Management and Training of the Young; or, The Principles on which a Firm Parental Authority may be Established and Maintained without Violence or Anger, and the Right Development of the Moral and Mental Capacities be Promoted by Methods in Harmony with the Structure and the Characteristics of the Juvenile Mind. A Book for the Parents of Young Children. By JACOB ABBOTT. Illustrated. 12mo, Cloth, $1 75.

☞ HARPER & BROTHERS *will send any of the above works by mail, postage prepaid, on receipt of the price.*

SCIENCE
FOR THE YOUNG.

By JACOB ABBOTT.

WITH ILLUSTRATIONS.

———

HEAT.   12mo, Cloth, $1 50.

LIGHT.   12mo, Cloth, $1 50.

WATER AND LAND.   12mo, Cloth, $1 50.

FORCE.   12mo, Cloth, $1 50.

———

Few men enjoy a wider or better earned popularity as a writer for the young than Jacob Abbott. His series of histories, and stories illustrative of moral truths, have furnished amusement and instruction to thousands. He has the knack of piquing and gratifying curiosity. In the book before us he shows his happy faculty of imparting useful information through the medium of a pleasant narrative, keeping alive the interest of the young reader, and fixing in his memory valuable truths.—*Mercury*, New Bedford, Mass.

Jacob Abbott is almost the only writer in the English language who knows how to combine real amusement with real instruction in such a manner that the eager young readers are quite as much interested in the useful knowledge he imparts as in the story which he makes so pleasant a medium of instruction.—*Buffalo Commercial Advertiser.*

Mr. Abbott has avoided the errors so common with writers for popular effect, that of slurring over the difficulties of the subject through the desire of making it intelligible and attractive to unlearned readers. He never tampers with the truth of science, nor attempts to dodge the solution of a knotty problem behind a cloud of plausible illustrations.—*N. Y. Tribune.*

———

☞ HARPER & BROTHERS *will send any of the above works by mail, postage prepaid, on receipt of the price.*

POPULAR HISTORIES

BY

JOHN S. C. ABBOTT.

HISTORY OF FREDERICK THE GREAT.

The History of Frederick the Second, called Frederick the Great. By JOHN S. C. ABBOTT. Elegantly Illustrated. 8vo, Cloth, $5 00.

THE FRENCH REVOLUTION.

The French Revolution of 1789, as Viewed in the Light of Republican Institutions. By JOHN S. C. ABBOTT. With 100 Engravings. 8vo, Cloth, $5 00.

NAPOLEON BONAPARTE.

The History of Napoleon Bonaparte. By JOHN S. C. ABBOTT. With Maps, Woodcuts, and Portraits on Steel. 2 vols., 8vo, Cloth, $10 00.

NAPOLEON AT ST. HELENA.

Napoleon at St. Helena; or, Interesting Anecdotes and Remarkable Conversations of the Emperor during the Five and a Half Years of his Captivity. Collected from the Memorials of Las Casas, O'Meara, Montholon, Antommarchi, and others. By JOHN S. C. ABBOTT. With Illustrations. 8vo, Cloth, $5 00.

By JOHN S. C. ABBOTT.

CHILD AT HOME.

The Child at Home; or, The Principles of Filial Duty familiarly Illustrated. By JOHN S. C. ABBOTT. Woodcuts.
16mo, Cloth, $1 00.

The duties and trials peculiar to the child are explained and illustrated in this volume in the same clear and attractive manner
in which those of the mother are set forth in the "Mother at
Home." These two works may be considered as forming a complete manual of filial and maternal relations.

MOTHER AT HOME.

The Mother at Home; or, The Principles of Maternal Duty
familiarly Illustrated. By JOHN S. C. ABBOTT. Engravings. 16mo, Cloth, $1 00.

This book treats of the important questions of maternal responsibility and authority; of the difficulties which the mother will
experience, the errors to which she is liable, the methods and plans
she should adopt; of the religious instruction which she should
impart, and of the results which she may reasonably hope will follow her faithful and persevering exertions. These subjects are
illustrated with the felicity characteristic of all the productions of
the author.

PRACTICAL CHRISTIANITY.

Practical Christianity. A Treatise specially Designed for
Young Men. By JOHN S. C. ABBOTT. 16mo, Cloth, $1 00.

It is characterized by the simplicity of style and appositeness of
illustration which make a book easily read and readily understood.
It is designed to instruct and interest young men in the effectual
truths of Christianity. It comes down to their plane of thought,
and, in a genial, conversational way, strives to lead them to a life
of godliness.—*Watchman and Reflector.*

It abounds in wise and practical suggestions.—*N. Y. Commercial
Advertiser.*